Studying Shakespeare

Studying Shakespeare

A Guide to the Plays

Laurie E. Maguire

Blackwell Publishing

BLACKWELL PUBLISHING
350 Main Street, Malden, MA 02148-5018, USA
108 Cowley Road, Oxford OX4 1JF, UK
550 Swanston Street, Carlton, Victoria 3053, Australia

First published 2004 by Blackwell Publishing Ltd.
Reprinted 2004 (twice)

Library of Congress Cataloging-in-Publication Data

Maguire, Laurie E.
Studying Shakespeare: a guide to the plays / Laurie E. Maguire.
p. cm.
Includes bibliographical references (p.) and index.
ISBN 0-631-22984-1 (alk. paper) – ISBN 0-631-22985-X (pbk. : alk. paper)
1. Shakespeare, William, 1564–1616 – Criticism and interpretation – Handbooks,
manuals, etc. 2. Shakespeare, William, 1564–1616 – Examinations –
Study guides. I. Title.
PR2976.M36 2003
822.3'3 – dc21

2002038481

A catalogue record for this title is available from the British Library.

Set in 10.5 on 13 pt Minion
by SNP Best-set Typesetter Ltd, Hong Kong
Printed and bound in the United Kingdom
by TJ International, Padstow, Cornwall

For further information on
Blackwell Publishing, visit our website:
www.blackwellpublishing.com

Contents

Illustrations

Acknowledgments

Andrew McNeillie first suggested this book to me in the summer of 2000. It was written between then and summer 2002. In a sense, however, it has taken twenty years to write as it is the product of every book and article I have read, every conference attended, every lecture heard or given, and every discussion with colleagues and students. I have taken care to track down and acknowledge the sources which have influenced my thinking; however, inadvertent omissions may occur in a work of this time span, and I should be grateful to be informed of any oversights.

In the meantime it gives me great pleasure to acknowledge my indebtedness to those critics, colleagues, and friends of whose influence I am most conscious. The frequency with which Alexander Leggatt, Ralph Berry, Brian Vickers, and Lynda Boose feature in the references speaks for itself. Dympna Callaghan has been the most patient of auditors, most challenging of interlocutors, and most supportive of friends. Anne Coldiron oversaw this project from its Ur-draft, and devoted precious time, energy, and enthusiasm to discussing all aspects of it. Katherine Duncan-Jones answered questions, and provided conversation and companionship on two continents. John Scholar offered helpfully Rhadamanthine readings of an early draft, and Danielle Sered provided exemplary research and secretarial assistance.

My students in Ottawa and Oxford have constantly stimulated and amazed; I am particularly grateful to Elisabeth Glover, Zoë Hopper, Ben Morgan, and Laurence Williams for permission to cite unpublished essays. Colleagues in Canada, the United States, and Britain have been endlessly helpful in matters theoretical, textual, and theatrical: Tom Berger, Philippa Berry, Ralph Cohen, David Carlson, Don Childs, Tony Dawson, Stephen Greenblatt, Werner Gundersheimer, Claire MacDonald, Andrew Murphy,

Randall Nakayama, Gail Paster, Ed Rocklin, Bill Sherman, Peter Stallybrass, Robert Weimann, Paul Yachnin, and Georgianna Ziegler.

I am indebted to the following libraries and librarians for their resources and assistance: University of Ottawa Library, Folger Shakespeare Library, Magdalen College Library, Shakespeare Institute Library, Shakespeare Centre Library, University College London Library, Oxford English Faculty Library, Bodleian Library, Centre for the Study of Cartoons and Caricature at the University of Kent, and University of Bristol Theatre Collection – in particular Betsy Walsh and her staff in DC, Susan Brock and Jim Shaw in Stratford, and Sue Usher, Christine Ferdinand, and Sally Speirs in Oxford.

Magdalen College Oxford, the University of Oxford, and the Arts and Humanities Research Board generously funded two terms' leave which enabled me to complete this book. I am grateful to them for their support, and to my English colleagues at Magdalen and the Oxford English Faculty for their extra labor during my absence.

I have published some of the arguments in this book in variant form in previous articles. Material on *Taming of the Shrew, 1 Henry IV*, and *Henry V* appeared in *Gloriana's Face: Women, Public and Private, in the English Renaissance*, ed. S. P. Cerasano and Marion Wynne-Davies (Brighton: Harvester Press, 1992). Material on *Comedy of Errors* appeared in *Comedy of Errors: Critical Essays*, ed. Robert S. Miola (New York: Garland Press, 1997). Material on *Romeo and Juliet* appeared in *Shakespeare: Text and Theater*, ed. Lois Potter and Arthur F. Kinney (Newark, DE: University of Delaware Press, 1999). Material on *As You Like It* appeared in *A Feminist Companion to Shakespeare*, ed. Dympna C. Callaghan (Oxford: Blackwell, 2000). Material on *Hamlet* appeared in *Performance Research* 7 (2002), ed. Claire MacDonald and William Sherman. Material on *Troilus and Cressida* appeared in *Renaissance Drama* 31 (2002), ed. Wendy Wall and Jeffrey Masten. I am grateful to the publishers – Harvester, Garland, University of Delaware Press, Blackwell, Routledge, and Northwestern University Press – for allowing me to reprint portions of these articles.

The portrait of the Moorish Ambassador (1600–1) is reproduced by kind permission of The Shakespeare Institute, University of Birmingham. The painting of *Santiago en la batalla de Clavijo* is reproduced by kind permission of the Museum of Fine Arts, Budapest. Pan books and Macmillan Publishing kindly gave permission to reproduce the cover of Minette Walters's novel, *The Scold's Bridle*. For permission to reproduce the cartoon of Elizabeth I and Shakespeare by Brian ffoulkes I am grateful to Elfa Kramers and the *Punch* picture library.

It has been a pleasure to work with the editorial and production staff at Blackwell at every stage. My thanks to Andrew McNeillie, Emma Bennett, Alison Dunnett, Jenny Hunt, Lisa Eaton, Laura Montgomery, Brigitte Lee, and Leanda Shrimpton.

Anyone who has written a book knows that it is a collaborative process, and the collaborative network extends beyond the field of specialization. Catharine Benson, Peter Friend, Michael Johnson, Kristine Krug, Candia McWilliam, Sarah Pantin, and Rebecca Whiting may not recognize their contributions in the following pages, but each enabled this book in crucial ways.

Conventions

All quotations come from the *Riverside Shakespeare*; for the name of the male protagonist in *Taming of the Shrew*, I have, however, adopted the spelling Petruccio from the Oxford *Shakespeare*. I have expanded all speech prefixes. In quotations from primary documents I have modernized spelling and punctuation. All italics are mine unless otherwise indicated. The dates of all Shakespeare plays are taken from the Oxford *Textual Companion*.

Introduction
Shakespeare: The Story

On June 17, 1994 a modernized Shakespeare tragedy took place on the freeway outside Los Angeles, playing live to a huge TV audience. A black man appeared to have murdered his white wife and now threatened to kill himself. The newspapers were full of *Othello* analogies. Like Shakespeare's Moor, who had overcome outsider status to become Venice's most revered military leader, O. J. Simpson had grown from inner-city poverty to super-star status, not on the fields of battle but on the football fields. Like Othello, he had done the state (or at least the world of sport, which in contemporary culture is almost the same thing) some service and they knew it. Like Othello, he suffered from jealousy, and his penchant for violence was to lead to tragedy. (Although he was acquitted of the murder of Nicole Brown Simpson, his history of wife abuse was well documented.) Like Othello, his excuse was loving not wisely but too well: Simpson's suicide note read, "If we had problems it's because I loved her too much."[1]

Seeing oneself or one's contemporaries in Shakespeare characters and situations is nothing new. In 1599 Shakespeare's acting company, the Chamberlain's Men, was paid by supporters of the Earl of Essex to perform an old Shakespeare play, *Richard II*, the central dramatic event in which is the enforced abdication of the eponymous king. Forty-one years into her reign, aged sixty-six, Elizabeth I was still unmarried, childless, and had not named a successor. The contemporary message in the historical drama was clear; Elizabeth told her councilors, "I am Richard II, know ye not that?" (Ure 1961: lix). During the long madness of George III, stage productions of *King Lear* were banned in England because the resemblance between the

---

[1]   Read at a press conference on June 17, 1994 and subsequently circulated in all the news media.

mad Lear and the reigning monarch was thought to be too close for comfort.[2] In the nineteenth century Coleridge felt he had a "smack of Hamlet" in him (i.e., he was a melancholy intellectual). T. S. Eliot's modernist Prufrock, on the other hand, confessed, "I am not Prince Hamlet, nor was meant to be" – that is, he was not destined for the role of hero (Eliot 1954: 15). The O. J. case was but the most public and dramatic of a regular phenomenon: identification with Shakespeare heroes.

Newspaper headlines regularly give us "real-life-Romeo-and-Juliet" stories. The compound adjective describes couples who marry despite family hatred (Serbian/Croatian romance is but the most recent of this genre), as well as stories of teenage love. Shakespeare characters are also invoked for purposes of propaganda. In the Falklands War of 1982, Mrs. Thatcher was, to some newspapers, a Fortinbras, a militant who fought "to gain a little patch of ground / That hath in it no profit but the name" (*Hamlet* 4.4.18–19). In August 2000 the British Conservative party branded the prime minister's wife, Cherie Booth, a Lady Macbeth. Booth's newspaper article on a contentious area of public policy, the new Human Rights Act, was seen as an attempt to direct power from behind the throne (White 2000a, 2000b; Anon 2000). In all three cases Shakespearean plays provide a convenient shorthand for personal characteristics and predicaments.

The phenomenon is not confined to Shakespeare. Before there was Shakespeare there was Chaucer: January–May marriages refer to the old husband and young wife of *The Merchant's Tale*. And before Chaucer there was Greek myth: Oedipus complex, Herculean task, Gordian knot. Using character names as a shorthand for personal characteristics and life's recurrent predicaments shows literature's capacity not just to tell stories and show characters but to tell *our* stories and show *our* selves. Lavinia illustrates this very point in *Titus Andronicus* when, having suffered egregious horrors – a double rape and the amputation of both her hands and her tongue – she is prevented by her injuries from revealing the crimes committed against her. Instead, she uses literature to speak for her, turning to "The Rape of Philomel" in Ovid's *Metamorphoses*. Ovid's gruesome tale of rape and violence parallels her own story.

---

[2] The resemblance was poignantly clear in Alan Bennett's play *The Madness of George III*, later filmed as *The Madness of King George*. King George arranges a reading of *King Lear* 4.7 ("Cure this great breach in his abused nature"; 4.7.14). When a late arrival, the lord chancellor, objects to the choice of play, the king's doctor protests, "I'd no idea what it was about" (Bennett 1992: 69; Bennett 1995: 63).

Lavinia's tragedy is extreme, but it portrays, as does so much of literature, normal life writ large.[3] You may not have suffered rape and amputation but you will have experienced loss, pain, and grief so deep you don't know how to articulate it. (Whether this is a three-year-old's broken toy, a teenager's broken heart, or an adult's broken family, the emotions are surprisingly consistent.) Your uncle may not have murdered your father and married your mother to gain a throne; but that is not what *Hamlet* is about. Or rather, it is what the *plot* of *Hamlet* is about. The *story* of *Hamlet* is less sensational and altogether more familiar: a young man's attempt to deal with the death of his father. Few of us would wish to identify with the Machiavellian murderer Richard III, but Freud's paraphrase of Richard's opening soliloquy rehearses the emotional logic which underlies it: "nature has done me a grievous wrong in denying me that beauty of form which wins human love. Life owes me reparation for this, and I will see that I get it." Freud points out that "Richard is an enormously magnified representation of something we can all discover in ourselves" (1953–74: 322).

This essentialist view of literature as a reflection of, and guide to, life is somewhat out of fashion among literary critics, partly because it invites one to focus on characters and assess their motivations. Character analysis, so popular in the first half of the twentieth century, quickly bordered on self-indulgent creative writing, and by the 1970s had fallen into disrepute. A. C. Bradley's influential *Shakespearian Tragedy* (1904) provides a typically excessive example of early twentieth-century expansionist approaches to character. Bradley writes of Gertrude in *Hamlet*:

> The Queen was not a bad-hearted woman, not at all the woman to think little of murder. But she had a soft animal nature, and was very dull and shallow. She loved to be happy, like a sheep in the sun; and to do her justice, it pleased her to see others happy, like more sheep in the sun. She never saw that drunkenness is disgusting till Hamlet told her so; and though she knew that he considered her marriage "oer-hasty" . . . she was untroubled by any shame at the feelings which had led to it. It was pleasant to sit upon her throne and see smiling faces round her. (p. 167)

---

[3] However, Lavinia's story cannot be safely confined to the fictional worlds of Ovid and Shakespeare. Alex Duval Smith's report on the late twentieth-century war in Sierra Leone describes a thirteen-year-old, Mariatu Kamara, pregnant as a result of rape. "When her child is born, she will not be able to hold it. She does not have hands with which to beg for food, let alone feed herself. After the crazed teenager who came to her village had raped her, his rebel friends hacked off her hands with a machete" (Smith 1999: 1).

Such intrusively inventive character study serves no critical function not least because, as the tell-tale present tense of "drunkenness is disgusting" shows, it confusingly conflates subjective moral judgment with analytical criticism.

Although such subjective pronouncements linger in some New Critical work such as Harold Bloom's *Shakespeare: The Invention of the Human*, in recent decades criticism has ventured into new terrain – the invigorating challenges of structuralism, poststructuralism, new historicism, cultural materialism, feminism. These innovative critical schools have brought with them new discoveries but also new dangers: their specialist vocabularies have made Shakespeare criticism less accessible to the ordinary reader and playgoer, and their theoretical basis has, as Alan Sinfield puts it, threatened to "make character a wholly inappropriate category of analysis" (1992: 58). Heather Dubrow writes that "character has virtually become a dirty word" (1987: 17). Once alerted to this creeping marginalization of what is dramatically essential, we can reach an accommodation which retains much of the new territory won by the theoreticians, for character is partly created, affected, and altered by the power structures and cultural contingencies (i.e., situation) to which the new scholarly *isms* have taught us to be attentive. The blunt reality of dramatic characterization remains. As recently as 1998 David Daniell could, without apparent embarrassment, devote thirty pages of his *Julius Caesar* edition (pp. 45–75) to character analysis. Statements like "Brutus is afraid of feeling" (p. 55) seem at home alongside historical discussions of tyrannicide.

Before Shakespeare was an author he was a dramatist; in reading Shakespeare's plays we are reading something that was first conceived for performance.[4] And character has never been an "inappropriate category of analysis" for those who perform Shakespeare – actors. If you speak to actors they will tell you that they approach Shakespeare's plays first through character and situation. David Tennant approaches Touchstone's Seven Degrees of a Lie monologue in *As You Like It* as "an audition. Touchstone, with his

---

[4] In his television series *Playing Shakespeare*, John Barton quotes a scholarly article about ambiguity, epistemology, and aesthetic problems in *Hamlet*, then turns to Michael Pennington in bemusement, challenging him to act it (Barton 1984: 101); not all academic aperçus have theatrical value. The pendulum occasionally swings in the other direction, however, as when Patrick Stewart credits Alan Dessen's article on Elizabethan stage Jews with providing "insight that transformed" his Shylock (Stewart 1989: 23).

new-found wife to support, will need a court to jest in, so the discovery of a benevolent Duke in the forest is an opportunity he can't miss out on" (1998: 42). An orthopedic surgeon explained to David Troughton that Richard III's breech birth might have led to a dislocated hip, a compensatory limp, and a crooked spine, with inevitable constant pain. Troughton's reaction: "In pain all his life? What an insight into a character. Here was one very simple explanation for Richard's malevolence" (1998: 74).

If you observe audiences you will see that they too respond first to character and situation. Robert N. Watson reminds us that "if dramatic characters are not really living people with full psychological histories, audiences still are" (1990: 327). Audiences do instinctively and recreationally what actors do professionally: try to explain the thoughts and character of the father who misunderstands a daughter, the son who rebels against a father, the husband who abuses a wife, the woman who loves a man who doesn't return her feelings, the politician who doesn't sleep at night, the ruler who invades a foreign country, the subject who questions the ruler's ethics, the soldier who is apprehensive on the eve of battle. I take the above examples from Shakespeare's plays,[5] but the approach is not confined to "high" literature. In a magazine interview Hugh Grant spoke of his sympathetically psychologized approach to Daniel Cleaver in the film of *Bridget Jones's Diary*, imagining the character as "a disappointed writer who had ended up as a publisher" (2001: 138).

Grant's approach, like that of Tennant and Troughton, is that of the Method actor. Method acting was devised by the Russian Stanislavski at the Moscow Arts Centre in the early twentieth century. It promotes an interiorized approach to character: actors construct their character's biography, tastes, attitudes, entire existence. Although associated with Stanislavski and drama, this kind of character analysis has a long literary history. Plutarch's *Parallel Lives of the Greeks and Romans*, a series of historical biographies, was one of Shakespeare's favorite sources: it supplied the base for the characters of Theseus, Julius Caesar, Brutus, Mark Antony, Coriolanus, Timon, Alcibiades, Pompey, and Cicero. Shakespeare could have consulted the Latin translation of the Greek original, although Sir Thomas North's

---

[5] The characters are, respectively, Lear; Hal; Petruccio and Iago; the Helenas in *Midsummer Night's Dream* and *All's Well that Ends Well* and the Jailer's Daughter in *Two Noble Kinsmen*; Henry IV; Henry V; Michael Williams, Alexander Court, and John Bates in *Henry V*.

English translation was published in 1579 and all the evidence indicates that Shakespeare worked from this translation, conveniently reprinted in 1595. As the title announces, the volume offers paired biographies (twenty-three in total) of a Greek hero and a Roman, and provides details of the heroes' personalities as well as their achievements. Plutarch is an historian and a biographer, and for him the two genres overlap. Historical events stem from personal decisions; and personal decisions are made by men. Plutarch's psychological interest is not confined to his *Parallel Lives*. His *Moralia*, a series of essays known to Shakespeare through Philemon Holland's translation in 1603, portray identity as flexible, multiple, and changeable.

Plutarch's (and Shakespeare's) interest in the flux of identity is extended by the French essayist Michel de Montaigne, whose *Essais* (1580) were posthumously translated into English in 1603. Ostensibly an autobiography, the book presents Montaigne's personality through the author's discontinuous responses; by trying out different attitudes and postures, Montaigne attempts to ascertain who he is and what he believes.

The Renaissance interest in character analysis is seen most spectacularly in Sir Thomas Overbury's *Characters*, a book of brief character sketches. There were five editions in 1614, one in 1615, three in 1616; there were further reprints in 1618, 1622, 1626, 1627, 1628, and 1630. Part of the initial commercial interest may have been due to the sensational nature of Overbury's death in 1613 (he was murdered in the Tower of London) and to his involvement in a court scandal of divorce and remarriage which made the original volume's *raison d'être* – a verse character of "a wife" – resoundingly topical. Subsequent volumes (regularly enlarged) were entirely in prose and comprised one- to two-page depictions of character: a wise man, an elder brother, a canting rogue, an ostler. Sometimes the characters border on stereotypes (a Jesuit, a drunken Dutchman, a braggadocio Welshman) but even in such xenophobic examples Overbury reveals nuances that go beyond mere types. This is partly because of his tendency to think metaphorically. Thus the braggadocio Welshman "is the oyster that the pearl is in, for a man may be picked out of him" (1890: 68); the creditor "racks and stretches gentlemen like English broadcloth, beyond the staple of the wool, till the threads crack and that causeth them with the least wet to shrink, and presently to wear bare" (p. 161).

Overbury notes gradation of character: there is a difference between "a whore" and "a very whore," between "a vertuous widow" and "an ordinary widow." His portrayal of the creditor moves from costume to attitude to custom (p. 160). The sympathetic depiction of a franklin contrasts the man's external with his internal attributes, and notes the significance of speech patterns: "His outside is an ancient yeoman of England, though his inside may give arms with the best gentleman and ne'er see the herald. There is no truer servant in the house than himself. Though he be master, he says not to his servants 'Go to field' but 'Let us go'" (p. 149). Overbury's imaginative detail extends even to the reading matter of a chambermaid: "She reads Greene's works over and over but is so carried away with the *Mirror of Knighthood*, she is many times resolved to run out of her self and become a lady errant" (p. 101). It is a short step from here to Stanislavski's *An Actor Prepares*.

Overbury's interest in characters as complex creatures with quirks and contradictions, beliefs and backgrounds – in short, with interiority – is an interest that most Renaissance dramatists shared. Thumbnail sketches in the manner of Overbury are frequent in Shakespeare: Hotspur's depiction of the foppish courtier, Ulysses's reading of Cressida's body language, Menenius's description of the vengeful Coriolanus, Lucio's gossip about the characters of Vincentio and Angelo.[6]

Thus, character study is a recurrent literary concern in the sixteenth century, nor should we expect otherwise in the century that saw the rise of humanism. Tudor humanism refers to the intellectual excavation of the classics by early sixteenth-century intellectuals. The humanist project emphasized translation (making classical authors available), style (improving vernacular literature through classical rhetoric and literary criticism), ethics (the timeless ideals of the ancients), education (the founding of schools and colleges, the writing of school textbooks), and civic values (mankind's behavior) (Carroll 1996: 246–65). The humanist worldview, unlike the medieval worldview, was androcentric rather than theocentric. Humans, and human potential, lay at the center of society. Androcentricity gave rise to questions about government, tyranny, the commonwealth, the court, responsibility, and how humans should contribute to the world – the so-called "civic humanism" of Cicero (sometimes called Ciceronian humanism). When books of literary and historical criticism tell us that the

---

[6] See Burns's illuminating and undervalued *Character* (1990) for further discussion of such episodes. In a study of those variant Shakespeare plays which were published in a short and a long version, Lukas Erne (2003) argues that the short text represents a stage version and the long text a revised reading version. The characters in the short texts are "functions or types indicative of orality" whereas those in the long texts have more personal and "life-like" identity (p. 242).

Renaissance was the era of the individual, they provide a shorthand definition of a crucial component of humanism. This focus on the individual is visible in the titles of the many humanist works that explore a particular aspect of a man's civic function: Castiglione's *The Courtier*, Sir Thomas Elyot's *The Governor*, Machiavelli's *The Prince*.

At the nonliterary level we can see the increased emphasis on the individual in changing funerary practice. Funeral sermons began to give biographical details of the deceased and to be printed in pamphlet form (a forerunner of the obituary). Funeral monuments, which had previously existed only for royals and aristocrats, now began to mark deceased individuals from lower classes, providing commemoration in an age in which tombstones were not yet widely used. Thus the sixteenth century, in both life and literature, emphasizes and legitimizes character study.

I am not advocating character study, and its companion, situation, as the aim of Shakespeare criticism, but I want to insist on their usefulness as a point of entry into all Shakespeare plays. Together character and situation constitute what one Shakespeare critic, Alice Walker, writing in the 1950s, called the New Realism. The New Realism has a significant advantage over all other scholarly *isms*: its nonspecialist vocabulary and subject matter can be accessed by everyone.

In the interval of a production of *Measure for Measure* I eavesdropped on two young women who were discussing the play. "What would you do if you were Isabella?" one asked the other. The question is ahistorical (not, for example, "What would a Jacobean audience expect Isabella to do?"), but its urgent involvement with character and situation is entirely appropriate, at least as an opening critical gambit. Exploring character and motivation is a quotidian activity for most people. If you have ever pondered your own insecurities, your partner's faults, your employer's strategies, your enemy's motives, your friend's childhood or your colleague's errors, you are equipped to analyze a Shakespeare play. This book does not give you critical tools to discuss Shakespeare; rather it shows that you already possess those tools, and illustrates how to use them to their best advantage.

If there is a difficulty with character study, it is that Shakespeare has set a standard by which other dramatists are measured and found wanting. Middleton and Jonson, in their city comedies, for example, provide characterization but they do not explore the characters, or provide the material for us to explore them, to the extent that Shakespeare does. Marlowe provides larger-than-life characters with recognizably human emotions and motivations (Faustus's interest in Mephistopheles seems as much due to loneliness as to necromantic ambition) but actors still puzzle over points of personal detail. Thomas Healy writes that Marlowe's dramatic characters "are vehicles for actions, they are not psychologically complex" (1994: 56). Stevie Simkin concurs: Marlowe's plays are "fairly intractable material for anyone determined to approach the text with a 'naturalistic' or 'realistic' methodology" (2001: 66–7). This does not mean that Middleton or Jonson or Marlowe are lesser dramatists; it means that they do something different from Shakespeare and do it very well. Shakespeare's dramatic values lie in human attitudes and actions. This, of course, is why he translates and endures; but it is also why we cannot take "Shakespeare" as a synecdoche for "Renaissance drama."

A character in a Russell Hoban novel muses, "I'd always assumed that I was the central character in my own story but now it occurred to me that I might in fact be only a minor character in someone else's" (1975: 186). Hoban's protagonist is an exception: we are always the major character in our own story. A theatrical anecdote has it that if you ask actors to summarize *King Lear* (for example), the actor of Kent will explain, "It's about this servant who . . ."; the actor of Goneril will say, "It's about this daughter who . . ."; the actor of Lear will begin, "It's about this king who. . ." (cf. Walter 1993: 201). All three accounts are correct. Tom Stoppard illustrates this point in a play based on another Shakespeare tragedy: in *Rosencrantz and Guildenstern are Dead* the two courtiers take center-stage while Hamlet assumes a walk-on role. In John Updike's novel *Gertrude and Claudius* events in Elsinore are presented from Gertrude's, and then from Claudius's, point of view. Life is always about our story, not someone else's. But, as life progresses, our story changes. Sometimes, like Hal in *Henry IV*, we're the rebellious child; fast forward a few years and we become King Henry IV, the worried parent. Sometimes our identity depends on our companions. A colleague reports that the experience of watching *King Lear* in the company of her children yielded a crucially different play from that watched in the company of her parents; on the first occasion she saw the play from the point of view of Lear, on the second from the standpoint of Lear's daughters. (Jane Smiley's novel, *A Thousand Acres*, chooses to tell the story from Goneril's point of view.)

In the following chapters I illustrate some of life's most familiar stories, drawn from all of Shakespeare's plays, and arranged in five broad chapters: "Private Life" (Shakespeare and Selfhood), "Marital Life" (Shakespeare and Romance), "Political Life" (Shakespeare and Government), "Public

Life" (Shakespeare and Social Structures), "Real Life" (Shakespeare and Suffering). This thematic arrangement, with its avoidance of a play-by-play approach, allows many of the plays to be discussed in two or three different places at different lengths. Because I approach characters and situations from a variety of critical angles, the revisiting of plays in different contexts results in both complementary and contradictory conclusions. This is a deliberate ploy, not a design fault; the answers given by texts depend on the kind of questions one asks them.

Although some recurrent motifs emerge, I have sought to avoid a polemical through-line, stressing an interrogative methodology rather than a committed ideology. The thematic organization of this book encourages overlap but I have avoided duplication. Thus, the financial motif of *Merchant of Venice* is considered briefly in chapter 2, "Marital Life," where I discuss financial investment and risk as a metaphor for marriage; it appears again, in greater detail, in chapter 4 in the section on "Money." The book works by a process of accretion; *Henry IV* and *V* may be classified generically as history plays, but their public, masculine world also revises the personal and romantic issues of some of the early comedies. Shakespeare did not load and close thematic programs like a human version of Microsoft Windows. The plays are in dialogue with themselves; so are the chapters of this book.

In the first two chapters I tend to concentrate on single issues in individual plays, but in the later chapters I juggle several plays as the private and personal themes of chapters 1 and 2 feed into the public and political themes of chapters 3 to 5. Each chapter has a short introduction. The chapter subsections, which deal with individual plays, generally launch straight into discussion of the respective play(s), although when background material is deemed necessary, as in parts of chapters 3 and 4, I have provided an introduction to the subsection. Sometimes plays are considered singly, sometimes they are discussed in a pair or a group, and sometimes a general discussion of a pair prefaces detailed discussion of the plays independently.

This book is an exercise in New Realism. It focuses on characters and situation, on human psychology, on Shakespeare's stories – all aspects of human life with which we are familiar. The aim is to show Shakespeare's accessibility. The book is designed for undergraduate students, for the intelligent playgoer, the enthusiastic novice, the admirer who wants a more nuanced and informed admiration, and the would-be admirer who needs a map through uncharted critical territory; it neither needs nor assumes prior knowledge beyond a reading of the play(s) under discussion.

This book is also a defense of Shakespeare's relevance in a century in which his place in the curriculum is increasingly challenged, and so, by extension, a defense of the relevance of literature to our lives today. In a recent survey of 700 senior business leaders, 55 percent chose fiction or poetry rather than a book on business or management as the work that most influenced their career (Hodson 2001). After September 11, 2001 theater groups began to perform on the streets of New York City. "Art is part of the answer," wrote Jeanette Winterson, "not as a panacea but because art has a way of going into the hurt place and cleaning it. Some wounds never heal but they need not remain infected." Shakespeare is, in my experience, a highly effective disinfectant.

1

Private Life:
Shakespeare and Selfhood

"Who is it that can tell me who I am?" (*Lear* 1.4.230)

Introduction

Shakespearean comedy typically has a tripartite structure: an opening predicament, a central section of confusion and dissolving identities, followed by restoration. We see this in *Comedy of Errors* (Egeon's death sentence; mistaken identities in two sets of twins; family reunion), in *Midsummer Night's Dream* (Hermia's enforced love choice; confusion and exchange of partners in the wood; marriage), in *As You Like It* (banishment; disguise and playacting in Arden; family reunion and marriage), in *Taming of the Shrew* (Baptista's condition that the wooing of Bianca depend on the marriage of her older sister; Petruccio's disorientation of Katherine; delayed marriage banquet), and so on. This dramatic structure has a long tradition. It is both pagan (anthropologists trace it to the three phases of the moon – waxing, waning, reappearing as a new moon) and Christian (the Friday of death, the Saturday of disappearance, the Sunday of resurrection [Frye 1986: 43]). In Shakespeare's plays it is also profoundly psychological, based on the paradox that in order to find oneself, one has to lose oneself.

This losing/finding always takes place in a different environment, in a holiday world: the Forest of Arden (*As You Like It*), a deserted island (*Tempest*), a tavern in Eastcheap (*1* and *2 Henry IV*). But holiday worlds can only ever be temporary, and Shakespeare characters, like real-life characters, must return from vacation to use their restored and renewed selves in the real world.

The loss that precedes finding is often profound, and Shakespeare's vocabulary for this disorientation ranges from melting to outright annihilation. In lacking his mother and his twin brother, Antipholus of Syracuse lacks a part of himself:

I to the world am like a drop of water,
That in the ocean seeks another drop,
Who, falling there to find his fellow forth
(Unseen, inquisitive) confounds himself.

So I, to find a mother and a brother,
In quest of them (unhappy), ah, lose myself. (1.2.35–40)

In *Midsummer Night's Dream* Helena uses images of seasonal extreme to describe the change of heart of her lover, Demetrius, who has fallen in love with Hermia:

For ere Demetrius look'd on Hermia's eyne,
He hail'd down oaths that he was only mine;
And when this hail some heat from Hermia felt,
So he dissolv'd, and show'rs of oaths did melt. (1.1.242–5)

The same image of melting characterizes Richard II's loss of identity as king when faced with Bullingbrook's takeover:

O that I were a mockery king of snow,
Standing before the sun of Bullingbrook,
To melt myself away in water-drops! (4.1.260–2)

The vocabulary of the elements and the seasons – sea, hail, snow, sun, thaw – illustrates drama's indebtedness to pagan celebrations in which the changing agricultural year was presented theatrically as a conflict between winter and summer. Francis M. Cornford's seminal study, *The Origins of Attic Comedy*, traces this theatrical structure from Greek drama to mummers' plays. The old season, autumn (often represented as an old king), is challenged by a newcomer; the two struggle for supremacy, and the old season is killed, its death being represented by winter; the new season/king (spring) ascends. It in its turn ripens (summer), decays (autumn), dies (winter), and is replaced (spring). This archetypal structure may explain why Shakespearean history and tragedy follow the same tripartite structure as Shakespearean comedy. But whereas comedy is triumphant and circular (the marriages with which it concludes represent the ascendance of the next generation and herald procreation and birth, the human equivalent of spring's ascendance), tragedy is linear and leads to extinction.

Although the self-discovery of characters in history and tragedy comes too late to create a harmonious resolution, the central section of loss is the same. "Who is it that can tell me who I am?" howls Lear (1.4.230); "I must nothing be" realizes Richard II (4.1.201). In *Othello* both the Moor and his ensign grieve over loss of identity: "Othello's occupation's gone" laments Othello (3.3.357); "I have lost my reputation! I have lost the immortal part of myself, and what remains is bestial" cries Cassio (2.3.262–4).

In this chapter I examine personal identity in nine Shakespeare plays.

1   The Divided Self

"How have you made division of yourself?" (*TN* 5.1.222)

Comedy of Errors (1594)

Comedy of Errors opens with Egeon, a Syracusan merchant, relating the events which have brought him to Ephesus. He and his wife, parents of identical twin boys both (implausibly) called Antipholus, adopted another set of identical twins, both called Dromio, to act as servants to the Antipholi. When the twins were still infants the family was separated in shipwreck, so that Egeon lost his wife, one Antipholus, and one Dromio. He brought up the surviving twin and servant in Syracuse until such time as Antipholus reached manhood when (accompanied by his Dromio) he set out in search of his lost brother and mother. Egeon is now traveling in search of his Syracusan son and servant, and finds himself in Ephesus. As it happens, Antipholus and Dromio of Syracuse have also landed in Ephesus where, coincidentally, the long-lost twins live, and where the lost mother/wife, Emilia, is abbess of a local priory. For four acts, the newcomer Syracusan twins are regularly mistaken for the resident Ephesian twins. Comic chaos is inevitable, until the entire family is reunited and misunderstandings cleared up in act 5.

Comedy of Errors is based on a Roman comedy, Plautus's *Menaechmi*, which gave Shakespeare the story of twins separated in infancy. In Plautus, there is only one set of twins; Shakespeare added the Dromios. Two sets of twins, bearing the same name, raise important questions about the location of identity. (Although Plautus gives the twins the same name, he provides a logical explanation: one inherits his brother's name when the brother is deemed lost. Shakespeare offers no explanation.) The characters in *Errors* assume, not unnaturally, that name confers identity. When Adriana, the wife of Antipholus of Ephesus, mistakes the Syracusan twins for her husband and servant, she identifies them by name; the astonished Syracusans take this as proof that she does indeed know them. However, as confusions escalate, both Antipholus and Dromio of Syracuse grow hesitant in assuming that name and identity are synonymous. "Do you know me, sir? Am I Dromio? Am I your man? Am I myself?" asks Dromio in anguish at 3.2.73–4. His master reassures him: "Thou art Dromio, thou art my man, thou art thyself" (75–6), but just 100 lines later he is unable to apply the same confidence to his own situation. "Master Antipholus," hails the goldsmith at 3.2.165; "Ay, that's my name" is Antipholus's guarded response. The duplicatability and detachability of names, the fact that they can have multiple referents, prevents them being a reliable marker of identity.

If names are unreliable, Dromio of Ephesus turns to the individual's body: "That you beat me at the mart, I have your hand to show," he tells the wrong Antipholus as proof that the two have indeed met recently (3.1.12). But any confidence in the fixity of the relation between body and the individual self is soon disrupted when the amorous Ephesian servant Luce claims Dromio of Syracuse as her fiancé on the basis of some "privy marks" on his body – marks that are not exclusively his because they are shared with his twin sibling. Other characters in the play repose trust in material objects – the goldsmith's chain, the courtesan's ring, the rope – whose detachability and transferability render them equally unsuitable as markers of a specific individual (Hopper n.p.). At one stage Adriana suggests that identity is not innate but reflected: she may be married but, if her husband frowns at her and visits prostitutes, she cannot feel like a wife because he does not act as a husband. *Errors* here anticipates the binary of the later *Tempest*, where Prospero can only be ruler of the island as long as there are subjects to rule; he and his slave Caliban are therefore symbiotically dependent on each other for their identities as master and mastered. Cassius points out a similar symbiosis in *Julius Caesar.* Caesar "were no lion, were not Romans hinds" (*JC* 1.3.106). Identities are mutually constitutive (cf. Lanier 1993: 90–101).

Errors does not resolve the difficult questions it poses, for, in the play's last moments, when all confusions have been explained, the twin Dromios cannot even tell themselves apart and have to draw cuts for seniority. This aleatory approach to hierarchy is seriously disruptive in the Elizabethan age, an age which liked to know – and to legislate – an individual's place, and hence social identity, by means of sumptuary legislation. "Sumptuary legislation" is the term given to the legal dress code that structured Elizabethan society: which class of people could wear expensive fabrics, what kind, what color, how much, who could carry a sword, etc. Identity was attached to dress; dress both created and confirmed status. In Marlowe's *Dr. Faustus*, Faustus's transgressive vision of dressing undergraduates in silk indicates his misuse of diabolic power. The rebel leader Jack Cade in *2 Henry VI* is equally anarchic in his plan to erase sartorial distinction: "all the realm shall be in common . . . and I will apparel them all in one livery"

(4.2.68–74). Similarly in the anonymous *Arden of Faversham*, a play written shortly before *Comedy of Errors* and *2 Henry VI*, the protagonist is outraged less by his wife's adultery than by the fact that her lower-class lover, a steward, is wearing a sword, an accessory to which he is not entitled.

Sumptuary legislation was coming unstuck in the 1590s when *Errors* was written. The dissolution of the monasteries in the 1530s, when real estate as we now know it began, had first enabled the *nouveaux riches* to acquire the trappings of inherited wealth: land. (Before the Reformation, England had only three categories of landowner: the crown, the nobility, and the church.) From land to coats of arms; from coats of arms to clothing . . . one challenge led to another as the financially successful refused to be restricted in class status.[1] In 1604 sumptuary legislation was repealed, having proved unable to stem the tide of capitalist individualism and self-creation. Apparel no longer proclaimed the man; identity was malleable. *Errors* extends this contemporary debate, moving from clothing to identity as a whole, asking where it resides and how it might be constructed.

As You Like It (1599–1600)

In *Comedy of Errors* the men travel in search of identity, whether physically like Antipholus of Syracuse or emotionally like Antipholus of Ephesus; the latter visits a prostitute and, on one occasion in the first printed text of the play (the Folio of 1623), is given the agnomen *erraticus* (wandering). The women stay physically at home. In *As You Like It* both the hero and heroine, Orlando and Rosalind, travel to the Forest of Arden.

In fact, Arden is the destination for all the characters. Rosalind's father, Duke Senior, is already in residence, having been banished from court by his usurping brother, Duke Frederick. When Rosalind grows up, she too is banished by Duke Frederick and flees to Arden (in male disguise), accompanied by her cousin Celia and the court clown, Touchstone. In the meantime, Orlando is in danger from his wicked brother, Oliver, and retreats to Arden with his aged retainer, Adam, where for several acts he is entertained by a young man, Ganymede (his beloved Rosalind, unrecognized by him). The villains eventually pursue the innocent to the Forest.

Juliet Stevenson recounts her impression of the play's woodland retreat: "What *is* Arden? Not Epping Forest, that's for sure. . . . Arden is a metaphor,

---

[1] See Duncan-Jones 2001: 82–103 for Shakespeare's attempts to acquire "gentleman" status – and the coat of arms and liveried uniforms that went with it.

a landscape of the imagination and a realm of possibility, a place where gender definitions can be turned on their heads" (Rutter 1988: 97).

Of all Shakespeare's comedies, *As You Like It* is one of the most sensitive to gender. Although Shakespeare heroines often don male disguise for self-protection or plot advancement (Julia in *Two Gentlemen of Verona*, Viola in *Twelfth Night*, Rosalind in *As You Like It*, Imogen in *Cymbeline*, Portia in *Merchant of Venice*), it is unusual to find the hero correspondingly feminized. In *As You Like It* Orlando's first appearance in the Forest of Arden is characterized in feminine fashion: he is a nurturing, maternal figure, caring for and feeding his octogenarian servant, Adam; at one point he carries him in his arms; and the vocabulary depicts Orlando as a "doe," looking after a "fawn" (2.7.1128; Rutter 1988: 105). *Mutatis mutandis*, the exiled Rosalind is in male attire with a "swashing and a martial outside"(1.3.120), and she adopts masculine behavior: she initiates conversations, negotiates finance, and arranges marriage. She enjoys her male attire and the freedom it affords her so much that she retains her disguise long after it has served its practical protective purpose in facilitating her flight with her cousin Celia. In act 1 Celia suggests that she and Rosalind go "to seek my uncle [i.e., Rosalind's father] in the forest of Arden" (1.3.103). This goal is accomplished in act 3, as Rosalind reveals in an incidental remark to Celia: "I met the Duke yesterday and had much question with him. He ask'd me of what parentage I was. I told him of as good as he, so he laugh'd and let me go" (3.4.35–8). Nonetheless, Rosalind retains her male disguise for a further two acts, giving up her masculine identity only because her lover Orlando says he can "live no longer by thinking" (5.2.50).

The experiment with selfhood extends into the epilogue where Rosalind plays with her identity as a female character ("It is not the fashion to see the lady the epilogue"; 1–2) and as a male actor ("If I were a woman I would kiss as many of you as had beards that pleas'd me"; 18–19). Her costume adds a third strand to the epilogue's juggling of gender. It is usually assumed that Rosalind is dressed as a bride – "I am not furnish'd like a beggar, therefore to beg will not become me" (9–11). But not dressed as a beggar does not necessarily mean dressed as a bride. Maura Kuhn points out that Rosalind is probably still costumed as Ganymede (1977: 42).

Unlike Shakespeare's other cross-dressed heroines, Rosalind is never given an opportunity in dialogue to reveal to her future husband that *she* has in fact been a *he*; her educative role in the Forest is thus left unacknowledged. Kuhn suggests that costume here reveals what dialogue does not, Rosalind choosing to wear male costume for her marriage to Orlando.

Juliet Stevenson's view of the play as one that allows characters to experiment with identity is amply borne out.

The personal experimentation with identity is not confined to gender. Rosalind's father, the banished Duke Senior, like the later King Lear, finds that he learns more about himself from exposure to the elements than he does from court life: "these are counsellors / That feelingly persuade me what I am" (2.1.5–11). (Productions often present the courtiers gazing at the Duke in amazement as a Siberian wind bellows around them. The Shenandoah Shakespeare Express production of 1995 presented the opposite extreme: evidently blistering heat, with the courtiers swatting mosquitoes from their faces.) Celia, too, changes. Characterized by her initiative in the court scenes, she is less prominent in the Forest. Whereas in 1.2 Celia was the one to cheer Rosalind, offer suggestions, initiate conversations, and prompt the cousins' flight, in Arden she is more passive. In 4.1, for example, the satirical wooing dialogue between Rosalind/Ganymede and Orlando, she is a silent spectator. Directors have to respond to this by giving Celia something to do during the 175 lines in which Rosalind and Orlando converse. In production Celia sleeps, reads, or less passively (and more comically) tries to retrieve a personal object – her shawl in the 1980 RSC production on which Rosalind and Orlando inadvertently, obliviously, stood and sat.

Even stereotypical villains change in Arden. Orlando's wicked brother, Oliver, needs no more than a therapeutic nap beneath one of the Forest's oak trees to metamorphose from bad to good:

> 'Twas I; but 'tis not I. I do not shame
> To tell you what I was, since my conversion
> So sweetly tastes, being the thing I am. (4.3.135–7)

The usurping Duke Frederick and his ill-intentioned military convoy get no further than the outskirts of the Forest before the Duke decides to become a monk and restore his brother's crown and land. Arden enables all the characters to unearth another part of themselves with surprising rapidity.

Personal exploration is not confined to the main characters. Touchstone the clown, a social inferior at court, (play)acts the urbane gentleman in the Forest. "Holla! you clown!" is how he summons Corin in 2.4.66, only to be reprimanded by Rosalind: "Peace, fool, he's not thy kinsman." (Touchstone uses clown in the sense of "low fellow"; Rosalind quibbles on the meaning "jester.") The rustic Corin is indeed socially inferior to a court clown, but in his repeated rhetorical play with the Forest's shepherds, Corin and William, Touchstone clearly aggrandizes himself. Away from the surveillance of his royal employers, Rosalind and Celia, Touchstone indulges in dazzling displays of pseudo-courtly rhetoric, only to find his adoption of a philosophical self exposed as superficial by Corin's ontological certainty. Unimpressed by Touchstone-as-courtier, and unashamed of his own profession of shepherd, Corin articulates the social and personal coordinates of his own life:

> Sir, I am a true labourer: I earn that I eat, get that I wear, owe no man hate, envy no man's happiness, glad of other men's good, content with my harm, and the greatest of my pride is to see my ewes graze and my lambs suck (3.2.73–7)

The country Corin knows who he is; the court characters have to find out.

In each personal journey, characters try out another part of themselves. (This pattern was aptly summarized in a *Guardian* theater review of *As You Like It* with the punning headline "Hello Jung Lovers.") Having united the male and the female, or the royal and the rustic, or the dominant and the submissive sides of their personalities, the characters take their unified selves back to court. There is still work to be done, for the flight to the Forest was precipitated by a political crisis (Duke Frederick's banishment), not a personal one (Oliver Hayes, personal communication). Nor do the characters totally shed urban values in their pastoral setting, for the first actions of Rosalind and Celia in the Forest are cued by capitalistic instinct: they buy a cottage, pasture, and flock intended for the lovesick shepherd Silvius, and raise Corin's wages. But Shakespeare is not so naive as to present a polarized opposition between court and country. The pastoral world has serpents, literal and metaphorical (Oliver is attacked by a literal one); it has a shepherd "of churlish disposition," Corin's employer, who, like the court villains Oliver and Frederick, "little reaks to find the way to heaven / By doing deeds of hospitality" (2.4.80–2); and it has characters like the narcissistic shepherdess Phebe who lack self-knowledge. The moralizing lament over the carcass of the hunted deer by the cynical courtier Jaques is enough to show that the pastoral world is not unequivocally kind.[2] But Shakespeare is not interested in environment as a repository of transcen-

---

[2] Hunting was not yet a target for animal rights activists, but Shakespeare, like More and Montaigne, seems to be unusual in the early modern period in empathizing with hunted animals. Julius Caesar, Lavinia (in *Titus Andronicus*), and Katherine (in *The Shrew*) are all presented sympathetically as cornered animals.

dental value so much as in how characters interact personally with their environment. With their personal identities in holistic health, the court characters are now equipped to return to their prior existence and cure (or attempt to cure) whatever is rotten in court civilization.

2   Naming the Self

"*As if a man were author of himself*" (*Coriolanus* 5.3.36)

Troilus and Cressida (1602)

Sometimes the self is imposed or inherited rather than discovered. This is unproblematic if the inherited self coincides with the evolved self; but if the two are in conflict the result can only be a divided self: "This is and is not Cressid" (5.2.146).

It always seems to me that one of the problems of being a member of the royal family is that no one is going to say in a tone of surprised admiration, "Our Charlie's done well for himself, hasn't he?" The problem of inheriting a life and identity that is pre-scripted is not confined to royal princes – ask any child of a famous parent, anyone who is expected to follow in a parent's or sibling's professional footsteps, anyone who has felt trapped by society's expectations. It is this problem that Shakespeare dramatizes in *Troilus and Cressida*.

Shakespeare's lovers, Troilus and Cressida, already have an identity outside Shakespeare's play: in Benoît de Sainte Maure's *Roman de Troie* (late twelfth century), in Boccaccio's *Il Filostrato* (ca. 1338), in Chaucer's *Troilus and Criseyde* (1385–7), among others. They and their love story do not exist in the earliest account of the Trojan war, Homer's *Iliad*, although it is likely that medieval authors drew their inspiration for Cressida from Homer's Briseis, the slave girl over whom Achilles and Agamemnon quarrel. Boccaccio named his heroine Criseida, Chaucer expanded the story, and by the time Shakespeare came to write his version in 1602 there were many Renaissance stories and plays about the tragic love story of Troilus and Cressida (none of the plays survive).

Troilus, a prince of the house of Troy, falls in love with Cressida, the daughter of a Trojan who has defected to the Greek camp. Immediately after Troilus and Cressida have pledged mutual love and fidelity, and have consummated their love, Cressida is sent for by her father, and the Trojans willingly exchange her for a military prisoner. Despite her earlier vows of fidelity, Cressida soon yields to the advances of her Greek guard, Diomedes. Consequently, her name becomes a byword for the faithless woman while Troilus's name becomes a synecdoche for the faithful lover. (In *Taming of the Shrew* Petruccio's faithful spaniel is aptly named Troilus.)

As Linda Charnes points out, these ghosts of the faithless and faithful haunt the scene in which Troilus and Cressida pledge themselves to each other. Troilus vows eternal loyalty to Cressida:

> after all comparisons of truth
> (As truth's authentic author to be cited)
> "As true as Troilus" shall crown up the verse. (3.2.180–2)

Cressida likewise vows loyalty, offering her name as a paradigm of infidelity if she should break her word:

> If I be false, or swerve a hair from truth, . . .
> Yea, let them say, to stick the heart of falsehood,
> "As false as Cressid." (3.2.184, 195–6)

This dialogue has a split-screen quality: it looks forward and back. Troilus cannot be the "authentic author" of his love story because his story has already been written (Charnes 1989: 416). Thus as the characters look ahead to the future they wish to inhabit, a future of faith and loyalty and love, the very iteration of their names points back to the already-written associations of Troilus (betrayed lover) and Cressida (faithless woman).

In this play the characters confront an insoluble dilemma. Their love propels them instinctively toward fidelity and romantic happiness. This is what it means to be true to themselves and their desires, to be Cressida in love with Troilus, and Troilus in love with Cressida. But their very names program them with an alternative behavior, a behavior that is at variance with what they themselves want. Their identity as autonomous characters in a Shakespeare play who want to live happily ever after conflicts with their inherited identity as characters whose love ends in betrayal (Charnes 1989: 418). Shakespeare's Cressida can only be herself by not being herself; she can only be Cressida (a faithful lover of Troilus) by not being Cressida (an emblem of infidelity).

Troilus and Cressida are torn apart, individually and as a couple, by the inherited burden of their names. Cressida is characterized, like Antipholus of Syracuse, by images of doubleness and division, although in her case the division refers not to herself and an absent twin but to herself in the play and the historical self whose behavior she resists:

Troilus: What offends you, lady?
Cressida: Sir, mine own company.
Troilus: You cannot shun yourself.
Cressida: Let me go and try.
        I have a kind of self resides with you;
        But an unkind self, that itself will leave
        To be another's fool. (3.2.144–50)

When Troilus later observes Cressida's behavior with Diomedes in the Greek camp, he comments, "This is and is not Cressid" (5.2.146). This is Cressida because it is how Cressida is supposed to behave in the play's sources; this is not Cressida because it does not correspond to the character he knows from acts 3 and 4. Although several Shakespeare plays are aware of the difficulty in finding and being oneself, *Troilus and Cressida* is unusual in presenting this dilemma metatheatrically: that is, the characters are aware of their status as characters in a play (Charnes 1989: 419). The dramatic self confronts the historical self; the individual fights against inheritance, striving for autonomy rather than action replay.

The ways in which names signify is seen in the number of early modern dictionaries and books that include glosses of proper names. The Geneva Bible of 1560 adds "A brief table of the interpretation of the proper names which are chiefly found in the Old Testament" (this "brief table" contains over one thousand personal names). Edward Phillips's *New World of English Words, or A General Dictionary* (1658) adds a list of "*the significations of proper names.*" Names, like words, required explication. We still accord proper names significance, even if we do not table them in dictionaries. The popularity of books of names to give one's baby caters to our interest in etyma. In November 2001 the Brazilian authorities intervened to prevent a father christening his son Osama bin Laden; he had previously been prevented from christening his first son Hitler. Such intervention is a direct acknowledgment of the fact that names carry baggage (some more so than others).

Romeo and Juliet (1595)

Troilus and Cressida is not the first Shakespeare play to juxtapose name with being. In the earlier *Romeo and Juliet* the lovers' patronymics – Montague and Capulet – carry feelings and codes of behavior (hatred, fighting). No longer identifying labels, Montague and Capulet, fetishized into icons of enmity, have become rallying cries to battle. As offspring of feuding families, Romeo and Juliet are expected to continue the feud. This they resolutely refuse to do, rejecting the associations of name ("What's in a name?"; 2.2.43) for an individuality that is entirely independent of family label. While both plays concern the relation between inherited name and the quest for personal identity, *Troilus and Cressida* focuses on behavior whereas *Romeo and Juliet* analyzes language.

We are linguistic beings; the self is rooted in language. When Mowbray is exiled in *Richard II* his anguish centers not on loss of family or friends but of language: "The language I have learnt these forty years, / My native English, now I must forgo, / And now my tongue's use is to me no more / Than an unstringed viol or a harp" (*RII* 1.3.159–62).

Names are a subset of language. One of the first human acts in Genesis is naming, an action whose significance perplexed Renaissance exegetes: did Adam's naming of the animals confer identity, or did it label a preexisting identity? They extended this question about the relation between name and identity to the relation between word and thing: does the word create the thing or vice versa? It is thus impossible to talk of naming without invoking language, and vice versa; indeed, the two subjects are often treated metonymically.

Romeo and Juliet embodies problems specific not to Verona or to sixteenth-century England, to young love or ancient grudge, but to language generally: the relation between word and meaning, and between name and being. It is the lovers' attempt to negotiate an identity independent of family name which leads to Juliet's famous antinominalist soliloquy: "What's in a name?" (2.2.43). "That which we call a rose / By any other word would smell as sweet" she responds to her own question (2.2.43–4). Oscar Wilde satirizes this view in *The Importance of Being Ernest* when Gwendolen declares, "My ideal has always been to love someone of the name of Ernest. There is something in that name that inspires absolute confidence. The moment Algernon first mentioned to me that he had a friend called Ernest, I knew I was destined to love you" (1.394–9).

It is significant that the hero and heroine are nameless when they meet and fall in love (Ryan 1988: 114; Weidhorn 1969: 678); their subsequent identification by family labels brings with it emotional and cultural baggage. As if trying to recreate the liberating and unprejudiced anonymity of their first meeting, Juliet muses on a Romeo who is not a Montague. But her speech is fraught with difficulties because of the extreme nature of her vision which posits a Romeo who is not simply not a Montague but also not a Romeo. Thus she moves from the prejudicial power of the patronymic to the limitations of all labels, and rejects both.

The name of Montague is not problematic *per se*; it is so only because Juliet bears the name of Capulet. Therefore one of the two lovers must relinquish a surname if their love is to be feasible.[3] It is this choice which structures the first few lines of Juliet's soliloquy:

> Deny thy father and refuse thy name;
> Or, if thou wilt not, be but sworn my love,
> And I'll no longer be a Capulet. (2.2.34–6)

However, Juliet's proposed alternative is not the namelessness implied by these lines, but another name. Even as Juliet is disassociating Romeo from Montague ("Thou art thyself, though not a Montague. / What's Montague? It is nor hand nor foot, / Nor arm nor face, nor any other part / Belonging to a man"; 2.2.339–42), even as she is avowing that names are irrelevant ("What's in a name?"), she is also paradoxically asserting their importance ("be some *other* name"; 2.2.42), even as she did in her rhetorical question "wherefore art thou Romeo?" (2.2.33). As Derrida points out (1992: 426), she does not say "Why are you called Romeo?"; she says "'why *are you* Romeo?' . . . his name is his essence." Romeo's response – to tear the written word of Romeo – shows his awareness of this Platonic point: since he is his name, his offer is synonymous with suicide, as his frantic rephrasing of the offer in 3.3 acknowledges:

> In what vile part of this anatomy
> Doth my name lodge? Tell me, that I may sack
> The hateful mansion.
> *Friar.* Hold thy desperate hand! (106–8)

In another play obsessed with names, *Julius Caesar*, the poet Cinna is murdered simply for bearing the same name as Cinna the conspirator:

> *Cinna:* I am not Cinna the conspirator.
> *Fourth Plebeian:* It is no matter, his name's Cinna. *Pluck but his name out of his heart.* (JC 3.3.32–4)

---

[3]   This problem did not exist during Romeo's infatuation with that other Capulet, Rosaline, as courtly love does not move toward marriage.

Problem: to pluck the name out of the heart is to kill the individual. Existence is predicated on a name, any name, as Romeo's statement in the orchard indicates. "Call me but love, and I'll be new baptiz'd" he says (2.2.50), offering to trade one offense-giving name for another. But when Juliet asks who is there, Romeo realizes his predicament: even if he does not call himself Romeo he still has to find some identifying label to answer Juliet's question about who he is (Lucking 1985: 8). Derrida (1992: 427) unpacks the paradox as follows: "Romeo is Romeo, and Romeo is not Romeo . . . [H]e would not be what he is, a stranger to his name, without this name." A similar predicament is faced in contemporary pop music by The Artist Formerly Known as Prince. In the city of Oxford a plaque identifies a street as "Pusey Street (formerly Alfred Street)," and a Bed and Breakfast sign proclaims "Heather House (formerly Hansa Guest House)." Shedding a name is clearly no easier for pop stars and places than it is for Shakespearean heroes.

Dr. Johnson described language as the dress of thought, a motif also employed by Juliet when she begs Romeo "Doff thy name." However, changing language or name is not as simple as changing hats. It signals the relinquishing of cultural memory, identity, history, the past, the familiar, and the crossing of tribal boundaries. Romeo and Juliet are prepared to give up such inherited identities in exogamous marriage, but their kinsmen are not. Arthur Brooke's long poem, *Romeus and Juliet* (Shakespeare's primary source for this tragedy), concludes by assigning punishments. Shakespeare's conclusion focuses on language: "Go hence to have more *talk* of these sad things; / Some shall be pardon'd, and some punished / For never was a *story* of more woe / Than this of Juliet and her Romeo" (5.3.307–10). The couple's marriage and tragic deaths will be translated into narrative.

In comedy, narrative is not a problem. Even in its most shorthand form, as in the reduction of Marina's life in *Pericles* to three nouns (a tempest, a birth, a death; 5.3.33–4), language is never problematic, and names unite families as quickly and easily as in *Romeo and Juliet* they divide them: "Is it no more to be your daughter than / To say my mother's name was Thaisa?" asks Pericles's daughter, Marina, as she is united with her long-lost father (5.1.209–10).

In tragedy language is dangerous, and equivocation undoes us. To Cordelia in *King Lear* "nothing" is a declaration of honesty, to Lear an instance of ingratitude. For Desdemona in *Othello* insistent questions about Cassio's reinstatement represent connubial intimacy, for Othello marital infidelity. In *Hamlet* stable family relationships collapse linguistically (the marriage of Hamlet's mother to his uncle makes Gertrude an "aunt-mother," her new husband an "uncle-father") just as in *Romeo and Juliet* "my only hate" becomes "my only love."

It may seem disconcerting then that *Romeo and Juliet* gives the last word to language but, as the grieving families prepare for narrative at the end of 5.3, the play registers a new civic attitude to names. "For never was a story of more woe / Than this of *Juliet* and her *Romeo*" says Escalus (5.3.309–10), identifying the young couple not patronymically as Capulet or Montague but as persons independent of family. The personal name still signifies, of course – Juliet means a woman born in July (she was born on "Lammas Eve" – July 31 – her Nurse tells us), Romeo means a pilgrim – but the signification is local and individual rather than historical and multiple. A play that began with "two households" ends positively (given the baggage attached to the two households) with two individuals. In this concluding focus on the personal rather than the patronymic, Verona takes a step closer to recognizing individuals rather than feuding tribes.

Taming of the Shrew (1590–1)

If Romeo and Juliet find selfhood to be independent of name, Katherine in *Taming of the Shrew* displays her selfhood by insisting on retaining her name. Katherine has a reputation as a "shrew," the label the Renaissance gave to any woman who talked too much. (Frances Dolan notes, incidentally, that there is no equivalent term for a man who talks too much; male speech is not a crime.) Petruccio, attracted to Katherine's dowry, and perhaps also to the challenge she represents, determines to woo her.

Petruccio's unorthodox tactic is to disorient Katherine by opposing everything she says and does:

> Say that she rail, why then I'll tell her plain
> She sings as sweetly as a nightingale;
> Say that she frown, I'll say she looks as clear
> As morning roses newly wash'd with dew. (2.1.170–3)

If she is silent, he will praise her "piercing eloquence" (2.1.176); if she rejects him, he will act "as though she bid me stay by her a week" (2.1.178). When Petruccio meets Katherine he proceeds rhetorically as planned, countering her shrewish reputation by claiming he has heard her praised for mildness and obedience.

The tactic is familiar in the psychology of behavior modification. It is a standard weapon in the arsenal of the parent or nursery teacher. "Who's the good boy/girl who wants to help me tidy the toys?" is more likely to elicit cooperation than the same request phrased as a command; the desire to match the description encourages the child to alter his/her behavior. Similarly, psychologists argue, Katherine will grow to match the praiseworthy woman Petruccio describes: "thy mildness prais'd in every town, / Thy virtues spoke of" (2.1.191–2). (This rhetorical ploy contrasts with that of his literary predecessors in shrew-taming who resort to physical violence.)

Petruccio's first linguistic tactic, however, is one he has not advertised: he renames Katherine. "Good morrow, Kate, for that's your name, I hear" (2.1.182). Katherine immediately corrects him, perhaps seeing in the diminutive an attempt to diminish her, perhaps feeling (understandably) defensive about her name: "They call me Katherine that do talk of me" (2.1.184). Undaunted, Petruccio bombards Katherine with her new name:

> You lie, in faith, for you are call'd plain Kate,
> And bonny Kate, and sometimes Kate the curst;
> But Kate, the prettiest Kate in Christendom,
> Kate of Kate-Hall, my super-dainty Kate,
> For dainties are all Kates, and therefore, Kate,
> Take this of me, Kate of my consolation – (2.1.191–4)

Petruccio here offers Katherine an alternative reality but whether the gesture represents a creative opportunity or sadistic oppression is debatable. Is he offering her a new identity or asserting his control over the old one? If the former, may that not equally be a form of control, challenging and overriding her autonomy? What is clear is that Katherine resists his revision, insisting on her name, her identity, on her way of being and seeing.

Relabeling someone without their invitation or agreement is a powerful statement, as the Bastard realizes in *King John* when he fantasizes about the social power to hurt which attends his elevation: "and if his name be George, I'll call him Peter; / For new-made honor doth forget men's names" (*KJ* 1.1.186–7). In *Henry V*, when Henry goes through a pro forma wooing scene with the French princess whose country he has just conquered, he addresses her unexpectedly as Kate; as invader and conqueror he can remake a nation, individuals, and names. *The Shrew's* Katherine, however, has her full name – and thus the independent identity associated with it? – restored to her on three occasions, all of them in scenes of apparent wifely submission.

On the road from Verona to Padua Petruccio willfully calls the sun the moon. Katherine corrects him. Asserting imperiously that it "shall be moon, or star, or what I list" (4.5.7), Petruccio prepares to return to Verona. Their traveling companion, Hortensio, advises Katherine to humor Petruccio: "Say as he says, or we shall never go" (4.5.11). Katherine now yields.

In performance Katherine's acquiescence often follows a moment's hesitation in which she assesses the situation and clearly decides to beat Petruccio at his own game. Certainly, she yields in terms so exaggerated as to suggest competitive playing: "be it moon, or sun, or what you please; / *And if you please to call it a rush-candle*, / Henceforth I vow it shall be so for me" (4.5.13–15). Petruccio quickly tests her, calling the sun the moon (Katherine agrees) and then the sun (Katherine agrees again). Again, her vocabulary is hyperbolic – if Petruccio says it is the moon, Katherine *knows* it is the moon. Her subsequent acknowledgment that Petruccio's mind is as changeable as the moon leads to her agreement that he can rename anything he wants.

However, the speech in which Katherine gives Petruccio this power slyly reasserts her preferred version of her name:

> What you will have it nam'd, even that it is,
> And so [therefore] it shall be so [thus] for *Katherine* (4.5.21–2)

This fluctuation in name should alert us to the possibility of Petruccio's bona fides in act 5 when he asks his wife to demonstrate uxorial obedience. He asks Katherine to display her new identity as an obedient wife (the non-shrewish "Kate" persona) but addresses her by the label associated with her old, independent identity, Katherine:

> Katherine, that cap of yours becomes you not;
> Off with that bable [bauble], throw it under-foot. (5.2.121–2)

> Katherine, I charge thee tell these headstrong women
> What duty they do owe their lords and husbands. (5.2.130–1)

The unexpected double reappearance of Katherine indicates that Katherine's identity is not extinguished in marriage, nor does Petruccio wish it to be. The dutiful "Kate" and the independent "Katherine" can coexist.

This conclusion is in accord with Petruccio's earlier avowed intent, as revealed in a soliloquy which describes his tactics: "And thus I'll curb her mad and headstrong humour" (4.1.209). "Curb" is the crucial word, for the plan is to restrain his wife, not to break her. Although the speech is structured round falcon-taming imagery (Petruccio's wife-taming tactics – sleep deprivation, starvation, disorientation – come from the world of falcon-taming), the verb "curb" belongs to the world of horse-training. The vocabulary of horse-training influenced that of wife-taming (Hartwig 1982; Roberts 1983; Wayne 1985). Wives, like horses, had to be broken in ("paced") and taught to respond to signals ("obey the manage"); in *Pericles* the Bawd explains to Lysimachus that the sexually uncooperative virgin Marina "is not pac'd yet, you must take some pains to work her to your manage" (4.6.63–4). Part of Katherine's erotic appeal must surely have been her wildness, and critics maintain that no man, then or now, would want to destroy this. Coppélia Kahn (1981: 117) speaks about "the most cherished male fantasy of all – that woman remain *un*tamed."

Margaret Loftus Ranald (1974: 153) makes a similar point in the context of *The Shrew*'s falcon-taming imagery:

> The falcon must be taught obedience to her master, but at the same time her wild and soaring nature must be preserved. This is a cardinal principle of hawk-taming. The bird must retain her hunting instinct; otherwise she is useless. But she must be taught to exercise her wild nature on command, to hunt under the government of her keeper/master.

Falcons can be trained; they cannot be tamed. And Katherine is not tamed, at least not in the sense made popular by shrew-taming tradition in which taming leads to extinction of identity. She conforms to a social norm for the sake of appearance, while retaining her own persona in private.

This point is made by Linda Bamber and Coppélia Kahn, neither of whom is happy with it. "Kate's compromise is distressing," writes Bamber (1982: 35); "Kate . . . is trapped in her own cleverness. Her only way of maintaining her inner freedom is by outwardly denying it, a psychologically perilous position," laments Kahn (1981: 113). We will consider these objections, and Katherine's potentially Pyrrhic victory, in chapter 2, but for now it suffices to note that Bamber and Kahn regularly deny Katherine her most basic request: her full name. Given the relation between name and identity, a play that ends with a husband addressing his wife as

"Katherine" bodes well for the heroine's retention of her own identity within marriage.

3   The Self and Language

"Language most shows a man: speak that I may see thee" (Jonson 1947: 625)

Measure for Measure (1603–4)

Isabella's language in *Measure for Measure* reflects both her personal spiritual commitment and her professional status as a nun (the former leads to the latter). Her lexicon is theological (grace, mercy, forgiveness, heaven), as are her thoughts: her analogies and references are to forfeited souls, martyrs' wounds, Christ's passion. When she is asked to plead a point of law with Vienna's acting governor, Angelo, her instinct is not to negotiate legal niceties but to appeal to Angelo's mercy, to awaken his Christ-like capacity to forgive. Isabella has only one language, and this language reveals her principles, her morals, her faith: in other words, who she is. No other Shakespearean character so clearly illustrates Jonson's equation between language and identity, above.

Isabella is sent to Angelo to beg for her brother's life. The situation is, in one respect, straightforward. Isabella's brother, Claudio, has fallen foul of a newly resurrected law which condemns lechery. But Claudio is not a lecher. He is what the Renaissance recognized as a married man and what we know as an engaged man. The Elizabethans had two or three stages of marriage: a promise in front of witnesses, a religious ceremony, and sexual consummation. Stages one and two could be combined, making the witnessed promise in church. Claudio and his fiancée Juliet have performed the first and third stages. As Claudio explains, they have delayed the church ceremony until they can win the support of Juliet's family (1.2.149–53). Technically, then, they should also have delayed consummation. The public promise is, however, legally binding. Claudio is no more a lecher than is any man who makes love to his lawful wedded wife, although a rigid interpreter of the law might judge otherwise, as has Angelo.

Angelo's judgment could easily be challenged; Claudio's case invites a debate about legal interpretation. But Isabella is no Portia. After a hesitant beginning in which she attempts a sophistical distinction – "Condemn the fault, and not the actor of it" – she admits defeat and is ready to exit

(2.2.42). Angelo has been curt and unencouraging (in the 1991 RSC production David Suchet opened his mail, only half attending to Isabella). But
then she recovers and tries to persuade Angelo in the only language she
knows: the language of theology. Pardon, mercy, remorse, mercy, God,
mercy, pity, merciful heaven follow in quick succession, and her sentences
grow in length and confidence. She is on familiar territory. Affected by the
passion of the girl, Angelo asks her to return the next morning.

In the second interview, Angelo introduces a new topic, presented as a
question: "Which had you rather, that the most just law / Now took your
brother's life, or, to redeem him, / Give up your body to such sweet unclean-
ness / As she that he hath stain'd?" (2.4.52–5). Isabella evades the question
of life versus body by introducing a third term, soul – "I had rather give
my body than my soul." There is clear exasperation in Angelo's response,
"I talk not of your soul" (2.4.57). Angelo suspects guile (2.4.74–5) but
Isabella's spiritual monolingualism is genuine. When Angelo indirectly suggests sex, she responds in bewilderment: "I have no tongue but one; gentle
my lord, / Let me entreat you speak the former language" (2.4.139–40). The
language she speaks is the language of mercy; she enters a legal situation
from a spiritual point of view.

The position is reversed, however, in the dénouement of act 5 when
Vienna's Duke asks Isabella to beg for Angelo's life – for the man who, she
believes, killed her brother and who attempted to seduce her (Angelo
believes he succeeded in the seduction but, in fact, his abandoned fiancée,
Mariana, substituted for Isabella in bed). Isabella's short argument
(11 lines) is entirely legal. Angelo meant well until he saw Isabella;
Claudio actually committed the sexual fault for which he died; Angelo
didn't (even if he thought he did); you can't punish someone for his
thoughts.[4] I do not recognize this voice of Isabella. The distinctive passion
of her faith is gone, and an opportunity to wax lyrical about mercy is
missed (Riefer 1984: 166).

The reason for this change, as Marcia Riefer observes (1984: 164–5, 168),
is the Duke, who interferes with Isabella's character in a manner as nefar-

---

[4]   In Sir Thomas More's ideal society, however, the Utopians do punish thought crime. "A
man who tries to seduce a woman is subject to the same penalties as if he had actually done
it. They think that a crime attempted is as bad as one committed, and that failure should not
confer advantages on a criminal who did all he could to succeed" (More 1978: 68). The gods
in *Pericles* act in the same way, killing Cleon and Dionyza for the intended murder of Marina,
as Gower explains: "The gods for murder seemed so content / To punish, although not done,
but meant" (5.3.99–100).

ious – and for reasons as selfish – as Angelo's attempts to interfere with her body. He plans Isabella's actions, directs her movements, withholds information (of Claudio's survival) from her; he tests her by making her beg for Angelo; he humiliates her by making her confess publicly to violation by Angelo (even though Mariana took her place). Isabella complies with all his plots, despite her reservations ("To speak so indirectly I am loath. / I would say the truth"; 4.6.1–2), because of his status: a figure of (apparent) religious authority. But his authority is directed, like Angelo's, to his own ends: he proposes to Isabella. Isabella's loss of voice is both personal (legalese usurps theology) and literal (she does not reply to the Duke's proposal). Her loss illustrates the threat to female individuality in a world ruled by strong but flawed men.

Troilus and Cressida (1602)

We are linguistic beings, as nominalist narratives such as Genesis and psychoanalytic authors such as Lacan remind us. Formed in and by language, defined in and by speech, we can therefore be injured by words. "Sticks and stones may break my bones / But words will never hurt me," asserts the children's playground chant, defiantly but erroneously. Quite simply, words wound. Hence censorship (in both early modern and contemporary society); hence the category of "verbal abuse"; hence Supreme Court action against racist speech, hate speech, "fighting speech." In *Troilus and Cressida* the scenes between men and women (Helen, Cressida, Cassandra, Andromache) illustrate a number of different ways in which speech can wound.

To readers of Greek drama, Hector, Trojan warrior-hero *par excellence*, is equally famous for his domestic role as beloved husband of Andromache. In *Troilus and Cressida* 1.2 we are offered a glimpse of Hector's private life, but it is a picture of masculine power and petulant temper rather than marital bliss. Cressida's servant Alexander reveals that the usually patient Hector was moved to anger because Ajax had defeated him in the previous day's battle. Hector's anger manifests itself as violence: "he chid Andromache and strook his armorer" (1.2.6). Verbal violence is directed at his wife, physical violence at the servant; but both are social subordinates, Hector's property, and we know from plays like *Taming of the Shrew* that violence directed at a servant functions as a reminder to the wife that "she, too, is his [the husband's] subordinate and that he could beat her if he chose" (Dolan 1996: 19). Nor, despite Alexander's depiction of Hector as an exemplar of patience, is this an isolated example of ill-temper. Act 5, scene 3 opens with Hector's brusque response to Andromache's petition that he unarm and shun combat: he orders her inside (5.3.4) and tells her to be quiet (5.3.7). David Bevington (1998: 32) speculates, not unreasonably, that Andromache leaves the scene in tears. Hector's peremptory verbal domination not only reflects social control, it "enacts it, becoming the vehicle through which that social structure is reinstated" (Butler 1997: 18).

Cressida, as we will see in detail in chapter 2, is similarly controlled by anger, whether by the explosions of her camp-guard, Diomedes, or by Troilus's admonitions and reprimands. She is also used to being verbally humiliated if her uncle Pandarus's conversation is any gauge: he talks about his niece and addresses her directly as "it," a pronoun used for children (3.2.33; 4.2.32–3), confronts her bluntly about sexual activity (4.2.23–4, 31–3), and tries to maneuver her into articulating sexual vocabulary (4.2.27–8). Although Cassandra is dismissed and ignored, her situation illuminates by its stark contrast Cressida's acceptance of verbal mistreatment, for, if we are constituted in language, derogation is preferable to "not being addressed at all" (Butler 1997: 27).

The languorous scene between Helen of Troy and her captor-seducer, Paris, in act 3, scene 1 is often dismissed as an example of Helen's frivolity, idleness, and disregard for the war conducted in her name. However, it seems an example of linguistic health when compared to the other male – female relationships and communications in the play. Paris, unlike Hector, listens and responds to his "wife": "I would fain have arm'd today, but my Nell would not have it so" (3.1.136 – 7). His homely use of the diminutive "Nell" here and at line 52 is in marked contrast to the other characters' talk of Helen and helps explain her interest in him: for Paris, Helen is a real-life woman, not an icon of beauty, not a disembodied "theme of honor," not an adjunct (or loss) representing sufficient (or inadequate) manhood (cf. Bevington 1998: 29). The couple *converse*: Paris shares a joke with Helen (3.1.52–3); they assess Pandarus's mood (3.1.127–30); Helen volunteers information in response to Paris's general question about Troilus (3.1.137–40); Helen compliments Paris (3.1.99–100), and he compliments her (3.1.150–4).

Paris's mode of address to Helen is permissive and petitionary rather than peremptory: "*Let us* to Priam's hall . . . / Sweet Helen, *I must woo you* / To help unarm our Hector" (3.1.148, 149–50). Given his position in Troy as Helen's lord, he might put his requests more into command than entreaty – as do Hector, Troilus, and Diomedes. Instead, we have a scene of conversational give-and-take remarkable in the play for its straightforward honesty. Stage productions offer many variants on this scene: indolence, love, foreplay, selfishness, hypocrisy (Paris does not fight in the war he began); a scene of conversation between Helen and Paris interrupted by Pandarus; a scene of conversation between Paris and Pandarus interrupted by Helen; a public scene; a private scene (in the 1996–7 RSC production, Helen and Paris entered naked from a Turkish bath).

Paris's concluding expression of love – "Sweet, above thought I love thee!" (3.1.159) – seems a "thank you" to Helen for her elegant speech at 3.1.155–8. Helen's speech is dutiful and would not be out of place in *Taming of the Shrew* – she believes a woman derives more beauty from dutiful service to a lord than from her physical appearance – but Paris's response shows that he does not take such statements for granted. The prince whose action prompted the Trojan war (his "rape" of Helen being abduction and perhaps also sexual violation) is presented by Shakespeare as the most verbally sensitive partner in the play.

In act 5 Troilus dismisses a letter from Cressida as "words, words, mere words" (5.3.108). The play, however, reveals that there is no such thing as a "mere" word. Words hurt emotionally. Injurious language enacts power relations as well as reflects them.

4   The National Self

"*What ish my nation?*" (*HV* 3.2.122)

Othello (1604)

The title of *Othello, the Moor of Venice* is an oxymoron: Moors do not come from Venice. Othello is a North African, who, as a resident of Venice, has only a partially Venetian identity. His martial expertise has given him both military and social prestige in Venice. He is invited to dine with senators and their families, he is the one to whom the Duke turns when Venice is under threat from the Turks, the one who is sent to Cyprus to thwart the Turkish invasion, the one in whom Venice reposes trust. Thus, Othello is securely and happily the Moor *in* Venice. That he can never be the Moor *of* Venice is brought home by Brabantio's reaction in the first scene to the news of Othello's secret marriage to Brabantio's daughter: "it is too true an evil" (1.1.160).

Brabantio's outrage, provoked by Iago's visually salacious images of difference ("an old black ram / Is tupping your white ewe"; 1.1.88–9) culminates in a complaint to the Duke. Like Egeus in *Midsummer Night's Dream* who can only explain his daughter's choice of husband by assuming she has been bewitched, Brabantio accuses Othello of employing magic. When Othello's magic charms prove to be none other than romantic eloquence, when Desdemona reveals that she was "half the wooer," and when the Duke admits that he himself would be proud of Othello as a son-in-law, Brabantio is defeated and rejects both Desdemona and Othello. Although Brabantio had admired Othello as a military leader, had entertained him regularly in his household and had trusted him alone with his daughter, he is now shown to be blinkered by a particularly complex form of racism, the kind that says "you can defend our state but you can't marry our daughters." Happily, the Duke sees beyond skin color, pointing out to Brabantio that Othello's "virtues" make him "far more fair than black" (1.3.290), and Desdemona reveals that she saw Othello's "visage in his mind" (1.3.252). Brabantio nonetheless remains unreconciled to his daughter's choice of husband.

The Elizabethans inherited from the middle ages an iconographic color-coding which equated black skin with the devil and hence with moral blackness (because God was light). In medieval plays the devil was portrayed as black (a stage effect achieved by soot, or, less messily, a black face stocking) and in the Elizabethan printing house the printer's assistant, covered in ink dust, was known familiarly as the "printer's devil." Black became a metaphor for evil, as in *Henry VIII* where the Chamberlain says of Cardinal Wolsey, "No doubt he's noble. / He had a black mouth that said other of him" (1.3.57–8). The Renaissance understood two categories of Moors. Tawny or "white" Moors were North Africans, like the Prince of Morocco who woos Portia in *Merchant of Venice*; "black" moors or black-amoors, with ebony skin, came from the south and west of Africa. With their predilection for theological symbolism the Elizabethans had little choice in the way they viewed these two groups of Moors. Tawny Moors, like the Prince of Morocco (dressed symbolically in white), were noble. Black Moors were lascivious, jealous, and villainous. Aaron the Moor in *Titus Andronicus* proudly lists his nefarious achievements, concluding "I have done a thousand dreadful things, . . . And nothing grieves me heartily indeed, / But that I cannot do ten thousand more" (5.1.141–3).

Iago talks about Othello as if he were a blackamoor: he is a sexually active "black ram," with a "sooty bosom" and "thick lips" (1.1.88; 1.2.70;

1.1.66. These descriptions presumably influenced Laurence Olivier's film interpretation in 1964). But there is a discrepancy between Iago's rhetoric and Othello's appearance. Othello is calm, dignified, noble in speech and behavior; he specifically counters lascivious stereotypes by explaining that his advancing years have reduced his interest in sexual intercourse. By the end of the play, however, Othello feels passionate sexual jealousy, commits barbaric violence, and speaks in a syntax which is reduced to expostulation ("Goats and monkeys"; 4.1.263) and which loses all grammatical structure ("Handkerchief – confessions – handkerchief"; 4.1.37). His behavior is now closer to that associated with the barbaric blackamoor than with the civilized Venetian. Iago's triumph is to break down the Venetian half of Othello's identity, making Othello match the earlier stereotypical description.

Othello's outsider position relates to more than variant skin color. Othello is doubly "Other" because of color and non-Venetian origin. The problem is not that he is a Moor but that he is not a Venetian. This makes him vulnerable to Iago's manipulations. Iago assures his general that, unlike Iago, he does not understand Venetian women. Venetian women, Iago says, are sexually cavalier:

> I know our country disposition well.
> In Venice they do let God see the pranks
> They dare not show their husbands; their best conscience
> Is not to leave't undone, but keep't unknown. (3.3.2001–4)

These generalizations are representative of contemporary Elizabethan attitudes: Venetian wives had a reputation for licentiousness (Ranald 1987: 147).

To complicate matters further, Othello is an older man, "declin'd / Into the vale of years" (3.3.265–6) married to a younger woman. Thus, Othello is triply insecure. He has a white wife; hence he feels insecure because he lacks civic social skills: "I am black, / And have not those soft parts of conversation / That chamberers [gallants] have" (3.3.263–5). He has a Venetian wife; hence it is easy for him to believe Iago when the latter insists that Venetian customs are unknown to him. He has a younger wife; hence it is easy for him to believe that his wife might ultimately prefer the youthful Cassio as a sexual partner. Certainly Roderigo is convinced that "she must change for youth" (1.3.349–50).

The play approves Desdemona's choice of the black Othello as husband by showing us the inadequacies of the white Venetian alternatives: the

Plate 1 This portrait of the Moorish Ambassador to Queen Elizabeth I (1600) bears little resemblance to Iago's deliberately misleading description of Othello, the Moor of Venice. Nonetheless, Iago's stereotypical description of a blackamoor influences most stage and film representations of Othello.

lovesick Roderigo is a gull, and Cassio, for all his charm, is someone who deifies Desdemona but who belittles Bianca, the woman with whom he sups and sleeps. Cassio's heroine-worship of Desdemona is evident early on. He describes Desdemona hyperbolically as "a maid / That paragons description and wild fame; / One that excels the quirks of blazoning pens, / And in th'essential vesture of creation / Does tire the ingener" (2.1.61–5); when she lands in Cyprus he enthuses, "The riches of the ship is come on shore!" (2.1.83). In a conversation between Cassio and Iago the latter attempts to steer the lieutenant into irreverent locker-room talk, which Cassio consistently resists:

> *Cassio*: Welcome, Iago; we must to the watch.
> *Iago*: Not this hour, lieutenant; 'tis not yet ten o'th' clock. Our general cast [dismissed] us thus early for the love of his Desdemona; who let us not therefore blame. He hath not yet made wanton the night with her; and she is sport for Jove.
> *Cassio*: She's a most exquisite lady.
> *Iago*: And I'll warrant her, full of game.
> *Cassio*: Indeed she's a most fresh and delicate creature.
> *Iago*: What an eye she has! Methinks it sounds a parley to provocation.
> *Cassio*: An inviting eye; and yet methinks right modest.
> *Iago*: And when she speaks, is it not an alarum to love?
> *Cassio*: She is indeed perfection. (2.3.12–26)

In the 1989 RSC production, this scene took place in the officers' mess with Ian McKellen's Iago indulging in the verbal equivalent of reading *Playboy*.

Cassio's attitude to his girlfriend, Bianca, is less respectful than his attitude to Desdemona. Although the text identifies Bianca in stage directions and speech prefixes as a courtesan, the Renaissance used this noun to label a woman who lost her virginity to a boyfriend as well as one who is paid for professional sexual favors (Wayne 1998: 192). Despite the fact that Cassio and Iago talk about her as if she belongs to the latter category, I think Bianca comes into the former: she waits for Cassio to come home for dinner; she embroiders for him; and she distinguishes herself from Cassio's "hobbyhorse" [prostitute]. However, Cassio describes her as a "bauble" [a plaything] at 4.1.135, and when she exits the scene in distress, his instinct is simply to shut her up:

> *Iago*: After her, after her.
> *Cassio*: Faith, I must, she'll rail in the streets else. (4.1.162–3)

Plate 2 Carreño de Miranda, *Santiago en la batalla de Clavijo*. Iconographic tradition depicts Santiago (St. James), the patron saint of Spain, during his greatest triumph: conquering the Moors. The name of Shakespeare's Iago means that his identity is inextricably bound up with the extinction of Othello, the Moor.

Like Othello he silences an innocent woman (we note that, in one of the play's many twists on color, her name, Bianca, means white). Thus, erroneous and extreme racial stereotypes (black = bad, white = good) are paralleled by erroneous and extreme gender stereotypes (women are either goddesses – Desdemona – or whores – Bianca).

In the nineteenth century Coleridge inaugurated an influential critical tradition when he described Iago as suffering from "motiveless malignancy"; that is, his evil does not have any specific cause or aim. But racism is its own origin and its own destination. That Iago's self is a racist self is seen in the associations of his name: Moor-hater or Moor-conqueror. Santiago (Saint Iago or St. James) is the military patron of Spain. One of his most famous exploits occurred in 939 CE when he helped King Ramirez deliver Castile from the Moors, killing 60,000 Moors in battle. Consequently "Santiago" became the war-cry of the Spanish armies, and Santiago is traditionally depicted on a white charger trampling the Moors underfoot.

Shakespeare's Iago targets not just the black but the non-Venetian. Cassio is denigrated as a "Florentine" (1.1.20), whereas Roderigo is valued as Iago's "countryman" (5.1.89). Iago hates all racial Others. His racism affects all Venice, causing social categories to disintegrate – father, husband, wife, lieutenant, general, governor. Robert N. Watson argues (1990: 339–40) that Iago's tactic is to annihilate both personal name and position: "Brabantio declares in anguish he no longer has a daughter, Cassio that he has lost his name and rank, Desdemona that she has lost her lord, and Othello that his occupation is gone, that he has no wife, and finally that he is no longer 'Othello.'" Racism leads to the destruction of identities beyond that of the outsider and to an assault on the society of which he is a fully functioning part.

King Lear (1605–6)

If Othello's identity is stripped away, so too is King Lear's. If Othello's identity is attacked in an adopted city-state, Lear's is stripped away on home territory. As in *Othello*, identity is analyzed in relation to nation and nationality.

"He hath ever but slenderly known himself" is the opinion of one of Lear's daughters (1.1.294) and her comment about her father is borne out by Lear's behavior in act 1. He fails to see that the exaggerated protestations of love for him voiced by his eldest daughters, Goneril and Regan, are insincere, and that the tongue-tied love of Cordelia, his youngest, conceals (and so reveals) true emotion. He fails to realize that one cannot give away the responsibilities of rulership and yet retain the title of king. And he fails to recognize that dividing a kingdom in three is a recipe for political disaster. The Renaissance audience had watched the rebels in *1 Henry IV* try to divide their kingdom in three just a few years before. Although the scene in *1 Henry IV* is full of exaggeratedly comic incompetence, it is impossible to imagine a sixteenth-century audience not taking it seriously given that the memory of civil war was so recent. For a king to initiate territorial division would be even more alarming.

Lear's poor judgments – staging a love-test among his daughters, dividing his kingdom, taking partial early retirement – have disastrous consequences for his family (some of which are discussed at greater length in chapter 5), and the first acts are full of blows to Lear's parental identity. In 1.4 he asks Goneril incredulously: "Are you our daughter?" (line 218). A few lines later incredulity increases to sarcasm – "I should be false persuaded / I had daughters" (1.4.233–4) – which Alice Walker glosses as "Am I your father?" (1953: 65). Identity is under threat.

As Lear moves closer to finding himself, he moves further from the court. By act 3 he is homeless, Regan having, in effect, denied him entrance to Gloucester's castle by denying entry to his knights; his entourage has been reduced from 100 to 0; he has stripped himself bare ("Off, off, you lendings"; 3.4.108). He is assaulted by the elements, welcoming them for the same reason as Duke Senior in *As You Like It*: they do not flatter, they "feelingly persuade me what I am" (*AYLI* 2.1.11). He is now close to poor Tom, the mad beggar he meets in the hovel: "the thing itself: unaccommodated man" (3.4.106–7). Thus reduced, he can begin to investigate the essentials of human nature. The question "Who is it that can tell me who I am?" (1.4.230) may be answerable.

Because he is a king, Lear's personal journey is also a national journey (history is what we make of our geography). Lear is one of the ancient kings of Britain, descended from the legendary Brute; his search for his own identity parallels Britain's search for its origin as a nation.

The sixteenth and seventeenth centuries were a period of significant achievements and advances in mapmaking (Gillies 1994; Mikalachki 1998). World maps had existed since the middle ages, but they were theological symbols not geographic representations: Jerusalem was at the center, Paradise at the top. Sixteenth-century England developed an interest in more detailed maps of smaller geographic units: English counties. In 1574 Christopher Saxton was commissioned to survey all the counties of

England and Wales and to provide detailed maps of them, a project he completed in 1579. The maps distinguished landscape (forests, rivers). Symbols were used: steeples and weather vanes for cities; sea-monsters and water-spouts for oceans; Aeolian gargoyles with puffed cheeks to indicate wind. So popular was the new cartography that maps were woven into tapestries, painted in the backgrounds of portraits, and printed on playing-cards (Morgan 1979: 150–3; Mikalachki n.p.).

Lear's journey in self-discovery is that of the mapmaker. He leaves the comfort of court and explores the land. As Mikalachki notes, Lear's wanderings trace the triangular shape of Britain, from Goneril and Albany in the north, to Regan and Cornwall in the southwest, to Dover in the east. Lear's anguished speech on the heath as he is buffeted by the storm comes from the language of cartography (Mikalachki 1998: 89):

> Blow, winds, and crack your cheeks! [Lear addresses the wind gods who decorated the borders of maps] rage, blow!
> You cataracts [the waterspouts of maps' sea-monsters] and hurricanoes, spout
> Till you have drench'd our steeples, drown'd the cocks! [the steeples and windcocks which are cartographic icons for cities]
> You sulph'rous and thought-executing fires,
> Vaunt-couriers of oak-cleaving thunderbolts,
> Singe my white head! And thou, all-shaking thunder,
> Strike flat [make one-dimensional; turn into a map] the thick rotundity [the three-dimensional globe] o' th' world! (3.2.1–7)

In getting to know his land – in experiencing its wild heath rather than its cartographic representation, its storms rather than their ornamental depictions – Lear is getting to know himself, not just as a human but as a Briton.

But Lear's encounter with the elements is not just local. His experience of deluging rain, and his attempt to divide his kingdom among his three children, replays the experience of an Old Testament ruler, Noah. In turn Noah's experience parallels that of Utnapishtim in the Babylonian epic *Gilgamesh*, of the Greek Deucalion, and of the hero in two separate Sumerian myths. These stories may share a common origin in some historical disaster (the flooding of the Tigris–Euphrates plain has been suggested). Seasonal flooding was a regular occurrence in the ancient Near East and is understandably allied to myths of origin. In Genesis the story of Noah offers a second creation narrative. God realizes His mistakes and begins again; the second creation inverts the first (the earth is covered with water rather than created from formlessness); Noah becomes a second Adam, commanded to "be fruitful and multiply" (Bowker 1998: 33; Davis 1998: 62, 64).

It is impossible to overestimate the importance of Genesis to the Renaissance mind: Genesis represented the beginning not just of the Bible (the first book of Moses), but of agriculture, domestic relations, political science, philosophy, law, history, geography, language. Adam was the first gardener, farmer, logothete, husband, father, negotiator, thinker; Nimrod was the first monarch, Noah the first vintner, Moses the first author, poet, historian, philosopher, astronomer, and Rebecca or Rachel the first dutiful wife (Williams 1948: 1–2). Renaissance histories of the world (those of Grafton and Ralegh, for example) begin with Genesis; Renaissance geographers plot the location of Paradise; Renaissance poets from Du Bartas to Milton turn to Genesis for inspiration in hexameron or theodicy. And Shakespeare's *King Lear*, a play about historical origins and geography, is, as Fred Flahiff reminds us (1986: 25), indebted to Genesis. Noah's history is Britain's history because British monarchs traced their ancestry to Noah; "Britain's history began when, after a great flood, an old man, the world's 'first Monarch,' called together his three children and divided the known world among them."

Theologians point out that, despite its narrative appeal, Genesis is hermeneutically one of the most difficult books of the Bible. Renaissance exegetes rose to the challenge: over forty commentaries on Genesis, ranging from three hundred to one thousand pages, in English and in Latin, were printed between 1525 and 1633. Arnold Williams (1948: 31) assesses these commentaries and their readership:

> Men merely felt a deep desire to know whence they had come. The remains of Greece and Rome told them much, but these remains were neither aboriginal in time nor divine in authority. The Book of Genesis was both, but it was not complete. The commentators completed it.

The commentaries show the finest metaphysical minds of the day – Babington, Luther, Calvin, Zwingli – wrestling with large questions: "What is meant by this: The earth was without form and void?"; "What waters are they which are above the firmament?"; "How do these lights in the firmament separate the day from the night?" (Gibbens 1601: B2r, C1v, C4r). Amongst such interrogatives Lear's demented question, "What is the cause of thunder?" (3.4.155), is not altogether fool.

Personal, national, and theological origins can be investigated through geography: Eden, the world, Britain. Lear's land, however, like Lear himself, is confused. *King Lear* is notable for the number of historical characters who have geographic names: (Earl of) Gloucester, (Dukes of) Albany and Cornwall, (Kings of) France and Burgundy. The titles are frequently omitted, the name reduced to its toponym. Where Shakespeare changed a name in his sources for *King Lear*, the change was in the direction of geography; the servant Kent is called Perillus in one of the sources, the anonymous play *King Leir*. The result is, in dramatic terms, the aural equivalent of Birnam Wood coming to Dunsinane in *Macbeth*. The characters literally enact the division of the kingdom. We hear of Kent going to Gloucester, of Albany to Cornwall, of Gloucester to Dover. The play unmakes the map (Flahiff 1986: 19).

Dover is, however, not a character name but a place name, and it is where British history begins. When Julius Caesar arrived in England, he arrived in Dover. When in the play we hear that King Lear is sent to Dover, that Gloucester is led to Dover, that the unnamed gentlemen meet at Dover, that the French invasion designed to rescue Lear begins at Dover, we might be inclined to ask with Regan, "Wherefore to Dover?" (3.7.53). One possible answer is: it's where a study of British identity, of the British nation, begins (Mikalachki n.p.).

In the play Dover and its famous cliffs are given the most detailed topographical description. There are flora, fauna, cliffs, danger:

> How fearful
> And dizzy 'tis, to cast one's eyes so low!
> The crows and choughs that wing the midway air
> Show scarce so gross as beetles. Half way down
> Hangs one that gathers sampire, dreadful trade!
> Methinks he seems no bigger than his head.
> The fishermen that walk upon the beach
> Appear like mice; and yond tall anchoring bark,
> Diminish'd to her cock; her cock, a buoy
> Almost too small for sight. The murmuring surge,
> That on th'unnumb'red idle pebble chafes,
> Cannot be heard so high. (4.6.11–22)

The irony, of course, is that this detailed topocosm has a purely rhetorical existence in the play. The blind, despairing Gloucester has asked a beggar to lead him to Dover so that he can commit suicide. The beggar is the disguised Edgar, Gloucester's son, who is intent on saving his father's life. The cliffs that he describes as being vertiginously, precariously close are false, none other than rhetorical creations. When Gloucester jumps, he jumps on flat ground, on the bare boards of the Globe stage. Origins are unreachable. The idea that you can find your national origins is as chimerical as the idea that one can control nature through cartography. In *King Lear* the map is divided, the heath inclement, Dover Cliff unreal. Rather than celebrating Britain, the play presents a pessimistic vision of man's attempts to master his land and find his historical origins (Mikalachki 1998: 94–5).

5   The Self at Play

"Go your ways and play" (*Merry Wives* 4.1.79)

Love's Labour's Lost (1594–5)

If the civilized world of court and of county maps does not aid Lear in finding himself, neither does academic life offer an adequate education in *Love's Labour's Lost* to those who commit themselves to its cloistral existence.

The play opens with the King of Navarre and his three friends vowing to devote themselves to study for a period of three years. They will fast, read books, sleep only three hours a night, and forswear the company of women. It sounds a lot like university, but Shakespeare had a healthy skepticism for such ascetic modes of study. In *Taming of the Shrew* the servant Tranio cautions his master, who has come to Pisa to study:

> Let's be no Stoics nor no stocks [blocks of wood and hence incapable of feeling], I pray,
> Or so devote to Aristotle's checks
> As Ovid be an outcast quite abjur'd. (1.131–3)

Love (as represented by the Roman love-poet Ovid) is important, he explains, because "no profit grows where is no pleasure ta'en" (1.1.39).

The King of Navarre could benefit from Tranio's advice. His vows are impractical – and not just because book learning isolated from life is impractical. It turns out that the French princess and her ladies are scheduled to visit Navarre's court. They must be entertained. And so the first of the men's visionary vows is broken.

In fact, in meeting, loving, and debating with the French ladies the men learn things they could not get from books: they learn about themselves. If the purpose of study is, as the King says, "that to know which else we should not know" (1.1.56), it is obvious that life and empirical experience are as educative as books. (Shakespeare himself did not attend university.) The women realize this and at the end of the play impose tasks on the men to help expand their experiences. Educative tasks are necessary because the men seem persistently unaware of reality. (Set in the 1930s, Branagh's film presented a countdown to war but the court of Navarre seemed naively unaware of the grave political situation.)

The vows the men make as lovers are as un-self-aware as the earlier vows they made as students. They send courtship presents to the princess and her three ladies. When the ladies swap the presents and reappear masqued with only the love-tokens to identify them, the men declare love to the wrong women. Once again their vows are broken of "necessity." Both roles – student and lover – turn out to be poses, in the Elizabethan sense of "supposes": pretense, playacting. But playing in the play repeatedly has to confront reality, from the arrival of the French princess's court to the arrival of Mercade (in which the men's wooing is forced to yield to the princess's public duty: she returns to France to mourn her dead father and inherit his crown).

Throughout the play the women are more astute than the men: they see through their lovers' games and affectations, from their pick-up lines to their proposals. "Did not I dance with you in Brabant once?" Berowne asks Rosaline. "Did not *I* dance with you in Brabant once?" Rosaline counters. With the ball back in his court Berowne admits, "I know you did." Rosaline now delivers the romantic put-down: "How needless was it then to ask the question" (2.1.114–17). Her point is: words must not just sound fine; they must serve a purpose. Thus at the end of the play Rosaline asks the witty Lord Berowne to work in a hospital for a year to see if he can "move wild laughter in the throat of death" (5.2.855). His jesting will now be put to use in the real world.

The women agree to meet the men again in a year to discuss love, but, as Berowne observes, "that's too long for a play" (5.2.878). Shakespeare thus denies his audience not one but four happy endings. Finding identity takes more time than a play can accommodate.

Identity change cannot come for the lords in *Love's Labour's Lost* through playacting, nor can it come in the two hours' traffic of the stage. But sometimes it can. Let's return to *Taming of the Shrew*.

Taming of the Shrew (1590–1)

In act 5 Vincentio, the father of Bianca's suitor, Lucentio, arrives in Padua, where he meets someone impersonating him. The audience has witnessed the reason for this impersonation early in the play: Lucentio, in need of a financial guarantor in marriage, tricks/persuades an anonymous passing merchant to act as his father, Vincentio. However, because his beloved, Bianca, has been forbidden to receive any suitors, Lucentio disguises himself as a Latin tutor to gain access to her. (Note the appropriateness of his disguised character's name: Cambio, Italian for "exchange.") While he acts the part of the Latin master he needs someone to maintain his Paduan household and existence, and to be an official suitor (in the form of financial competitor) in Bianca's household; so he seconds one of his servants, Tranio, to pose as Lucentio; another servant, Biondello, therefore has to act as servant to Tranio/Lucentio. By the time Vincentio walks on stage in act 5 he is almost the only character in the play not to have assumed a false identity.

Vincentio immediately recognizes his household servants, Biondello (impersonating Tranio) and Tranio (dressed as Lucentio), but the servants deny all knowledge of him. Like the Syracusans in Ephesus, Vincentio insists on the primacy of name in confirming identity: "as if I knew not his name! I have brought him up ever since he was three years old, and his name is Tranio" (5.1.81–3). From name he moves to biographical fact – Tranio's father is "a sailmaker in Bergamo" (5.1.77–8) – but his repeated insistence on what he knows only results in the police being called to take him to prison as an impostor. Nothing he can adduce can convince anyone that he is the real Vincentio. Juliet Dusinberre observes that

> Vincentio almost doubts his own identity under reiterated accusations of impersonating the man he is. In the concrete world in which these people move, so many of the characters are impersonating someone else that those who are not impersonating anyone have as tenuous a hold on reality as those who are. (1975: 107)

In other words, Vincentio's real world is affected by others' playworld. Although he is simply minding his own business he is still at risk of losing his identity.

The play began with Christopher Sly's identity being affected by others' playacting. The first two scenes – labeled "Induction" in all modern editions but scene 1 and 2 in the first printed edition, the Folio of 1623 – introduce Sly, a comatose, drunken tinker who is the victim of a trick. While out hunting, a lord and his fellows come across Sly, decide for their aristocratic amusement to take him home, dress him in rich clothes, and convince him that he is a lord. As part of this ploy, the Lord and his companions perform the role of servants, with one commanded to impersonate Sly's wife. The plan is to change Sly's reality by playacting: "we will play our part / As he shall think by our true diligence / He is no less than what we say he is" (Ind.1.69–71).

The trick is successful. Convinced by material surroundings ("I smell sweet savors, and I feel soft things"), by the servants' reiteration of his title, and by their insistence that he is who they say he is, Sly rejects his previous self: "Upon my life, I am a lord indeed" (Ind.2.72). Nor is this change of identity entirely fictitious: Sly now speaks in verse. Theater has the power to alter reality.

In the taming plot Petruccio's playacting similarly interferes with and alters Katherine's identity. His ludic buffoonery and Petrarchan exaggerations provide a verbal picture of a new personality which Katherine grows to match; the mild, obedient woman Petruccio describes in act 1 is very much in evidence in act 5. Vincentio's reality is also affected by characters' impersonations. Sly, Katherine, Vincentio . . . the sequence continues to us, the audience: our lives and selves will be changed by our experience in the theater.

But although these transformations are similar they are not identical. Katherine's transformation may or may not be permanent, and it may or may not be genuine. Since the induction's first scene gives elaborate instructions about how to impersonate a dutiful wife (curtsy, speak softly, shed tears – assisted by an onion in a handkerchief, if necessary), we are entitled to be suspicious of Katherine's performance in act 5. Sly's position is more (unhappily) straightforward: his elevation to the aristocracy can only be temporary.

Oddly, Shakespeare does not complete the Sly framework. Perhaps he never wrote a Sly ending; perhaps he wrote one and it has not survived; perhaps practical reasons enforced a change of mind: it squanders a good actor to have him watch the action from above for four acts, as the stage direction at the end of act 1, scene 1 instructs – "they sit and mark." The question of whether Shakespeare completed the Sly framework arises because of the existence of a play published in 1594 called *The Taming of a Shrew*. The play is a derivative adaptation of Shakespeare's play (Miller 1998: 260–2), intermittently close in language and almost identical in plot. *A Shrew* extends and completes the Sly plot. *A Shrew*'s Sly interrupts the play from time to time: he gets very excited about the fool, and he objects to the imprisonment of Vincentio (obviously an experience which is rather close to home). In act 5 he falls asleep, and when the play is over the Lord returns Sly to the wood. When Sly awakes he, like Bottom in *Midsummer Night's Dream*, remembers his metamorphosis as a dream, from which he has learned "how to tame a shrew" (Dolan 1996: 153).

Although *A Shrew* provides structural symmetry, it reduces subtlety. Sly interprets the title literally, taking only a plot-related message from the play – how to tame a wife. Shakespeare's plot is shrew-taming but his theme is theater: the ways in which life and personal identity can be transformed by drama. His refusal to revert to the Christopher Sly story leaves us suspended in the world of drama; the play's five acts have usurped reality's two scenes. Theater has the power to overtake life.[5]

At least, this is one way of approaching the play. In chapter 2 I offer a less benign interpretation, for one of the joys of reading Shakespeare plays is that their identities, like those of the characters who read them, change in different times and circumstances. If we turn our critical lens to the reality of marriage rather than the transformative power of drama, *The Shrew*, post-1960 at least, is a very different play. To marriage we now turn.

---

[5] The theatrical motif was to the fore in Gale Edwards's RSC production in 1995. Tranio's elevation to Lucentio was every understudy's dream: the chance to play the romantic lead. (The occasion was not without its attendant nerves: after his first encounter with Baptista, Tranio had urgent recourse to his asthma inhaler.) Petruccio's blustering "Have I not heard lions roar" speech was obviously his best audition piece (behind him, Grumio mimed Petruccio's gestures – rehearsed movements with which he was clearly all too familiar). Katherine's long speech of obedience in act 5 was not the recitation of a dutiful wife but a long-awaited moment in which one actor upstaged another.

2

Marital Life:
Shakespeare and Romance

"*a pair of stairs to marriage*" (*AYLI* 5.2.37–8)

Introduction

Shakespeare is celebrated as the poet of romantic love. Emma Thompson's screenplay of *Sense and Sensibility* uses sonnet 116 ("Let me not to the marriage of true minds admit impediments") to illustrate the shared romantic sensibilities of Marianne Dashwood and Willoughby. Greetings card websites offer 3D sonnets for Valentine's Day (see http://www.bluemountain.com in which the lines of sonnet 116 oscillate, save for those lines that describe the emotional stability of love). The city of Verona thrives on tourists' visits to Juliet's "balcony" even though Romeo and Juliet were fictional characters who never loved except on the stage of the Globe (and before that in the pages of the poem from which Shakespeare borrowed their love story, Arthur Brooke's *Romeus and Juliet*). Shakespeare's works provide us with convenient aphoristic wisdom about love and its hazards ("the course of true love n'er did run smooth"; *MND* 1.1.134) as well as lyrical verses for use at weddings. But for all the Romeos and Juliets, the Hermias and Lysanders, the Rosalinds and Orlandos who fall lyrically in love and commit themselves to marriage, there are antiromantic reminders of love's darker aspects: Beatrice in *Much Ado* who was once, it seems, jilted by Benedick: "he lent it [his heart] me awhile . . . he won it of me with false dice, therefore your Grace may well say I have lost it" (2.1.278–82); Lavache in *All's Well that Ends Well* who marries because the flesh drives him to it; Antipholus of Ephesus in *Comedy of Errors* who neglects his longsuffering wife and visits a prostitute; Orsino in *Twelfth Night* who seems more in love with the role of the lover (lounging on floral banks, listening to melancholy music) than with Olivia, the ostensible object of his desires; the Jailer's Daughter in *Two Noble Kinsmen* who runs mad when her love for Palamon is not returned.

Even when couples love passionately and reciprocally, happy endings are not guaranteed: the Pyramus and Thisbe story in *Midsummer Night's Dream* parallels Hermia's and Lysander's predicament and provides a sobering, albeit travestied, reminder of how the Athenian lovers' story might have ended. Shakespeare had more reason than most to know about the hazards of love. His shotgun wedding at the age of 18 to Anne

Hathaway, a woman eight years his senior, presumably curtailed his teenage freedoms. More significantly, it put paid to his chances of a university education in an age when Bachelor of Arts degrees were literally limited to bachelors.

Even when romance goes well, there is no single paradigm of romantic love. We see this most visibly in *As You Like It* which juxtaposes different attitudes to love. Not much happens in this play after the first act. In act 1 the good characters flee to the Forest of Arden. After this, the action is over; from now on, it's all attitude. By act 5 no fewer than four couples agree to marry – the highest number in any Shakespeare play – a fact noted wryly by the satirical Jaques: "There is sure another flood toward, and these couples are coming to the ark" (5.4.35–6). But although the destination is the same for all eight lovers – marriage – the route by which they reach it is very different, for each has a different perspective on love.

In this chapter I want to look at Shakespeare's celebratory and cautionary tales of love and marriage in thirteen plays. When Rosalind describes the love of Celia and Oliver in *As You Like It* she says they "no sooner met but they look'd; no sooner look'd but they lov'd; no sooner lov'd but they sigh'd; no sooner sigh'd but they ask'd one another the reason; no sooner knew the reason but they sought the remedy: and in these degrees have they made a pair of stairs to marriage" (5.2.33–8). The first part of this chapter looks at the positive side of romance as characters ascend the stairs to marriage. But marriage, in Shakespeare as in life, isn't always a happy ending; sometimes it's an unhappy beginning. Accordingly, the remainder of this chapter looks at what happens when love goes wrong.

In his one-man show on Shakespeare, which played in London and New York in the early 1980s, Ian McKellen challenged his audience to find a happy marriage in Shakespeare. It couldn't be done. "Portia and Brutus in *Julius Caesar*?" someone proffered. "Oh, yes, very happy," McKellen agreed sarcastically, "especially when she swallows the burning coals." "Hotspur and Kate in *1 Henry IV*?" suggested another audience member. "But Hotspur hasn't shared her bed for two weeks and won't tell her he loves her." And on we went, through the canon. Is Shakespeare really the playwright of romance?

1   Love and Hazard

"*Who chooseth me must give and hazard all he hath*" (MV 2.7.16)

Merchant of Venice (1596–7)

In 1615 Alexander Niccholes, the author of *A Discourse of Marriage and Wiving,* offered this piece of cautionary wisdom:

Marriage is an adventure, for whosoever marries, adventures; he adventures his peace, his freedom, his liberty, his body. (D1r)

Niccholes was writing in an age which regularly exploited the dual meanings of adventure, which, as noun and verb, meant both venture (=risk) and adventure (= [embark on] an exciting undertaking). In 1596–7 Shakespeare anticipated Niccholes's view of marriage and his language of hazard. *Merchant of Venice* is a play about risk; it is also a play about love. The two, as Shakespeare shows, are one and the same.[1]

The merchant of the play's title, Antonio, is a wealthy businessman. So wealthy is he that he can afford to be generous; consequently, he lends money without charging interest. His friend, Bassanio, borrows from Antonio to finance a love-venture: he wishes to travel to Belmont to win the hand of the rich lady Portia. This is not the first time that Bassanio has borrowed money from Antonio. In fact, Bassanio cheerfully admits that he is a bad risk, having lost all the money that Antonio has lent him on previous occasions. He justifies his new request for funds with a sporting analogy: shooting another arrow after a lost arrow often enables you to retrieve both (1.1.147–52). Antonio lends Bassanio the money, not because it is a potentially profitable venture nor because it will be a reliable return of capital, but because he loves his friend (1.1.153–7).

Bassanio's motive in wooing Portia, like that of many Shakespearean wooers, is initially financial. Petruccio in *Taming of the Shrew* comes "to wive it wealthily in Padua; / If wealthily, then happily in Padua" (1.2.75–6). Fenton in *Merry Wives of Windsor* confesses to Anne Page that, although he first loved her for her wealth, he has now progressed beyond such super-ficialities to the greater treasure of Anne herself (3.4.13–18). In *Merchant of Venice* Bassanio stresses Portia's wealth; it occupies first place in his rhetorical priorities, eclipsing Portia's beauty (which comes second) and her virtues (which come third):

(1) In Belmont is a lady richly left
(2) And she is fair and fairer than that word
(3) Of wondrous virtues. (1.1.161–3)

The play's imagery supports Bassanio's fiscal interests, dignifying the finan-cial motive with mythology: Bassanio is a second Jason in search of the golden fleece.

---

[1]   Cf. Berry 1972: 114. On the relation between passion and risk in the context of drama as well as romance see McDiarmid 1988: 47.

But unlike Fenton in *Merry Wives*, for whom riches become metaphorical, Bassanio always speaks in material terms; for him romance, debt, and bridging loan are inextricably linked. He tells Antonio that his courtship is a plot "to get clear of all the debts I owe" (1.1.134). His description of Portia is unremittingly fiscal: "richly left," "nothing undervalu'd / To Cato's daughter" (1.1.165–6), "Golden fleece" (1.1.170), "her worth" (1.1.167). When he expresses his confidence that he will be "fortunate" in love, the adjective is surely double-edged.

Bassanio's financial difficulties have been caused by his lavish lifestyle, by "something showing a more swelling port / Than my faint means would grant continuance" (1.1.124–5). His impecuniousness does not prove a cautionary experience, however. Having been granted a loan by Antonio, we see Bassanio immediately ordering new clothes (2.2.116–17). Launcelot Gobbo relishes the prospect of employment by Bassanio because he "gives rare new liveries" (2.2.109).

It therefore seems a little hypocritical of Bassanio to reject the gold casket in Belmont. His choice of the lowly bronze casket may indicate that he has finally seen the difference between external and internal values (this is the hint given by the song which plays while he muses on the caskets), but it is hard to forget his earlier pragmatism, and, in the later trial scene in act 4, "judging others by himself" (Stewart 1989: 24), he assumes that Shylock's only motivation is financial. "Thou gaudy gold, / Hard food for Midas, I will none of thee" (3.2.101–2) he tells the casket. None? – apart from the gold I've borrowed from Antonio – to repay all the gold I've squandered (also borrowed from Antonio) – and, of course, the gold I'm trying to win now in the form of the golden fleece, a rich wife. But apart from that, I won't have anything to do with gold (cf. Goddard 1951: II, 86). I am skeptical of Bassanio's sincerity here, as was the director of the Vancouver production in 1976, who presented Bassanio as a blatant opportunist. In this production Bassanio went to Belmont disguised first as the Prince of Morocco then as the Prince of Arragon (Dawson 1978: 6–7n.).

Such a satiric presentation is understandable, not least because all the characters in this play seem to be intent on pecuniary gain. Jessica steals money; Portia inherits it; Lorenzo and Bassanio marry it; Antonio trades in it; Shylock lends it; Launcelot Gobbo changes jobs for more of it (see chapter 4, "Money," for lengthier analysis of these activities). The casket test devised by Portia's father, in which his daughter's suitors must choose one of three caskets (gold, lead, or bronze), would seem to protect

Portia from suitors who are mere fortune hunters. However, like the hierarchically fiscal color-coding of the caskets, the play's mercantile imagery simply expresses, in language we all understand, what love is: a venture, an adventure, a hazard, a risk. We invest ourselves emotionally. And as with all investments, we may ruin ourselves or we may find ourselves enriched beyond measure. The motto on the lead casket – the winning casket – defines love and marriage: "Who chooseth me must give and hazard all he hath." (In the Shenandoah Shakespeare Express production of *Merchant of Venice* in 1992, the song which accompanies Bassanio's deliberations over the caskets was hummed to the theme tune of the American quiz show *Jeopardy*.)

Thus, when Portia offers herself to Bassanio, she does so in a rhetorical gesture which moves quickly from giving 50 percent of herself to giving 100 percent:

> One half of me is yours, the other half yours –
> Mine own, I would say; but if mine, then yours,
> And so all yours. (3.2.16–18)

Love, like friendship, does not apportion affection. It operates like Antonio's business: it gives generously.

The question of Antonio's generosity is, however, a moot one. It is true that he does not charge interest, "not as you would say / Directly int'rest," observes Shylock (1.3.76–7). But there are other ways of exacting interest (Berry 1988: 45). Shylock offers the Old Testament story of Laban's sheep as an example:

> When Jacob graz'd his uncle Laban's sheep . . .
> Mark what Jacob did:
> When Laban and himself were compremis'd [agreed]
> That all the eanlings [new-born lambs] which were streak'd and pied
> Should fall as Jacob's hire, the ewes being rank
> In end of autumn turned to the rams,
> And when the work of generation was
> Between these woolly breeders in the act,
> The skillful shepherd pill'd me certain wands [stripped some branches],
> And in the doing of the deed of kind,
> He stuck them up before the fulsome ewes,
> Who then conceiving did in eaning time
> Fall [give birth to] parti-color'd lambs, and those were Jacob's.
> This was a way to thrive, and he was blest. (1.3.71, 77–89)

Jacob, in other words, leaves nothing to chance. Instead of letting nature take its course, creating a random number of piebald lambs – his payment as Laban's shepherd – he practices genetic engineering. The veterinarian gynecological details are questionable (as are the details in most parables), but the point is clear: Jacob's cooperative acceptance conceals his self-interested manipulation. For Jacob read Antonio. Shylock hints that Antonio is as self-interested as other usurers; he is just less overt in his usury.

Antonio's language and actions bear out Shylock's insinuation, showing that he, like Laban, has found an indirect way of making a return on his investment. When the day of reckoning comes and Antonio is due to pay Shylock his pound of flesh, Antonio sends an emotional letter to Bassanio, requesting Bassanio's presence at his death:

> Sweet Bassanio, my ships have all miscarried, my creditors grow cruel, my estate is very low, my bond to the Jew is forfeit; and since in paying it, it is impossible I should live, all debts are clear'd between you and I, if I might but see you at my death. Notwithstanding, use your pleasure; if your love do not persuade you to come, let not my letter. (3.2.315–22)

The letter is an elegant form of emotional blackmail. Antonio expects love and loyalty in return for his financial investment in Bassanio (Berry 1972: 129–30).

Marriage is always a time of potential crisis in friendships (as in *Much Ado, Two Gentlemen of Verona*) and in families (as in the opening of *King Lear*). It disrupts the status quo: relationships may remain healthy but they cannot remain the same. Thus it is easier if friends embark on marriage at the same time: "get thee a wife, get thee a wife" is Benedick's not entirely altruistic advice to Don Pedro (*Much Ado* 5.4.122). Antonio's letter to Bassanio tests his friend's allegiance to friendship over marriage. Portia defuses the conflict by supporting Bassanio's visit to Antonio. The accommodation of friendship and marriage enables the play's happy ending. The ending is nonetheless only technically happy inasmuch as Antonio is left single (unlike Gratiano who is paired off with Nerissa), and is presumably as inexplicably melancholy as he was in act 1 ("In sooth, I know not why I am so sad"; 1.1.1).

Antonio's love for Bassanio and his sadness are often presented in production as causally connected: Antonio suffers from unrequited homosexual love. This interpretation is facilitated by Shakespeare's text which omits the emotional specificity of its source, Ser Giovanni's *Il Pecorone* (late fourteenth century, printed in Italy in 1588), where the Antonio character is an avuncular godfather to the Bassanio character. Shakespeare's Antonio enables financially the marriage he seems emotionally reluctant to promote. Love is thus for him as much of a risk as marriage is for the main characters, but although Antonio appears to give as freely as does Portia he only pays lip-service to the concept of emotional hazard.

2   Love and Friendship

> "*Friendship is constant in all other things*
> *Save in the offices and affairs of love*" (*Much Ado* 2.1.175–6)

Two Gentlemen of Verona (1590–1)

Shakespeare's plays belong to a period which values male friendship as highly as romantic love. The epithet "male friendship" is often used as a euphemism for homosexuality although the two may not be equivalent; it is a mistake to impose contemporary categories of sexuality on to earlier periods or to equate sexual preference with sexual practice. "Homosocial," "homoerotic," and "homoromantic" are thus more useful terms than "homosexual." The first three may be temporary and dilettante, whereas the last implies a lasting orientation, exclusivity of preference and intensity of predilection, although clearly the terms can overlap. Some of Shakespeare's sonnets fit all four adjectival descriptions; Antonio's affection for Bassanio is homosocial and conceivably homosexual; the relationship of Valentine and Proteus in *Two Gentlemen of Verona* is homosocial, as close a friendship as that between Rosalind and Celia or Hermia and Helena.

Proteus meets Silvia, the beloved of his best friend, Valentine, only to find himself instantly in love with her. Proteus's love for Silvia quickly overturns his friendship and loyalty to Valentine to say nothing of his earlier affection for his own beloved Julia. He tells Silvia's father of Valentine's plan to elope with Silvia; Valentine is consequently banished; Silvia flees to the forest to look for him; and Proteus follows Silvia to the forest. Silvia reminds Proteus of his friendship to Valentine but Proteus dismisses this consideration with a glib rhetorical question: "In love / Who respects friend?" (5.4.53–4). Unable to get Silvia to accept his love suit (she remains loyal to Valentine), Proteus resorts to rape: "if the gentle spirit of moving words / Can no way change you to a milder form, . . . / I'll force thee yield to my desire" (5.4.55–6, 59). As one critic observes, at this point there are *no* gentlemen in Verona.

Valentine fortunately arrives on the scene in time to prevent the rape, at which point Proteus's shame and contrition are as extreme as his earlier disloyalty. Valentine accepts his friend's apologies and, to show there are no hard feelings, offers to give up Silvia to Proteus: "And that my love may appear plain and free, / All that was mine in Silvia I give thee" (5.4.82–3). Friendship is now more important than love, and Silvia is reduced to a pass-the-parcel exchange.

Two Gentlemen of Verona is performed infrequently today, partly because its characters lack the psychological depth and motivation we have come to expect of Shakespeare, partly because the convention it drama-tizes, whereby male friendship takes priority over romantic love, can be difficult to portray convincingly.[2] David Thacker negotiated these difficul-ties brilliantly in his 1991 RSC production. He set the play in the 1930s – all cocktails and tennis parties and dinner jackets and flying gear – and suffused it with songs from Cole Porter ("Night and Day," "In the Still of the Night"), the Gershwins ("Love Walked In," "Somebody Loves Me"), Irving Berlin ("What'll I Do?"), Rogers and Hart ("My Heart Stood Still," "Blue Moon"), and others. The onstage chanteuse who performed the songs framed the action with Ray Noble's "Love is the Sweetest Thing," the refrain of which stresses "love's story." By substituting one convention (the Broadway romantic musical) for another (the male-friendship narrative), Thacker transposed the play to a genre we all recognize. Robert Beard's production at Stratford, Ontario, in 1988 was equally successful for similar reasons. The back wall of the set featured a giant children's storybook, through which characters made their entrances. The set primed us to expect narrative convention and the traditions of story-telling rather than psychological realism: the characters were literally performing a story.

Two Gentlemen of Verona extols male friendship as one of the highest forms of love, but the play places the love/friendship opposition in the context of a larger debate about human loyalty. "Were man / But constant, he were perfect," moralizes Proteus in the last act (5.4.110–11). Proteus's

---

[2]   Shakespeare revisits this convention in *Much Ado About Nothing* where he handles it much less stereotypically.

treachery to his friend, Valentine, and Valentine's willingness to sacrifice his love, Silvia, to his friend are different but equally reprehensible displays of inconstancy.

Launce, the clown, reveals the shallowness of the heroes' behavior. Launce's primary stage relationship is with his dog, Crab. Launce tells a story of an occasion on which Crab got loose in Silvia's family dining room, stole the dinner meat, urinated under the table and then again on exit, this time against Silvia's skirt. To save his dog from whipping, Launce took Crab's transgression upon himself, saying that it was he, Launce, who urinated. Launce is therefore whipped, instead of his dog. This, it emerges, is not the first time that Launce has intervened on behalf of his pet: "I have sat in the stocks for puddings he hath stol'n, otherwise he had been executed; I have stood on the pillory for geese he hath kill'd, otherwise he had suffer'd for't" (4.4.30–3). Now that's *amore*.

Winter's Tale (1609); Two Noble Kinsmen (1613–14)

Shakespeare revisits the topic of love versus friendship in *Winter's Tale* where King Leontes's Edenic memories of the boyhood friendship he enjoyed with King Polixenes are shattered by the serpent of sexuality when he suspects his wife, Hermione, of infidelity with his old friend. The confidence of the two courtiers who open the play with admiration of their monarchs' deep-rooted affection – "there is not in the world either malice or matter to alter it" (1.1.33–4) – is quickly overturned. One is never quite sure, in reading or performance, if Leontes is more outraged at the betrayal of friendship or of marriage.

The same confident belief in friendship is voiced at the beginning of *Two Noble Kinsmen* where Palamon tells his kinsman "I do not think it possible our friendship / Should ever leave us," to which Arcite, continuing his trope from line 139 – "We are one another's wife" – responds with nuptial solemnity, "Till our deaths it cannot" (2.1.173–4). However, when both men fall in love with the same woman, Emilia, they renege on their vows: "Friendship, blood /And all the ties between us I disclaim" (2.1.233–4).

Although discord is inevitable when "two at once woo one," as Puck puts it, friendship is equally jeopardized by a more conventional one-to-one wooing as Arcite realizes when (pre-Emilia) he extols the advantage of the kinsmen's imprisonment in Thebes: "Were we at liberty / A wife might part us" (1.1.147–8). The Theseus plot illustrates his point. The play opens with a celebration of Theseus's wedding to the Amazon Queen, Hippolyta. The feast is interrupted when Theseus exits to confront Creon, King of Thebes; he instructs his friend Pirithous to remain in Athens to continue the festivities. When Hippolyta's sister, Emilia, observes Pirithous's devotion to Theseus, Hippolyta responds confidently (defensively?) that "we more than his Pirithous, possess / The high throne in his heart" (1.3.95–6). Between the women's discussion of Theseus's friendship and Hippolyta's assertion of her emotional priority comes Emilia's lengthy autobiographical narrative of her childhood friendship with Flavina. No mere reminiscence, like that in *Midsummer Night's Dream* where Helena invokes the amity of her childhood with Hermia – "so we grew together, / Like to a double cherry, seeming parted, / But yet an union in partition" (*MND* 3.2.208–10) – Emilia's story leads to a general principle: that "the true love 'tween maid and maid" exceeds heterosexual love ("more than in sex dividual"; 1.3.81–2) and that she will never love a man. Thus *Two Noble Kinsmen* introduces three pairs of friendships: Theseus–Pirithous, Palamon–Arcite, Emilia–Flavina. It is the only Renaissance play to highlight same-sex friendship among women, and thus makes doubly ironic Palamon and Arcite's enmity over a woman who expresses no interest in men.

If marital coupling is the desired ending – desired not just in terms of comedic convention but in terms of social convention and procreation – one of the same-sex members in the triangular relationships must be removed (Mallette 1995: 44). Flavina has been disposed of before the play began (she died at the age of eleven; 1.3.53–4), thus making Emilia technically, if not emotionally, available (although the question of to what extent an Amazon is ever available is a moot one). Arcite, although the victor in the competition for Emilia, is killed by his horse; thus Palamon wins by default. Emilia appears happy in neither case. She greets Arcite's victory with regret for Palamon's consequent death – "Is this winning?" (5.3.138) – and Palamon's victory with silence. Both kinsmen are aware of loss in their respective moments of triumph. "Emily, / To buy you I have lost what's dearest to me / Save what is bought," says Arcite (5.3.112–13). Palamon is more mournful: "That we should things desire which do cost us / The loss of our desire! That nought could buy / Dear love but loss of dear love!" (5.4.109–11). Marriage in this play comes at a high price. As Richard Mallette points out, matrimony "triumphs . . . institutionally, if not emotionally" (1995: 44). The dominant attachments are to the dead, to same-sex friends (ibid.: 29, 36, 47).

3   Love and Madness

"*Love is merely a madness*" (*AYLI* 3.2.400)

Midsummer Night's Dream (1595); *Cymbeline* (1610)

Financial logic, not love, was the impetus behind Bassanio's initial approach to Portia in *Merchant of Venice* but other Shakespeare characters display little logic of any kind in love. "Reason and love keep little company together now-a-days," muses Bottom in *Midsummer Night's Dream*, "the more the pity that some honest neighbours will not make them friends" (3.1.143–6). Love and reason are not always compatible and nowhere is this more apparent than in the opening of *Midsummer Night's Dream* where Hermia's choice of husband – Lysander – clashes with that of her father, who insists on his daughter marrying Demetrius.

This is a classic dramatic situation from Roman comedy onwards. In Shakespeare the consequences, or threatened consequences, for the dis-obedient daughter – and it is always the daughter who loves against her parents' wishes – can be severe. Hermia's father invokes Athenian law, which offers her one of two alternatives: death or life as a nun. In *Othello* Desdemona marries against her father's wishes and is cut off emotionally by him (1.3.189–98), as is Jessica in *Merchant of Venice* for marrying a Gentile (3.1). In *Merry Wives of Windsor* Anne Page's parents plot to marry her by force to the wealthy husband of their choice (a situation compli-cated by the fact that the parents have different choices). In all these situ-ations Shakespeare supports the daughter, for reasons he presents at length in *Midsummer Night's Dream*.

In this play Hermia laments that her father does not see things from her point of view: "I would my father look'd but with my eyes." Theseus admonishes Hermia, "Rather your eyes must with his judgment look" (1.1.56–7). The daughter's irrational love must cede to parental reason ("judgment").

But Egeus's vision is not reasonable or even remotely justifiable. In insisting on Demetrius as a husband, Egeus insists on a young Athenian who is to all intents and purposes indistinguishable from Hermia's choice, Lysander. Demetrius is from the same background as Lysander, as rich as Lysander, and as handsome. Hermia can therefore have no logical reason for preferring Lysander. And that's the point: love is irrational.

Love's irrationality is further illustrated in the Helena plot. Before he turned his attentions to Hermia, Demetrius, we are told, wooed Helena, "and she, sweet lady, dotes, / Devoutly dotes, dotes in idolatry, / Upon this spotted and inconstant man" (1.1.108–10). Shakespeare's word for a love that is irrationally pursued is "doting"; and loving someone who doesn't love back is obviously irrational. In lines that do not admit any subtext, Demetrius tells Helena, "I do not nor I cannot love you" and "I am sick when I do look on thee" (2.1.201, 212). The situation is even more complexly irrational, for, if Demetrius and Lysander are equally attractive, so are Hermia and Helena. The baffled Helena acknowledges, "Through Athens I am thought as fair as she / But what of that? Demetrius thinks not so; / He will not know what all but he do know" (1.1.227–9). The revealing sequence of verbs – "thinks," "know" – highlights the dichotomy between love (thought/imagination) and reason (knowledge) which the play examines. Demetrius's transfer of affection to Hermia is as illogical as Helena's persistent love for Demetrius.

Helena concludes, as Bottom does later, that reason and love keep little company together: "Love looks not with the eyes but with the mind; / And therefore is wing'd Cupid painted blind. / Nor hath Love's mind of any judgement taste" (1.1.234–6). Theseus makes the same point in act 5 when he links the madman with the lover and the poet:

> The lunatic, the lover, and the poet
> Are of imagination all compact.
> One sees more devils than vast hell can hold;
> That is the madman. The lover, all as frantic,
> Sees Helen's beauty in a brow of Egypt.
> The poet's eye, in a fine frenzy rolling,
> Doth glance from heaven to earth, from earth to heaven;
> And as imagination bodies forth
> The forms of things unknown, the poet's pen
> Turns them to shapes, and gives to aery nothing
> A local habitation and a name. (5.1.7–17)

The beautiful Helen referred to here is, of course, Helen of Troy. "Helen" in the early modern period was a metonymic shorthand; it could only mean one Helen. A man in love, Theseus says, will believe his beloved to be as beautiful as Helen of Troy even if his loved one is a dark-skinned Egyptian (Elizabethan standards of beauty privileged fair complexions). Theseus identifies the common denominator of the lunatic, lover, and poet

as imagination. Whereas the lunatic's imagination causes him to halluci-
nate and the poet's to invent, the lover's imagination sees beauty where
others do not. Even though he had begun the play unsympathetically insistent that Hermia realign her romantic gaze to comply with her father's
wishes, Theseus here acknowledges the illogic of love, the power of imagination, and the relation between the two.

If Demetrius has transferred his affection from Helena to Hermia before
the play begins, Lysander transfers his affection from Hermia to Helena in
the course of the play. Thus, the play repeats the situation of act 1, with the
position of the women reversed: Helena rather than Hermia is now wooed
by two men. This second change of allegiance is caused by accident and
artifice. Puck applies the magic love-juice, which has the power to make
man or woman "madly dote / Upon the next live creature that it sees"
(2.1.171–2), to the wrong Athenian. Instead of Demetrius's gaze being redirected to Helena, as Oberon helpfully intended, it is Lysander's gaze that is
diverted. Lysander's new emotion is as irrational as Demetrius's change of
affection, although he, like Helena, tries to find explanation in logic:

> Not Hermia, but Helena I love.
> Who will not change a raven for a dove?
> The will of man is by his reason sway'd;
> And reason says you are the worthier maid. (2.2.113–16)

It is in the nature of post-Enlightenment subjects to invoke logic to explain
actions and emotions, but Shakespeare's pre-Cartesian characters are no
exception.

The fusion of taste with logic, or rather the sleight of hand which disguises the former as the latter, exposes the unease we feel when gripped by
what Shakespeare calls the imagination and what Immanuel Kant calls the
singular judgment. Here is Kant: "I describe by a judgment of taste the rose
that I see as beautiful. But the judgment which results from the comparison of several singular judgments, 'Roses in general are beautiful,' is no
longer described simply as aesthetical, but as a logical judgment based on
an aesthetical one" (1964: 289). In changing "I find a rose beautiful" to
"roses are beautiful," we perform the same act of syntagmatic ratiocination
as Lysander when he justifies his change of affection in the lines quoted
above: "Who will not change a raven for a dove?" He later justifies his rejection of Hermia in similar terms, telling Helena "I had no judgement when
to her [Hermia] I swore," to which Helena replies curtly, "Nor none, in my
mind, now you give her o'er" (3.2.134–5).

That reason and judgment are far from operative in this play is shown by the ingredient of the magic love-potion: pansy, not persuasion. Through the intervention of Puck, Oberon, and the magic love-juice the lovers' eyesight is redirected, and Demetrius explains that he now finds Helen to be his beautiful beloved:

all the faith, the virtue of my heart,
The object and the pleasure of mine eye,
Is only Helena. (4.1.169–71)

But this was also his view before the play began (see 1.1.106–10; 4.1.171–2). We have no guarantee that his romantic apostasy will not recur.

That the happy ending of this play is caused by external intervention – floral eyedrops applied by fairies – has caused much critical concern. Most Shakespeare comedies end with the characters achieving a new vision because they have been self-reflecting and consequently self-correcting (cf. Hunter 1983: 120). Thus, as we saw in chapter 1, they have the personal wherewithal to emerge into the new life – marriage – beyond act 5. But the lovers in *Midsummer Night's Dream* are simply lifted wholesale from one emotional state to another by Puck and Oberon. In Lysander's case, the love-juice returns him from an accidental aberrant vision to a prior reality; it corrects a mistake which it itself has caused. But Demetrius is returned to the pre-play situation in which he loved Helena; the specter of emotional impermanence remains. It is further underlined by the play's mythological references, most of which refer to betrayal, and by the play's ruler, Theseus, a figure renowned, *inter alia*, for his infidelity to females.

For reassurance we must return to the love-juice. R. W. Dent points out that, etymologically, the pansy ("paunsy" in one variant Elizabethan spelling) comes from the French *pensée*, which means not just "thought," as it does today, but "imagination," "vision." Thus, Cotgrave's French/English *Dictionary* of 1611 offers the following definition: "A thought, supposal, conjecture, surmise, cogitation, imagination; one's heart, mind, inward conceit, opinion, fancy, or judgement; also, the flower Pansy" (Dent 1983: 129). Demetrius vows to love Helena not because of an external event (the application of juice from the pansy) but because of an internal event: the reordering of his vision, a change in perception, *pensée*. The love choices of the conclusion are no more rational but they are at least not external.

The imaginative irrationality of love is not a bad thing. Nick Bottom the weaver, who is temporarily turned into an ass and wooed by a Fairy Queen, remembers his metamorphosis only as a dream. He gives us a garbled account of the experience:

> I have had a dream, past the wit of man to say what dream it was. . . . The eye of man hath not heard, the ear of man hath not seen, man's hand is not able to taste, his tongue to conceive, nor his heart to report, what my dream was. (4.1.205–6, 211–14)

Bottom's speech, with its misaligning of the senses, is a parody of 1 Corinthians 2:9: "The eye hath not seen, nor the ear heard, neither have entered into the heart of man, the things which God hath prepared for them that love Him." Bottom is here to remind us of St. Paul, to tell us that there is a love beyond human comprehension, beyond logic, beyond rational explanation. That love is divine love. The irrationality of romantic love is a window on divine love for it touches a part of us that is beyond daily logic.

Nowhere is the value of romantic illogic better illustrated than in *Cymbeline*. Imogen marries Posthumus, a good and noble gentleman, who is soon misled into bad and ignoble behavior: he suspects Imogen of infidelity, accuses her, arranges to have her killed. Throughout her emotional tortures Imogen never stops loving Posthumus, and her love is expressed in terms of visual blindness: "nor here, nor here, / Nor what ensues, but have a fog in them" (3.2.78–9). In other words: "I can't see to this side or to that side or what's ahead; I can only see what is right in front of me." And what Imogen sees is that she loves Posthumus. Her love survives because she ignores all the rational reasons why it shouldn't (Lewis 1992: 78–9). Sometimes the blindness and shortsightedness of love – its irrationality and its madness – are its greatest strengths.

All's Well that Ends Well (1604–5)

Irrationality can, however, have an unhealthy flipside when one persists in loving someone who doesn't reciprocate. The Jailer's Daughter in *Two Noble Kinsmen* goes mad because of her love for Prince Palamon. Helena in *All's Well that Ends Well* follows her man across France, Spain, and Italy, even though he has made his rejection clear in a letter.

In the first scene of *All's Well that Ends Well* Bertram departs for the King's court in Paris, for, as an underage count, he is a ward of court. (Bertram's father has just died; the King assumes guardianship of him until he comes of age.) Hence his mother's double loss and double grief in the play's first line: "In delivering my son from me, I bury a second husband," i.e., now I really know what it means to lose a husband: I lose my son as well. Throughout this scene Helena is unnoticed by Bertram. His indifference is partly due to considerations of class for, as the daughter of a doctor, Helena is socially inferior. In the Renaissance doctors, like barber-surgeons, were tradespeople. Bertram, on the other hand, is an aristocrat. Although the couple have bereavement in common (both have recently lost their father) and have been brought up in the same household, they have little to do with each other and Bertram treats Helena as a household attendant. (In the BBC film Angela Down's Helena moves with quiet efficiency, preparing Bertram's luggage; Bertram treats her as a domestic.)

With Bertram's departure Helena is now separated from the object of her desire geographically as well as emotionally and socially, but her ardor is no whit lessened. Unable to view Bertram in person, she simply gazes on the picture she has drawn in her "heart's table":

> 'Twas pretty, though a plague,
> To see him every hour, to sit and draw
> His arched brows, his hawking eye, his curls,
> In our heart's table – heart too capable
> Of every line and trick of his sweet favor [face].
> But now he's gone, and my idolatrous fancy
> Must sanctify his reliques. (1.1.92–8)

The language of idolatry is not only unhealthy and irreverent: it smacks of obsession. (On this last line Harriet Walter's Helena in the 1981–2 RSC production smothered a framed photograph of Bertram with kisses as if it were a religious icon.) Helena's concentration on superficials – Bertram's brows, eyes, curls – is also disquieting. Didn't an earlier Helena tell us that "love looks not with the eye but with the mind" (*MND* 1.1.234)?

The French King is so ill that his physicians have abandoned hope: "Galen and Paracelsus . . . all the learned and authentic fellows . . . gave him out incurable" (2.3.11–14). Helena has inherited medical skills and prescriptions from her father. Together these circumstances provide her with a bona fide reason to follow Bertram to the King's court where she presents her medical knowledge and spiritual powers. Part of the scene with the invalid King (2.1) is presented in incantatory rhyming couplets, suggesting that magic as well as medicine is involved; in true fairytale fashion, Helena miraculously heals the King. In gratitude, he grants Helena her choice of husband – Bertram. Bertram is understandably appalled: "I cannot love her, nor will strive to do't" (2.3.145).

I confess to some sympathy for Bertram here. In asking the King for "leave to use / The help of mine own eyes" in marriage (2.3.107–8), he requests no more than did Hermia in *Midsummer Night's Dream*. Marriage is far from his thoughts: he is young, underage, and has just left a house of mourning, a house of women. Just as his thoughts turn to court life and masculine military endeavors (he is keen to join the French courtiers in the Italian wars), he is forced by the King into marriage. "Undone, and forfeited to cares for ever!" is his first marital line (2.3.267).

Bertram's reluctance turns to rebellion, and he feigns a business trip to cover his planned escape to the Tuscan wars, an escape financed by his wedding gift from the King. In the scene before he sneaks away, he behaves coldly and cowardly. He leaves Parolles to do his dirty work, informing Helena of Bertram's departure. In his conversations with Parolles, he cannot even name Helena (Lower 1998: 244):

Bertram:	Is she gone to the King?
Parolles:	She is.
Bertram:	Will she away to-night?
Parolles:	As you'll have her. (2.5.20–3).

When Helena enters to bid farewell, Bertram is impatient to have her gone ("Let that go. / My haste is very great. Farewell; hie home"; 2.5.76–7). He lies to her, telling her he will see her again in two days. In a dialogue of indescribable pain and poignancy for most audiences, Helena makes a hesitant and circumlocutory request for a kiss:

Helena: I am not worthy of the wealth I owe,
   Nor dare I say 'tis mine; and yet it is;
   But like a timorous thief, most fain would steal
   What law does vouch mine own.
Bertram: What would you have?
Helena: Something, and scarce so much; nothing indeed.
   I would not tell you what I would, my lord.
   Faith, yes:
   Strangers and foes do sunder, and not kiss. (2.5.79–86)

Whether Bertram grants her request is at the discretion of the director, for Shakespeare does not provide a stage direction. The single-line response suggests he declines, but if he does oblige, he does so perfunctorily: "I pray you stay not, but in haste to horse" (2.5.87).

After Bertram's departure Helena opens a letter he has left her, informing her of the conditions under which he'll acknowledge her as his wife: "When thou canst get the ring upon my finger, which never shall come off, and show me a child begotten of thy body that I am father to, then call me husband; but in such a 'then' I write a 'never'" (3.2.58–60). The subtext of this letter is clear: when pigs fly. Most women would be daunted and deterred by such blatant rejection. Not Helena. She interprets the letter (obstinately? courageously? blindly?) not as rejection but as challenge. With marvelous ingenuity and determination – and the help of another woman – she tricks Bertram into giving her his ring and having sex with her; her ensuing pregnancy completes the fulfillment of all epistolary conditions.

Even so the play does not offer a neat conclusion. In a long and dramatic dénouement which causes as much frustration to the onstage characters as it does to the audience, Bertram lies and tries to wriggle out of the situation, before being forced by overwhelming evidence to acquiesce. Bertram is as shallow as he was at the beginning; he gives in not because he is converted but because he is cornered. He and Helena, I imagine, live unhappily ever after. Samuel Johnson, writing in the eighteenth century, speaks for many of us:

> I cannot reconcile my heart to Bertram; a man noble without generosity, and young without truth; who marries Helen as a coward and leaves her as a profligate: when she is dead [believed dead] by his unkindness, sneaks home to a second marriage, is accused by a woman whom he has wronged, defends himself by falsehood, and is dismissed to happiness. (Wimsatt 1960: 113)

That Helena succeeds in gaining her love object is undeniable. That her object is not worth gaining is beside the point. Even Shakespearean heroines fall in love with reprobates.

For Elizabethans the traditional definition of a comedy was a play that ends in marriage. In *All's Well that Ends Well*, however, the marriage occurs in act 2: boy gets girl. The problem Shakespeare poses is what happens when boy doesn't want girl. Unlike *Midsummer Night's Dream* where this situation is resolved in positive and romantic ways, *All's Well* tempers the romance with realism. The world of *All's Well* is irreducibly realistic: a world where fathers die and a mother loses guardianship of her son, where even a king can languish of an unglamorous ailment (a fistula – an abscessed gland tract in the anal region). It is a world where the French King allows his courtiers to fight for whichever side they please in the war between Florence and Siena, simply because they "are sick / For breathing and exploit" (1.2.16–17). In other words, war serves aerobic needs rather than ethical principles (a point well brought out in Trevor Nunn's 1981–2 production at the Royal Shakespeare Company where the scene opened with the confined courtiers lifting weights and doing press-ups). It is a world where Bertram's battalion ignominiously charges its own side, where his closest friend, Parolles, cowardly betrays him, and where the best slanders Parolles can invent against Captain Dumaine are somatic: he is licentious and, when inebriated, he wets the bed (Leggatt 1971: 22):

> For rapes and ravishments he parallels Nessus. . . . Drunkenness is his best virtue, for he will be swine-drunk, and in his sleep he does little harm, save to his bed-clothes about him; but they know his conditions, and lay him in straw. (4.3.251–8)

Bertram is promoted to Captain and returns from war with a facial bandage, but the clown suggests that the wound it covers may be a syphilitic sore rather than a scar (4.5.94–101).

Helena's quest for Bertram comes straight from the world of fairytale and folklore – the Clever Wench, the Curing of the King, the winning of a husband by Passing a Test. It is not surprising that, in the play's realistic world, Helena's fairytale devices should meet antiromantic resistance. Bertram resists not just marriage but genre, the comic convention that says "all's well that ends well," that marriage is a happy ending (Kastan 1985: 581). From acts 3 to 5 he proves the opposite, and the peace that concludes the play is fragile and conditional, anticipated in the future rather than cemented in the present. Helena may be pregnant but the condition imposed by Bertram was "show me a child begotten of thy body that I am father to." That child, as any lawyer would point out, is still in the future (a future known for neonatal risk). This uncertain ending is in marked contrast to the triumphant atmosphere of the Boccaccio tale from which Shakespeare took the Helena–Bertram story, where the Helena character enters not pregnant, not holding one child, but bearing healthy twin infants in her arms.

The uncertain ending of *All's Well that Ends Well* is not just physical but verbal. The last lines are fraught with conditionals – no fewer than five in four speeches. The last appears in the epilogue where the actor playing the King reaches out beyond the fabric of the play to ask us, the audience, to create a comic ending, by registering our approval with applause: "All is well ended, if this suit be won, / That you express content" (Epilogue.2–3). As David Kastan observes (1985: 584–5), we are being asked to do what a few lines earlier the characters in the play failed to do: create a comic ending.

All's Well that Ends Well is, as one critic has said, the work of a man who wants to write tragedy. However, Helena's situation is neither tragic nor comic but bleakly realistic. She wants Bertram; he doesn't want her; she wants him anyway. Probably more of us are empirically familiar with this type of situation than we are with love at first sight. Love's madness can be unmitigated folly as well as positive cecity.

Measure for Measure (1603–4); *Troilus and Cressida* (1602)

Helena is not the only Shakespeare character to persist in loving irrationally. Mariana in *Measure for Measure* feels the same way as Helena. Mariana was engaged to Angelo before the beginning of the play; Angelo broke the engagement when her family did not manage to provide the required dowry. As we saw in chapter 1, betrothal was binding in the Renaissance, a stage of marriage rather than an engagement in our sense (where we mean engaged *to be* married). Renaissance marriage had two legal stages – promise and consummation; hence the value of the bedtrick in drama to capture men like Bertram who have undertaken the first stage but reneged on the second. Note Bertram's vocabulary as he splits marriage into its two components: "Although before the solemn priest I have sworn, / I will not bed her" (2.3.269–70); "I have wedded her, not bedded her, and sworn to make the 'not' eternal" (3.2.21–2). Breaking a betrothal was essentially breaking a marriage. In *Measure for Measure* Angelo compounds his crime by offering slanderous justifications for his broken betrothal: he "swallow'd his vows whole, pretending in her discoveries of dishonour" (3.1.226–7). He thereby renders Mariana unmarriageable.

This is Angelo's pre-play activity. In the course of the play's five acts he behaves no better, and is shown to be a sexual harasser (see chapter 4), a liar, a coward, and a hypocrite. Mariana loves him nonetheless and, after a bedtrick in which she secures the marriage through sex, joyfully claims him as her husband in act 5. The Duke offers Mariana money and land "To buy you a better husband" (5.1.425). She refuses his offer with the simple state-ment, "I crave no other, nor no better man" (5.1.426). Mariana, like Helena in *All's Well that Ends Well*, here demonstrates the positive side of persis-tent love: acceptance of a flawed individual.

Troilus and Cressida ends with the two lovers parted for ever. Cressida eventually rejects Troilus, albeit at considerable emotional cost. Troilus is a self-indulgent lover who bodes ill as romantic protagonist. His love affair with Cressida is "sport" (1.1.115). He views women as goods, and sexually soiled goods at that (2.2.69–72). He finds marriage fit only for violation (he sanctions the Trojans' retention of Helen of Troy at 2.2.148–9) or for rhetorical illustration ("I take to-day a wife"; 2.2.61). Troilus does not talk of love (Lyons 1964: 111), although he talks much of passion and desire, of truth and faith, nor does he talk of marriage to Cressida. He talks, as he thinks, of self and the senses. He wants to "wallow" in the lily beds of Cressida's environment (3.2.12). His "imaginary relish" is not of the spiri-tual but the sensual (3.2.18–29). Even as he and Cressida exchange confes-sions of love, he turns the conversation to himself. With six personal pronouns in thirteen lines (3.2.158–70), he extols his personal merits and belittles women's constancy (and thus Cressida's). Not one of his romantic speeches can match the simple sincerity of Cressida's "I have lov'd you night and day / For many weary months" (3.2.114–15). He is indeed full of "brave oaths," but if we look ahead to act 4, scene 2 we see how little substance there is behind his sentimental protestations.

In this scene Aeneas announces the immediate exchange of Cressida for a Trojan prisoner-of-war. Troilus's question, "Is it so concluded?" (4.2.66), may be the dazed response of a devastated lover. However, he makes no protestation, no denial (contrast Cressida's anguished and determined lines at 94–109: "I will not go . . . I have forgot my father"; 4.2.94, 96), and his first thoughts (line 69) are typically of himself: "how my achievements mock me!" (two personal pronouns in one line). Is this all Cressida is to him – an "achievement"? His second thoughts are similarly unsentimental, a quick priming of Aeneas in protective mendacity: "and, my Lord Aeneas, / We met by chance, you did not find me here" (4.2.70–1). He exits; no thoughts of Cressida; no farewell; no comfort. (The BBC film, clearly uncomfortable with Troilus's exit, follows act 4, scene 2 with scene 4, so that Troilus and Cressida can react together after the news of her exchange for Antenor.)

When Troilus returns in 4.4, it is as part of the official Trojan delegation to accompany Cressida to the Greek camp. The brief private goodbye with

Cressida is embedded in an atmosphere of mistrust: five commands to "be true," which distress rather than reassure Cressida ("O heavens! 'be true' again?"; 4.4.74). Critics rightly condemn Troilus for insensitivity here. "At this moment when Cressida surely needs comfort and sympathy, he again insults her integrity with a series of imperatives" (Okerlund 1980: 9). These imperatives prompt Cressida's most poignant cry, "O heavens, you love me not!" (4.4.82), a clear-eyed interpretation of the evidence.

Troilus's language and attitude in leave-taking continue to be as narcissistic as they were in love-making. The separation is seen as affecting only him, as divine punishment for his love. Like many egoists, Troilus loves the victim role:

> Cressid, I love thee in so strain'd a purity,
> That the blest gods, as angry with my fancy,
> More bright in zeal than the devotion which
> Cold lips blow to their deities, take thee from me. (4.4.24–7)

His next speech is similarly fanciful but, as Howard Adams points out (1991: 85), the elaborate phrasing is unambiguous in intent: "Chance / . . . strangles our dear vows / Even in the birth of our own labouring breath" (4.4.33–8). The relationship is over. Troilus accepts an externally imposed conclusion, leading several critics to believe that he grasps this opportunity with relief. Cressida is now remainder viands; apparently one night's "sport" has satisfied his sense of "achievement." These reactions confirm the "monstrous" nature of his earlier vows: Troilus has (as Cressida feared) the voice of a lion and the act of a hare (3.2.79).

It is hard to give up someone just because you know they're no good. (Love is irrational, as we saw above.) Cressida never falls out of love with Troilus; she just falls into reason. Unique among Shakespearean heroines, she makes the decision to follow her head not her heart. This does not guarantee her happiness but it does guarantee emotional survival.

4   Marriage and Identity

Comedy of Errors (1594)

As we saw in chapter 1, twins, particularly separated twins, provide an obvious starting point for any examination of identity. *Comedy of Errors* extends its investigation of identity, however, from siblings and selfhood to wives and womanhood: Adriana struggles to reconcile her sexual and spiritual roles in marriage.

Adriana's predicament derives in part from a duality in Renaissance attitudes to women. Viewed as both divine and dangerous, women and their beauty could lead men to an appreciation of higher things (the spiritually beautiful, the celestial) or to physical temptation (lust, gratification, damnation). Both extremes of these female stereotypes are represented in *Errors*. The love-stricken Antipholus of Syracuse employs the vocabulary of worship in wooing Luciana: she is "divine," "a god" (3.2.32, 39). In the next scene, his servant, Dromio of Syracuse, uses the language of demonology to describe his pursuit by the sexually forward maidservant, Luce: Luce "haunts" him (3.2.82), she is a "diviner" [witch], she knows "what privy marks" he has, so that he "amaz'd, ran from her as a witch" (3.2.140–4). The common root of these two women's names (Luce and Luciana) shows that the demonic female (the "diviner" who would possess the male) and the divine female (the goddess whom the male wishes to possess) are but two sides of the same female stereotype.

Adriana attempts to unite both extremes, attending to her husband's body and soul: she offers private dinner (a euphemism for sex) and confession ("Husband, I'll dine above with you to-day, / And shrive you of a thousand idle pranks"; 2.2.207–8). Adriana sees her identity as a wife as a fusion of two opposing female stereotypes.

Shakespeare departed from Plautus's setting of Epidamnum, situating his action in Ephesus. Historically, Ephesus offers two polarized female role models. The first is the independent unmarried pagan Amazon (tradition held that Amazons founded Ephesus). The second is the submissive Christian servant (St. Paul's letter to the Ephesians sets out the standards of Christian marital behavior in which the wife defers to her husband as head of the household). It is because of Ephesus's tradition of Amazon women that St. Paul directs his letter about wifely submission not to the Galatians, Corinthians, or Colossians, not to the Philippians, the Hebrews, or the Romans, but to the Ephesians. It is the Ephesians who are most in need of Paul's advice: "Wives should be subject to their husbands as to the Lord, since, as Christ is head of the Church and saves the whole body, so is a husband the head of his wife; and as the Church is subject to Christ, so should wives be to their husbands in everything" (Ephesians 5:21–33). Shakespeare's change of location was presumably designed to exploit the dual associations of Ephesus.

At the beginning of the play Adriana is clearly equated with the Amazon Ephesian, Luciana with the Christian. Adriana chafes at the restrictions marriage imposes on women ("Why should their liberty than ours be more?"; 2.1.10). Luciana knows Paul's lesson by heart:

> There's nothing situate under heaven's eye
> But hath his bound in earth, in sea, in sky.
> The beasts, the fishes, and the winged fowls
> Are their males' subjects and at their controls:
> Man, more divine, the master of all these,
> Lord of the wide world and wild wat'ry seas,
> Indu'd with intellectual sense and souls,
> Of more pre-eminence than fish and fowls,
> Are masters to their females, and their lords. (2.1.16–24)

In Trevor Nunn's RSC production in 1976–7 Luciana read the speech from a book (presumably the Bible or a Bible commentary) in which she showed her sister the relevant passage, indicating that the subject is non-negotiable.

Having introduced this opposition between the Amazon and the Pauline female, the play immediately begins to question it. Adriana can hardly be an independent woman since, as a wife, she has legally promised submission, while Luciana, who preaches submission, can do so only because (as Adriana points out) she is independent (2.1.38–41). The identities of Adriana and Luciana, like those of the twins, begin to merge, become confused. Despite her rhetorical question, "Why should their liberty than ours be more?"(2.1.10), Adriana seems to want not liberty but the right to love and be loved as a wife. When next we meet the women it is Adriana who has the long Pauline speech on marriage as she lyrically, passionately tells Antipholus that husband and wife are "undividable incorporate" (2.2.122; cf. Ephesians 5:31). Luciana's subsequent speech on marriage is strangely unspiritual, full of knowing advice to her (supposed) brother-in-law about how to conduct an extramarital affair: "Look sweet, speak fair, become disloyalty; / Apparel vice like virtue's harbinger; / Bear a fair presence, though your heart be tainted; / Teach sin the carriage of a holy saint: / Be secret-false" (3.2.11–15). Throughout *Errors* we see Adriana and Luciana trying to work out which type of Ephesian woman to be (pagan or Christian, independent or submissive), and experimenting with whether it is possible to be both. Can women be both divine (the spiritual goddess) and a "diviner" (a sexual bewitcher)? Can female identity synthesize polarities?

These questions arise in part from a contemporary debate, *la querelle des femmes* ("the debate about women"), which reached its high point in the 1590s. Female identity had long been characterized in bipolar terms: women were fickle or constant; they lacked a soul (Genesis only said God made a second body) or were goddesses to be worshipped; they were shrewish or silent; devious or dutiful. The debate began with the early church fathers for whom there were only two models of womanhood (Eve or the Madonna), but it was reopened in the sixteenth century with pamphleteers, prose writers, and dramatists all weighing in with an opinion for or against women. The reopening was prompted in part by the fact that a woman was on the throne and seemed to be doing rather a good job of governing the country; by the 1590s it was not possible to dismiss female ability as blithely as had once been the case. In *Comedy of Errors* Shakespeare links the contemporary debate about women with the contemporary debate about identity (see chapter 1). It used to be customary to dismiss *Errors* as apprentice work, perhaps Shakespeare's first play (short, farcically physical, full of end-stopped rhyming couplets and puns), but its investigation of identity – the individual's, the twin's, the married woman's – seems to me remarkably sophisticated. The recent confident placing of this play in 1594 seems eminently justifiable.

All's Well that Ends Well (1604–5); Taming of the Shrew (1590–1)

Like Adriana, Helena in *All's Well that Ends Well* faces a conflict relating to her identity in marriage as she tries to combat society's stereotypes. Her play enlarges the exploration of selfhood to encompass the struggles faced by both Helena and her young husband, Bertram, as they develop from boy and girl to man and wife.

Bertram's father has died just before the play begins; because Bertram is too young to inherit, he is sent to the French court in Paris, to complete his minority under the guardianship of the King. Bertram is understandably eager to experience the world, but is frustrated when his youth renders him ineligible for the Italian wars: "I am commanded here [ordered to stay here], and kept a coil with, / 'Too young' and 'the next year' and ''tis too early'" (2.1.27–8). Further restricted by an arranged marriage to Helena, he runs away to war.

Military activity, under the jurisdiction of Mars, is traditionally where boys become men. Bertram enthusiastically invokes the god of war:

Great Mars, I put myself into thy file;
Make me but like my thoughts, and I shall prove
A lover of thy drum, hater of love. (3.3.9–11)

Bertram achieves great honors on the battlefield, thus coming of age as a
man. He is promoted to general of the horse and the Florentines say "the
French count has done most honorable service" (3.5.3–4). But war is not
the only arena for proving manhood; sex is also an important *rite de passage*
(Parker 1984: 101–2; Ranald 1987: 45; Stanton 1992: 160). Although he is
resistant to marriage and is a "hater of love," Bertram is not averse to sex,
and in Florence he tries to seduce a young virgin, Diana. His attempted
seduction is described in terms of siege warfare (he "lays down his wanton
siege before her [Diana's] beauty"; 3.7.18), but Diana, we are told, "is arm'd
for him, and keeps her guard / In honestest defense" (3.5.73–4). For
Bertram, sex and battle merge, both activities under the auspices of Mars,
both arenas in which he can aggressively prove himself a man.

For Elizabethan men, masculine honor was synonymous with
military glory. For Elizabethan women, "honor" had a different meaning:
virginity (Parker 1984). When Bertram denies Diana's request that he
give her his family ring, justifying his refusal on the grounds that the
ring represents ancestral honor, Diana turns his logic and terminology
against him:

    Mine honor's such a ring,
My chastity's the jewel of our house . . .
Which were the greatest obloquy i'th'world
In me to lose. Thus your own proper wisdom
Brings in the champion Honour on my part,
Against your vain assault. (4.2.445–6, 448–51)

Diana, as befits her namesake the goddess of chastity, wishes to retain her
virgin honor.

Helena, however, has a different attitude. In the play's first scene she
engages in a conversation with Parolles, one of Bertram's followers, about
how a woman may (1) barricade her virginity against the enemy, man; and
(2), failing that, how a woman may "lose it to her own liking" (1.1.150–1).
Elizabethan women were not supposed to have a "liking" for sex. Critics
have condemned Helena for her frankness, and for her tenacity in pursuing Bertram to the bedroom. (She encourages Diana to agree to Bertram's
sexual request, but it is actually Helena who spends the night with

Bertram.) Milton Shulman described her as "a heroine with the brash moral standards of a strumpet" (cited in Styan 1984: 14). Throughout the play Helena pursues Bertram in France, in Italy, in Spain, at the French court, and in the bedroom. As a result she is in danger, as she herself realizes, of being charged with "impudence [immodesty], / A strumpet's boldness, a divulged shame" (2.1.170–1). Simply put, a determined woman must be shameless. "Impudence" today has no severer a meaning than impertinence; however its Latin root, *pudere* (to cause shame), which it shares with pudenda, was very much to the fore in the Renaissance. Impudence was a carnal transgression: sexual immodesty, something to be ashamed of.

Literature, like life, knows how to categorize the modest virgin, and it knows how to categorize her opposite, the whore. What Helena wants is the pleasure of lawful married sex – and Elizabethan society had no category in which to slot this legitimate desire. Bertram's journey to selfhood in the field of Mars is thus easier than Helena's in the field of Venus, for he at least does not encounter a societal double standard. His sexual peccadilloes are viewed as adolescent experiment: "Certain it is I lik'd her," he says of Diana and his supposed tryst, "And boarded her i'th'wanton way of youth" (5.3.210–11). Diana, on the other hand, is viewed as a "common customer" for her putative sexual encounter.

Contemporary events remind us of the prejudices faced by Helena and Diana. (The William Kennedy-Smith rape trial made much of the fact that the victim wore underwear from the American lingerie store Victoria's Secret.) Shakespeare's careful choice of female names in the play points out the reductive sexual stereotyping of women in his age: he gives Diana the name of the mythological goddess of chastity and gives Helena the name of the mythological queen whose sexual activity led to the Trojan war. (For the early modern period Helen of Troy was not just an icon of shame but an emblem of unrestrained sexual desire. The forms of her name, Helen and Helena, are used interchangeably in the period, just as Shakespeare abbreviates Diana to Dian.) But between these extremes lies a healthy halfway house: female enjoyment of, and desire for, married sex. Men are from Mars, women are from Venus. The problem is that Venus was not simply associated with loving marital intercourse: Renaissance slang used "nuns of Venus" as a euphemism for whore. When Helena seeks Bertram as a husband ("Dian, from thy altar do I fly"; 2.3.74), the problem she encounters is how to fly from Diana's altar to Venus's without being viewed as a slut (Parker 1984: 100; Stanton 1992: 158).

Helena's desire for Bertram leads her into paradox. On the one hand, her bold pursuit brands her as a shameless woman. On the other hand, it identifies her as masculine: publicly active, desiring, choosing. In becoming an active participant in the choice of her husband, Helena seeks an identity that her society does not sanction. Katherine in *The Shrew* similarly objects to society's codes: she wants freedom of speech in an age that does not permit her this liberty. Her crime is linked with Helena's via sex. In a simple metalepsis the early modern period viewed the mouth as a sexual surrogate: if a woman opened one orifice (her mouth), how could men be sure she would not indiscriminately open another (her vagina)? A woman who could control her desire for speech could also exercise sexual control. Helena does not want indiscriminate sex; she simply wants to choose her marriage partner, just as Katherine does not want indiscriminate speech: she simply wants to be permitted to protest:

> My tongue will tell the anger of my heart,
> Or else my heart concealing it will break.
> And rather than it shall, I will be free,
> Even to the uttermost, as I please, in words. (4.3.77–80)

Being true to yourself when society's values are in opposition to yours is a struggle, as the predicaments of both Helena and Katherine reveal, but Katherine's second line above shows the consequences of not being true to oneself: emotional damage. Katherine says simply that speech is "psychologically necessary for her survival" (Kahn 1981: 108). There are no more heartrending lines in Shakespeare.

5   Love and Abuse

"Fortune is a woman, and it is necessary to beat her and maul her when you want to keep her under control" (Machiavelli 1977: 123)

Introduction

Abuse is a contemporary term with a very long practical history. Obviously, any culture that views women legally as objects owned and traded by men, that views women spiritually as evil and in need of subjugation and physical correction, that views women intellectually as inferior and institutionalizes this view in education, politics, and law, that views women physically as substandard versions of men, and that views marriage as a hierarchy rather than a partnership, is likely to lead to abuse. Misogynist cultures that deem women inferior in all these areas have brought exceptional creative ingenuity to bear on the development of physical cruelty to women: in the West we have chastity belts, infanticide, femicide, rape, witch-burning, wife-beating, branks, and cucking (Lerner 1986: passim; Wilson 1997: 252).[3] Legal systems and societal custom have long been on the side of the abuser. An Elizabethan proverb proclaimed "A woman, an ass, and a walnut tree: the more they're beaten, the better they be" (Tilley 1950: W644), and until 1891 British husbands were legally permitted to keep their wives under lock and key (Morgan 1982: 6). Although the insidious hallmark of abuse today is privacy, early modern domestic violence was public – even when carried on at home, for the household was a public place. The "branked" wife was paraded in the street, the charivari was a public event; crowds assembled to watch cucking of scolds (Dolan 1996: 14–24, 218–25, 244–303). Even if the husband lacked witnesses to his physical control over his wife, he had no need to conceal the means by which he achieved domination, for his mastery was a matter for celebration not secrecy. Abuse was simply a blunt reality of early modern life.

Taming of the Shrew (1590–1); Merry Wives of Windsor (1597–8)

Katherine in *The Shrew* is the most obvious Shakespeare example of an abused woman. Although New Criticism may interpret Petruccio's contradictions ("Say that she rail, why then I'll tell her plain / She sings as sweetly as a nightingale"; 2.1.170–1) as a game, a loving tease with the positive psychological aim of behavior modification (see chapter 1), in the twenty-first century it is difficult to find the subjugation of a woman a suitable subject for comic treatment.

Early modern society divided women into two categories: those who are silent (and therefore desirable) and those who are talkative (and therefore unmarriageable). In the first acts of the play Katherine's sister, Bianca, is

---

[3] Not all patriarchal cultures are misogynist. "Although the earliest writings of Greece, Rome and Israel contain and justify female subordination, they are not misogynous. This attitude came later in the Greek poetry of the seventh and sixth centuries BCE, in the satires and poetry of the first century AD in Rome, and in the Jewish and Christian interpretations of the Old Testament from the second century BCE to the third century AD. Women would then be stigmatized as innately evil" (Wilson 1997: 252).

Plate 3 The brank, a head harness with a sharp spur which lay on the tongue, was applied to women who talked too much. If the woman tried to talk, she lacerated her tongue (swallowing had the same effect). The design similarity between this instrument and a horse's bridle is obvious; the vocabulary of shrew-taming has much in common with that of horse-training. This picture comes from the cover of Minette Walters's detective novel, *The Scold's Bridle* (1994).

praised for "silence" and "mild behavior and sobriety" (1.1.70–1), while Katherine is described as a wild animal, a "wildcat," a "wasp," a "devil," a "fiend of hell" (1.2.196, 2.1.209, 1.1.66, 1.1.88). Coppélia Kahn points out (1981: 107–8) that Katherine does very little to earn her wild and diabolic epithets; the mere fact of her speech – twelve lines in 1.1 – is sufficient to brand her.

Enter Petruccio, a young man in search of money and a challenge (he confesses the former; we infer the latter). Katherine provides both. Her desperate father offers a huge dowry to the man who can win Katherine's love. His proviso that her suitor gain Katherine's love is a redeeming feature, given the transactional nature of early modern marriage; Katherine's feelings need play no part in Baptista's negotiations. Petruccio undertakes to tame Katherine and turn her into a model wife. This he does, as we saw in chapter 1, by a calculated process of verbal and physical disorientation. He contradicts Katherine in an example of what today's mental health professionals call "countering"; he deprives her of food and sleep; and he behaves unpredictably – he hits the priest, swears in church, rejects designer clothing that he has ordered for Katherine, and beats his servants for nugatory reasons. Eventually Katherine gives in to this contrary man, agreeing that the sun is the moon and the moon the sun.

Taming of the Shrew belongs to the subgenre of comedy known as farce. Farce has certain stock ingredients. In farce characters react rather than reflect. In *The Shrew* Katherine simply responds to stimuli whereas the lovers in *Midsummer Night's Dream* compare their experiences in the woods. *The Shrew* is not a meditative play: Katherine has no soliloquies, Petruccio only two, and the purpose of these is to relay information rather than reveal psychology. Michael Siberry, who acted Petruccio at the RSC in 1995, points out that "Petruccio is someone who never explains himself: he may tell you what he is doing, but he won't explain why" (1998: 45). Farce centers on confusion and contradiction; characters mistake and are mistaken, "yes" is opposed to "no." Act 5 of *The Shrew* presents two Vincentios (the onstage characters' automatic reaction is to arrest the second Vincentio rather than ascertain which of the two is the legitimate bearer of the name). In farce the plot moves fast, a strategy designed to prevent us thinking, for if the action were slow, we'd have time to realize how silly it was. Farce is violent at the slightest provocation (Petruccio beats characters from his servant to the priest) and the violence lacks consequence; thus Katherine can break Hortensio's lute (an expensive instrument) over his head and no one need ask him if he is hurt or has insurance (cf. Heilman

1963: xxxii). Farce often employs domestic or marital plots (Punch and Judy is simply farce transferred to the puppet world, as Dolan points out, 1996: 296–9). These generic ingredients in *The Shrew* cue us to view the play as farce not as realism, to expect puppets not psychology.

But, as John Mortimer once remarked, farce is simply tragedy played at two hundred revolutions per minute. In real life, violence is tragic not comic. In real life, repeated angry outbursts by a man for the purpose of controlling a woman are far from funny. In real life, denying a human being food and sleep constitutes cruelty not comedy. These are the tactics of brainwashing cults and political torture, the substance of petitions to governments and letters to Amnesty International. In the 1940 Thorold Dickinson film *Gaslight*, the husband contradicts the wife continually, convincing others that she is mad. His manipulations are terrifying, not comic.

In defense of Petruccio, we may note, as critics frequently do, that he never actually hits Katherine. This restraint is in marked contrast to one of the play's sources, *A Merry Jest of a Shrewd and Curst Wife Lapped in Morel's Skin for her Good Behaviour* (published in 1594). In this long ballad, the husband kills the family horse (Morel), salts its hide, beats his wife until her skin bleeds, wraps her in the salted horsehide, and then locks her in the basement. Such tactics are typical in shrew-taming literature, and Petruccio is unusual in eschewing them. However, no husband is a decent chap just because he behaves less badly than he might. In current medical usage, "abuse" is not confined to physical assault: it includes repeated verbal and emotional mistreatment and belittlement ("psychological abuse"). There is no denying that Petruccio is psychologically cruel. When Petruccio shouts, beats his servants, and behaves unpredictably, he reminds Katherine that he has power to hurt his subordinates and property – and hence her (Dolan 1996: 19), for in Renaissance culture a wife was, like the furniture and the servants, "household stuff" and could be treated the same way.

Contemporary case studies suggest that if a man puts his fist through the drywall or kicks the furniture, he will eventually transfer his violence to his partner. Farce may be a world without pain but real life is not. Real-life women need to get help and get out. Katherine does not get help, nor does she get out. Sixteenth-century women couldn't. However, in some interpretations and stage presentations of the play Katherine is not at risk. Petruccio's manipulations, contradictions, and imposed deprivations are seen as a game – a loving tease with the positive psychological aim of behavior modification. Changed behavioral patterns will enable

Katherine to find her true identity, receive societal approval, and live happily ever after.

There is much to support this line of argument. Petruccio's strategy is obviously to teach Katherine to see beyond exteriors. Thus his outrageous attire on his wedding day is accompanied by the explanation "to me she's married, not unto my clothes" (3.2.117), a motif restated in the next act when he insists that they travel to her father's house in old clothes:

> For 'tis the mind that makes the body rich;
> And as the sun breaks through the darkest clouds,
> So honor peereth in the meanest habit.
> What, is the jay more precious than the lark,
> Because his feathers are more beautiful?
> Or is the adder better than the eel,
> Because his painted skin contents the eye?
> O no, good Kate (4.3.172–9)

Thus we should look beyond Petruccio's external – abusive – behavior.

Petruccio's syntax suggests that he falls genuinely in love with Katherine, for the two parenthetical comments on her beauty constitute departures from his preconceived spiel:

> Hearing thy mildness prais'd in every town,
> Thy virtues spoke of, and thy beauty sounded,
> *Yet not so deeply as to thee belongs,*
> Myself am mov'd to woo thee for my wife. (2.1.191–4)

> For by this light whereby I see thy beauty,
> *Thy beauty that doth make me like thee well.* (2.1.273–4)

Editors punctuate the italicized comments variously – with dashes, commas, brackets – but in all instances their ad hoc nature – and hence their genuineness – is clear. In the BBC film John Cleese's Petruccio dropped his voice and put his hand on Katherine's shoulder, moved by the sight of her, before exaggeratedly resuming his chirpy spiel. She, in turn, was moved by the tactile contact (clearly foreign to her) and the seeds of their relationship were sown.

All the deprivations Petruccio subsequently imposes on Katherine – lack of sleep, lack of food – he also imposes on himself (Cleese's Petruccio could hardly complete his soliloquy in 4.1 without yawning). In the ridiculous demands of the sun–moon scene, Petruccio is not asking Katherine to submit but to play: to join with him in a game of playfully transforming reality. At this point Katherine not only enters into the world of play but goes one better through exaggeration (see chapter 1). When Petruccio asks Katherine to address an old man as a woman, she addresses the man not just as a woman but as a "young budding virgin" (4.5.37), then continues in a salacious nudge-nudge wink-wink extravaganza: "Happy the parents of so fair a child! / Happier the man whom favorable stars / Allots thee for his lovely bedfellow!" (4.5.39–41). By the time Petruccio chooses to correct her ("this is a man"; 4.5.43) Katherine is rhetorically in command, and a piece of brilliant stagebusiness has become the norm. She apologizes:

> Pardon, old father, my mistaking eyes,
> That have been so bedazzled with the [*Katherine looks at Petruccio for guidance*] – sun? –
> That every thing I look on seemeth green. (4.5.45–7)

We are now prepared for the same tone of teasing exaggeration in Katherine's 45-line speech of submission in act 5.

Additional support for viewing Petruccio's tactics as a positive invitation to play come from the Induction. As we saw in chapter 1 ("The Self at Play"), what the Lords do to Sly in a temporary way Petruccio does for Katherine at a psychological level. Sly is given a new identity as a lord and, like Katherine, is bombarded with a new name ("your lordship," "your honour"). As a result, his behavior changes: he speaks in blank verse.

I like this interpretation a lot because it enables me to read and teach the play without feeling abject misery. Deep down, however, I know that such an interpretation actually makes matters worse for it says that a woman can only find herself with the help of a man, or worse, that a man is entitled to overrule a woman's life and behavior choices. Furthermore, it makes Katherine's lengthy final speech dubiously triumphant. She is applauded by all on stage, including Petruccio; paradoxically, she has achieved what she always wanted – the right to speak – and she ends the play doing what she was doing at the beginning – scolding Bianca, only this time with male approval. But it is surely a Pyrrhic victory for Katherine if her freedom of speech as a woman is dependent on male cues and party-line patriarchal content. She can achieve what she wants only by appearing to do what her husband wants. She can be who she is only by not being who she is. What profits it a woman if she gain a voice but lose her identity?

Part of the intellectual attraction of *Taming of the Shrew* is that its misogyny is open to debate. As a literary critic I can see both sides of the interpretive coin. As a woman, however, I cannot find the subjugation of a wife fit matter for comic treatment. Shakespeare, I think, was dissatisfied too. He avoided farce in future plays (with one exception, *Merry Wives of Windsor*, which was written in special circumstances), and his next two abused women appear in tragedies: *Othello* and *Troilus and Cressida*. Before we turn to these tragedies, let us consider the *Merry Wives*.

The *Merry Wives* was allegedly written to command when Queen Elizabeth expressed a desire to see Falstaff in love; Shakespeare adapted a play-in-progress by inserting a plot in which Falstaff simultaneously woos the two eponymous wives as a get-rich-quick scheme. As it stands, the play has many loose ends, and the integration of farcical revenge with Italianate intrigue and topical allusion is clearly not complete. Nonetheless, the play is thematically coherent and has much to say about domestic behavior, marital trust, and bourgeois citizen values.

Seeking revenge for their recent dismissal, Falstaff's men inform the Windsor husbands, Ford and Page, of Falstaff's designs on their wives. Page is confident of his wife's honesty; the pathologically suspicious Ford, however, visits Falstaff in disguise where Falstaff boasts that Mistress Ford has already made a tryst with him. The tryst is actually a set-up: outraged at Falstaff's overtures to them, the wives have joined forces to humiliate Falstaff. By arranging for the rendezvous between Mistress Ford and Falstaff to be interrupted, they plan to have Falstaff unceremoniously removed. The staged interruption becomes reality, however, when the jealous Ford returns unexpectedly and Falstaff, hiding in the laundry basket, is dumped in the river. He fares no better on the second assignation when, disguised as the fat woman of Brainford, Ford beats him out of the house.

Falstaff is not the only "female" to be beaten by Ford. When Mistress Ford's emissary, Mistress Quickly, visits Falstaff to arrange a third assignation, she reveals that Mistress Ford "is beaten black and blue, that you cannot see a white spot about her" (4.5.112–13). Falstaff's response defuses this moment of potential alarm by turning it into comic competition – "What tell'st thou me of black and blue? I was beaten myself into all the colors of the rainbow" (4.5.114–16). Quickly's story may be a fiction, of course, for by this time Ford is in on the plot, and the two couples, plus the rest of Windsor, unite to arrange Falstaff's third and public humiliation. But if not a true account of events, Quickly's statement is emotionally true: violence is often a consequence of jealousy, as Shakespeare shows a few years later in *Othello*.

Ford's jealous suspicions of his wife are partly borne of his attitude to her as property: "Money buys lands, and wives are sold by fate" (5.5.233). Only what is owned or possessed can be stolen; if one views a wife as property, one fears loss of that property. Ford's mercantile approach to matrimony – shared by Fenton, at least initially, and by Slender and Caius who woo Anne Page for her dowry and inheritance prospects – is analogous to Falstaff's attitude to fornication: "She [Mistress Page] bears the purse too; she is a region in Guiana, all gold and bounty. I will be cheater [escheator] to them both and they shall be my exchequers [treasuries] to me. They shall be my East and West Indies, and I will trade to them both" (1.3.67–72). In a sense, the wives' comic revenge on Falstaff stands for their punishment of all men (White 1991: 17), their repudiation of the commodification of women and the cleansing of middle-class Windsor society.

Othello (1604); *Troilus and Cressida* (1602)

In *Othello*, Iago's wife, Emilia, fits the typical profile of the abused wife, just as Iago fits the classic profile of the abuser. Susan Forward observes that "no-one who feels good about himself needs to control another human being" (1986: 226); and Iago clearly does not "feel good" about himself. He is envious of Cassio for the "daily beauty" in his life; he is sexually suspicious of Othello (he believes that Othello has slept with Emilia); and he is a misogynist, belittling women in general and Emilia in particular (2.1.100–61). His mercurial moods further mark him as a dangerous man.

Emilia's personality is well-nigh effaced in her desire to please and placate her husband. It is not until the final act, when she realizes that Iago is responsible for Desdemona's death, that she finds the courage to speak out. However, as is so often the case in abusive relationships, this new-found knowledge of the nature of her husband, and her threat to leave ("Perchance, Iago, I will ne'er go home"; 5.2.197), endangers her safety. Iago kills her before she can reveal further truths about his character and actions.

One of the most painful demonstrations of abuse comes in a short scene in *Troilus and Cressida*, a play written just before *Othello*. The Trojan Cressida is forced to leave her lover, Troilus, and, immediately on arrival in the enemy Greek camp, is "wooed" by her guard, Diomedes. The scene is traditionally viewed as a scene of seduction, with Cressida being blamed by critics for giving Diomedes the love-pledge which Troilus had given her just twenty-four hours before. In fact, the scene is a textbook example of abuse.

Shakespeare presents Diomedes as a bully, *tout court*. Diomedes ignores Cressida's evident pain, ambivalence, and reluctance to give him a love-token. He uses a simple tactic – anger – thereby making the episode one of male coercion rather than female agreement. Psychologists tell us that, when faced with anger, the sensitive and the insecure will apologize for things for which they are not to blame, abase themselves, agree, submit, concede, do anything – including relinquishing Troilus's love-token – to stop the angry attitude or rhetoric. "Nay but you part in anger," says Cressida, and Troilus, who is eavesdropping, asks rhetorically, "Does that grieve thee?" (5.2.45). His interpretation could not be more wrong. It does not grieve Cressida; it frightens her, bewilders her.

Note how the dialogue between Diomedes and Cressida repeats one pattern throughout the scene: she makes a request, he breaks off in evident anger, and she capitulates. Note how Diomedes is on the point of exit several times in the scene, but Cressida cannot let him part in anger; how he gets what he wants, even though it is obvious that this is not what she wants; how he overrules her; how her "No" goes unheard because she falls into self-denying submissive behavior. (I omit all asides from the three eavesdroppers and add implied stage directions.)

> *Cressida:*   . . . tempt me no more to folly. . . .
> *Diomedes:*   Nay then – *[he offers to exit]*
> *Cressida:*   I'll tell you what – (5.2.18–21)

> *Cressida:*   I prithee do not hold me to mine oath,
>   Bid me do any thing but that, sweet Greek.
> *Diomedes:*   Good night. . . . *[he offers to exit]*
> *Cressida:*   Diomed –
> *Diomedes:*   No, no, good night, I'll be your fool no more
>   *[he offers to exit]* . . .
> *Cressida:*   Hark a word in your ear. . . . (5.2.26–34)

> *Diomedes:*   And so good night. *[he offers to exit]*
> *Cressida:*   Nay, but you part in anger. (5.2.44–5)

After these exchanges, Cressida gives Diomedes the love-pledge from Troilus – the sleeve – but instantly regrets the gift and recalls it. Diomedes insists on having it, and aggressively questions Cressida about its original owner. It is clear from an earlier conversation between Diomedes and Troilus that Diomedes can be in no doubt about the identity of his rival, but, as one critic points out, his insistent "Whose was it?" beginning at 5.2.90 (he repeats the question four times) indicates his need to prove his conquest by having Cressida surrender utterly. Cressida tries to defy Diomedes – "I will not keep my word" – but Diomedes's angry threat of exit, his fifth, is more than she can cope with: "You shall not go. One cannot speak a word / But it straight starts you" (5.2.98, 100–1). She accurately identifies his behavioral pattern (i.e., "I can't say anything without you reacting with anger and withdrawal"). He ignores her diagnosis-cum-plea, uttering only a terse and menacing response: "I do not like this fooling" (5.2.101).

That abuse has a literary Shakespearean precedent is scant consolation to anyone. Real-life victims do not become heroines – at least, not until they are dead (Nicole Brown Simpson is an obvious example). For Shakespeare, abuse is a story with only one ending – extinction. Katherine loses her personality, Emilia her life, and Cressida her autonomy.

3

Political Life:
Shakespeare and Government

"*Always in Shakespeare political attitudes stem from personality*" (Humphreys 1984: 36)

Introduction

Politics and politicians are treated pejoratively in the Shakespeare canon, at least where *en passant* references are concerned. For Lear, politicians are "scurvy" tricksters who "seem / To see the things [they do] not" (4.6.171–2); Hamlet considers a politician someone who "would circumvent God" (5.1.79); Hotspur condemns Bullingbrook as a "vile politician" (*1HIV* 1.3.241). In all three quotations "politician" is synonymous with "schemer." Of course, in a period that saw the first political "how to" manual – Machiavelli's *The Prince* (ca. 1513) – it was impossible to view politicians favorably. Although the modern meaning of politician as "statesman" was current in the late sixteenth century, Machiavellian trickster was the dominant definition.

Machiavelli's pragmatic conduct book demonstrates how to gain and consolidate power. Throughout, the stress is on appearance rather than truth, and the book promotes cruelty, treachery, violence, and irreligiosity. It promotes these not as ends in themselves but as means to secure a strong state, a teleology overlooked by early modern English readers. Consequently *The Prince* was (mis)interpreted as a cynical work of unabashed immorality. Little wonder that in the sixteenth century "Old Nick" denoted both Niccolò Machiavelli and Satan.

In fact, *The Prince* was a description of "what men do" rather than a prescription for "what they ought to do" (Bacon 1966: 190). Nonetheless the book was banned by Tudor politicians, and its practical cornerstone creeds were interpreted negatively and reductively. "Policy" became a byword for crafty intrigue, "political" a synonym for "Machiavellian." In *Merry Wives of Windsor* the Host protests his innocence with a series of rhetorical questions: "Am I politic? Am I subtle? Am I a Machivel?" (3.1.101) All three terms are synonymous.

If the Machiavel is a negative political figure, a "politic" and "subtle" man, he is also creative and theatrical. In Renaissance drama our appreciation of a character's theatrical presentation of himself often conflicts with our moral condemnation. Richard III's insolent wooing of Lady Anne is a typical example: our horror at the brash audacity with which Richard woos the grieving woman whose husband and father-in-law he has murdered (Prince Edward and Henry VI) gives way to zest for his bravura performance over the coffin of Henry VI. Richard encourages our positive reaction with his self-congratulatory coda, addressed to the audience:

> Was ever woman in this humor woo'd?
> Was ever woman in this humor won? . . .
> What? I that kill'd her husband and his father,
> To take her in her heart's extremest hate,
> With curses in her mouth, tears in her eyes,
> The bleeding witness of my hatred by,
> Having God, her conscience, and these bars against me,
> And I no friends to back my suit at all
> But the plain devil and dissembling looks?
> And yet to win her! All the world to nothing! (1.2.227–8, 230–7)

By focusing on the odds against him ("all the world to nothing"), he foregrounds technical accomplishment and sidesteps ethics.

That political figures should also be performers comes as no surprise in our age of spin-doctors and speech writers. Ronald Reagan provides the most obvious example of the symbiosis of theater and politics but analogous cases are numerous. Bill Clinton's charisma is presented as performance skill rather than genuine quality in *Primary Colors* (book and film). Margaret Thatcher took voice lessons to lower her tonal pitch. Saddam Hussein proved a master of sartorial manipulation during the Kuwait crisis of 1990: Arab dress – the patriot; Western suit – the statesman; combat uniform – the military hero. Tony Blair matches his props to his audience (a civilized china cup for tea at the Women's Institute Conference; a no-nonsense earthenware mug for tea with the trade unions; a mug with a sentimental transfer of his children for an impromptu weekend interview outside 10 Downing Street). But to an early modern audience whose political figures were regal ones, divinely appointed rather than democratically elected, the notion of authority as performative was incongruous. In *Macbeth* King Duncan's body is "the Lord's anointed temple" (2.3.68); Shakespeare's anachronism, given the elective thanist succession in medieval Scotland, illustrates how deeply entrenched is the notion of divine rulers.

"Not all the water in the rough rude sea / Can wash the balm off from an anointed king" states Richard II (*RII* 3.2.54–5). Richard's medieval worldview is about to be deposed, as is Richard himself, by Henry Bullingbrook, the future Henry IV, a man who knows how to manipulate image and play roles. In a graphic alimentary metaphor, Henry IV explains that the public will sicken if it consumes too much; he therefore rations his appearances to ensure greater public appreciation (*1HIV* 3.2.55–84). His son, Hal, takes this policy from a gastronomic to an economic trope. In his first soliloquy in *1 Henry IV* he outlines a policy known to economists as "increasing . . . marginal utility" (Fischer

1989: 161). By creating scarcity (of grain, food, property etc.) one can artificially inflate value. Hal proposes to do this – with himself. He will absent himself from court, associate with wastrels in taverns, behave in an unprincely way; because the public expect so little of him, his later emergence as a responsible king will therefore "show more goodly." This is a highly sophisticated strategy of image manipulation.

Two plays later, Hal, as Henry V, presents a variety of images in a variety of situations: he is more a consummate actor than a hereditary monarch.[1] In this pragmatic world, a world which leads directly to ours (as the epithet "early modern," in preference to the older term "Renaissance," recognizes), the man who can act the role of king is the man who deserves to be king. This is simply a theatrical inflexion of Machiavellian *realpolitik*, which Shakespeare summarizes elsewhere: "They well deserve to have / That know the strong'st and surest way to get" (*RII* 3.3.200–1). (That this approving definition of *The Prince*'s philosophy comes from that staunch believer in the divine right of kings, Richard II, is an irony worth pursuing. Cf. Leggatt 1988: 66.)

With the exception of Titus Andronicus, Shakespeare's earliest political figures belong to English history plays. The English history play enjoyed a brief vogue from the 1580s to the early 1600s, and during those decades the public could experience a relatively unbroken sequence of English history over four centuries from the Normans to the Tudors. There were often several plays on the same reign (at least four plays on the reign of Henry V, for instance), many of which are no longer extant.

The appeal of the history play was multiple. It satisfied a need for information about one's own country: its rulers, their actions, and the consequences. English historiography was a relatively recent phenomenon. The first history of England, *Anglia Historia*, was published in 1534; it was commissioned by Henry VII and written by the Italian-born writer Polydore Vergil. In 1548 and 1550 appeared Edward Hall's *Union of the Two Noble and Illustre Families of Lancaster and York*. By 1577 Raphael Holinshed had written the two-volume *Chronicles of England, Ireland and Scotland*, enlarged in 1587 to three volumes. These imposing volumes were known as "Chronicle histories," and "Chronicle" became a shorthand for "history book." In Ben Jonson's comedy *The Devil is an Ass*, Fitzdottrel is complimented on his historical knowledge: "By m' faith, you are cunning i'the Chronicle, Sir." "No," protests Fitzdottrel, "I confess I ha't from the playbooks, / And think they are more authentic" (2.4.12–14).

History plays also catered to a post-Armada patriotism. Sometimes patriotism was allied to anti-Catholic proselytizing. In the late 1580s and early 1590s, for example, the repertory of the Queen's Men, a company in which Shakespeare probably acted and whose plays dealt with topics he was later to rewrite (King John, Richard III, Henry IV,

---

[1] Although Henry inherited the crown from his father, he is only a first-generation Lancastrian king. Thus, political uncertainty threatens his reign, as both he and his father acknowledge (*2HIV* 4.5.212–19; *HV* 4.1.292–305).

and Henry V), is nothing less than Protestant propaganda. The history play also reflected the humanists' androcentric interest, analyzing the role of man in the moral maze of history.

Above all, the appeal of the history play is the appeal of soap opera: glamorous figures and larger-than-life personalities; internecine feuding across several generations; spectacular success and spectacular failure; villains we love to hate; crimes committed and concealed; betrayal and double-crossing; politics and politicians; extravagant costumes (in *2 Henry VI* Queen Margaret views Eleanor's sartorial excesses as an attempt to humiliate her; Richard II's court was famous for its conspicuous consumption of clothing); sex (Queen Margaret's affair with Suffolk in *2* and *3 Henry VI*; Joan of Arc's night with the Dauphin in *1 Henry VI*; Lady Faulconbridge's infidelity with Richard I in *King John*); royal romance (Henry V and Princess Katherine of France); scandal (the Duchess of Gloucester's trafficking with conjurors and spirits in *2 Henry VI* is the material of tabloid headlines). Think Oliver Stone (*JFK*); think TV serial (*Dynasty*); think mythical, cyclical epic (*Lord of the Rings*). The Elizabethan history play combines all three.

Shakespeare's nine history plays divide neatly into two tetralogies hinged by *King John*. They were not composed as sequences, nor were they written in chronological order of reign (*2* and *3 Henry VI* precede *1 Henry VI*, for instance, and the plays on *Richard II*, *Henry IV*, and *Henry V* were written several years after the historically prior *Henry VI* plays), but it will be convenient to consider them here as two tetralogies. The first tetralogy, composed in 1591–3, deals with the Wars of the Roses and their causes: *1 Henry VI*, *2 Henry VI*, *3 Henry VI*, *Richard III*.[2] Shakespeare then turned his attention to the reigns which led up to that of Henry VI; *Richard II*, *1 Henry IV*, *2 Henry IV*, *Henry V* were composed between 1595 and 1599. *King John*, which stands alone, was composed in the middle of the decade (1596). The issue of identity, which preoccupied Shakespeare in the plays discussed so far, is still to the fore but it receives a new twist, for individual identity has far-reaching public and national consequences.

Furthermore playacting – that other Shakespearean obsession, expressed throughout the canon in both theme (see *Taming of the Shrew*, *Midsummer Night's Dream*) and technique (chorus, induction, play-within-the-play, metaphor) – is more complexly inflected. Whereas in comedies like *Taming of the Shrew* and *Midsummer Night's Dream* drama and imagination are positively associated, in the English histories theater and the theatrical are tools for public image and political manipulation. Shakespeare analyzes the king as actor and the politician as performer.

---

[2] The order of composition was probably *2 Henry VI*, *3 Henry VI*, *1 Henry VI*, *Richard III*; Shakespeare seems to have worked with a collaborator on all three *Henry VI* plays. In the 1590s *2* and *3 Henry VI* were known as *The First Part of the Contention between the Houses of York and Lancaster* and *The Tragedy of Richard, Duke of York*, respectively.

1   Acting Politics

"*A King is as one set on a stage*" (James I, *Basilikon Doron*, p. 163)

3 Henry VI (1591); *Richard III* (1592–3)

Handicapped by a limp and a hunchbank, Richard of Gloucester is not an obvious candidate for social or military success. Nonetheless, he emerges at the end of *3 Henry VI* as a valiant soldier; in *Richard III* he systematically murders his kindred to gain the throne of England. His is the story of a man who maneuvers and manipulates to achieve his goals, and he does so with self-conscious theatricality: "Richard is a great role, as Richard himself was the first to discover" (Blanpied 1988: 61).

At the end of *3 Henry VI* Richard of Gloucester reveals himself in a psychologically honest soliloquy (5.6.61–93) in which he denies human emotions ("pity, love, . . . fear"), human bonds ("I have no brother"), and declares himself a thing apart: "I am like no brother," "I am myself alone." Severance of family bonds is always a cause for alarm in Shakespeare, not least because of the family's emblematic role as a microcosm of the bond between ruler and subject and between God and man. From the beginning of the *Henry VI* plays we have seen families sundered by political ambition and civil war. Winchester conspires against his brother, Gloucester; their servants feud (domestics were, like wives and children, social subordinates and hence part of the family); Joan of Arc rejects her father; the apprentice Peter Thump challenges his ersatz father, his master; Clarence betrays his father and brothers; an anonymous son accidentally kills his father and an anonymous father accidentally kills his son; even Henry VI entails his estate to the Yorks rather than to his own son, Prince Edward of Lancaster. And in *3 Henry VI*, a play which concludes with the triumph of the united York clan, Richard detaches himself psychologically from the family for which he has fought.

In one sense he has always been marked apart. He tells us that he is congenitally misshapen and that he was born with teeth ("which plainly signified / That I should snarl, and bite, and play the dog"; 5.6.77). A few lines previously Henry VI had listed these and other ominous portents: "the owl shriek'd at thy birth, an evil sign" (5.6.44). The young Duke of York later discusses these rumors with his grandmother in *Richard III* 2.4. Clearly we are not meant to forget that "these signs have mark'd [Richard] extraordinary," as another rebel, the superstitious Glendower, claims in *1 Henry IV* (3.1.40).

But if later plays dismiss the importance of perceived ontological portents – Hotspur points out that the earth would have quaked at the time of Glendower's birth had his mother's cat "but kitten'd" (*1HIV* 3.1.19), and Edmund in *King Lear* asserts that he would have been what he is "had the maidenl'est star in the firmament twinkled" at his conception (*Lear* 1.2.132–3) – *Henry VI* and *Richard III* explore the way in which an individual like Richard is "determined." "Since I cannot prove a lover / . . . I am determined to prove a villain," announces Richard punningly at the start of *Richard III* (1.1.28, 30). Determination (resolve) masques as determination (destiny).

This fracture between seeming and being is visible in a contradiction in Richard's last soliloquy in *3 Henry VI*. Having claimed an automatic relation between birth appearance and behavior (the snapping personality of the dentally equipped baby), he prays that his mind may match his deformed body: "Then since the heavens have shap'd my body so, / Let hell make crook'd my mind to answer it" (5.6.78–9). If Richard is a villain, the role is clearly not congenital. One suspects, then, that the earlier disavowal of emotion (pity, love, fear) is a gesture of denial rather than a statement of truth.[3] As Blanpied notes (1988: 63), Richard never says "I am a villain" but "I will try myself out in the role of villain."

At the beginning of *Richard III* the family rejection which concluded *3 Henry VI* has been replaced by the family unity of the first-person plural (Leggatt 1988: 35): "Now is the winter of *our* discontent / Made glorious summer by this son of York; / And all the clouds that low'r'd upon *our* house / In the deep bosom of the ocean buried" (1.1.1–4). The grammatical union is suspiciously ironic[4] for at line 14 we meet the contrasting conjunction "But" and the assertive individual pronoun "I":

But I, that am not shap'd for sportive tricks, . . .
I, that am rudely stamp'd, and want love's majesty . . .
I, that am curtail'd of this fair proportion, . . .

---

[3] In the RSC production of 1995–6, David Troughton interpreted a similar line in *Richard III* in this manner, "Tear-falling pity dwells not in this eye" (4.3.65); see Troughton (1998: 92).

[4] This was how it was played in the 1987 ESC production, which extended the irony by using the first two lines of *Richard III* at the end of *3 Henry VI*.

> Why, I, in this weak piping time of peace,
> Have no delight to pass away the time. (*RIII* 1.1.14, 16, 18, 24–5)

Peace is not congenial to Richard because he is not equipped for pacific pursuits: music, love, sex. Envy of his brother Edward's erotic success seems at the forefront of this speech (the stress is on sex not love: "lascivious," "sportive tricks," "strut before a wanton ambling nymph" [1.1.13, 14, 17; cf. Neill 1988: 21]) and, in a defiantly overcompensatory gesture, Richard moves to the other extreme: villain rather than lover.

> And therefore, since I cannot prove a lover
> To entertain these fair well-spoken days,
> I am determined to prove a villain
> And hate the idle pleasures of these days. (1.1.28–31)[5]

This rhetorical trick is typical of Richard: he presents alternatives which are extreme. We see this again in *Richard III* in the scene in which he woos Lady Anne, telling her to murder him or marry him: "Take up the sword again, or take up me" (1.2.183). Like the lover/villain binary, these are not logical alternatives, nor are they the only alternatives. But Richard is a master of theatrical and rhetorical manipulation.

We accept his perspective partly because we are complicit with Richard. His primary relationship is not with Buckingham but with the audience; we are cast as accomplices through his confidences, a technique which derives from the figure of the Vice in the medieval morality. Furthermore, Richard dominates the first act, and by the time we are given a scene without him (1.4), we are conditioned to his way of thinking. When we start to resist Richard, as we inevitably do,[6] his political power wanes, for in this play he who is in control of theater is in control of politics.

Richard introduces the theatrical vocabulary in his first soliloquy: "Plots have I laid, inductions dangerous" (1.1.32). In the next scene, having engaged in an extended stichomythic exchange of insults with Lady Anne, whom he attempts to woo, he metatheatrically acknowledges genre and controls pace:

---

[5]   The quid pro quo villainy for sexual inability is Shakespeare's addition to his sources (Barber and Wheeler 1988: 111).
[6]   David Troughton (1998: 91) locates the first split between audience and protagonist in 3.7 when the audience laughs "*at* Richard and not *with* him."

> But, gentle Lady Anne,
> To leave this keen encounter of our wits
> And fall something into a slower method. (1.2.114–16)

Richard here turns a scene of mourning into a scene of romantic comedy. Theatrically self-conscious throughout, he stages detachable playlets – The Witty Lover, The Loving Brother, the Reluctant Prince (Neill 1988: 27) – and there is a chirpy theatrical artifice to the way in which characters and episodes are introduced: "here Clarence comes" (1.1.41); "but who comes here? the new-delivered Hastings" (1.1.121); "and in good time, here comes the sweating lord" (this last from Richard's assistant director, Buckingham; 3.1.24). We cannot take this seriously. Richard is playing, playing with history.[7]

Other characters share Richard's theatrical vocabulary, as they vie with him for theatrical, and hence political, control. The marginalized Margaret sees herself as a "chorus" to a "frantic play" (4.4.68). Buckingham cunningly offers a theatrical metaphor to suggest Hastings's desire for promotion from a supporting political role: "Had you not come upon your cue, my lord, / William Lord Hastings had pronounc'd your part" (3.4.26–7). This sense of politics as play was subtly brought out in Jane Howell's BBC film of the tetralogy, with a set resembling a child's adventure playground. Walkways, planks, doors, destruction, graffiti: playground as theater, war as playground, politics as performance.

Good actors, successful actors are those in whom the person and the role are seamless ("He did not act King Lear; he *was* King Lear"). Richard can never be a successful king because he is too aware of the division between himself and the role (and, hence, of the division within himself). On the eve of the battle of Bosworth he wakes from a bad dream, asking "What do I fear? Myself? There's none else by. / Richard loves Richard, that is, I am I" (5.3.183–4). This, at least, is the reading of the second edition (1598), a reading accepted by almost all editors. The first edition (1597) reads "What do I fear? Myself? There's none else by. / Richard loves Richard, that is, I and I." The first edition stresses a divided Richard, whereas the second edition assumes an integrated Richard. The divided Richard was portrayed in the RSC production in 1995–6, where David Troughton's Richard used

---

[7] John Blanpied points out that although Richard lists the many "obstacles between himself and the crown, . . . they all come down readily" (1988: 66). Too readily: claimants and enemies die on cue, as if in a well-rehearsed play.

the audience as his conscience ("My conscience hath a thousand several tongues"; Troughton 1998: 95).

Henry V, by contrast, spends two plays rehearsing an invisible interface between self and role. He is, arguably, a less attractive character than Richard theatrically, partly because we see less and less of the man behind the mask; but he is without question a more successful monarch and politician.

1 Henry IV (1596–7); 2 Henry IV (1597–8); Henry V (1598–9)

In Alan Bennett's *The Madness of George III*, the Prince of Wales complains "To be heir to the throne is not a position; it is a predicament" (Bennett 1992: 55). It is this predicament which Shakespeare dramatizes in *1* and *2 Henry IV*. Although the plot of the plays presents the threat to Henry IV from the northern rebels, the story is quite different: the growth of Hal, the Prince of Wales. In *Henry V* we see the fruits of Hal's apprenticeship when the new king leads his country to war.

When Hal first introduces himself in soliloquy to the audience in *1 Henry IV* 1.2, he lays his cards on the table. For him kingship is a strategy, and the strategy begins long before ascending the throne:

> herein will I imitate the sun,
> Who doth permit the base contagious clouds
> To smother up his beauty from the world,
> That when he please again to be himself,
> Being wanted [missed], he may be more wond'red at. . . .
> So when this loose behavior I throw off
> And pay the debt I never promised,
> By how much better than my word I am,
> By so much shall I falsify men's hopes,
> And like bright metal on a sullen ground [background],
> My reformation, glitt'ring o'er my fault,
> Shall show more goodly and attract more eyes
> Than that which hath no foil to set it off. (*1HIV* 1.2.197–201, 208–15)

It is a supremely pragmatic plan. By "falsifying men's hopes" – leading them to expect the worst of his reign by spending his time in an Eastcheap tavern – he will augment his value as king. In the world of the future Henry V, royalty is like currency: its value can be artificially lowered and inflated. Hal's vocabulary, here and elsewhere, is tellingly material and mercantile – *debt, bright metal, foil.*

In essence, his strategy is no different from that of his father, who in the conference between father and son in 3.2 explains

By being seldom seen, I could not stir
But like a comet I was wond'red at . . .
Thus did I keep my person fresh and new,
My presence, like a robe pontifical,
Ne'er seen but wond'red at, and so my state,
Seldom but sumptuous, show'd like a feast. (3.2.46–7, 55–8)

The difference between Henry IV's and Hal's strategies is that the latter's involves using and disposing of people. Hal's soliloquy begins with two lines in which he announces that he will tolerate his frivolous friends in Eastcheap until such time as his kingly sun chooses to break through the clouds. It is one thing to view kingship as currency; it is quite another to view people as such. This is the attitude that will lead to the public rejection of Hal's Eastcheap companion, Sir John Falstaff, in *2 Henry IV*, even though Hal and the discarded Falstaff have much in common, for Falstaff's attitude to his conscripts is not significantly different from Hal's to his friends. They are expendable: "food for powder, food for powder" (*1HIV* 4.2.66).

Shakespeare, like Hal, has three plays in which to develop (in theory) and demonstrate (in practice) this postmedieval and unsacramental concept of kingship. Authors rarely set out to write three-part plays, and the chances are high that Shakespeare initially envisaged a dramatic diptych: one play dealing with the reign of Henry IV and another dealing with the reign of Henry V. At some stage during the writing of what became *1 Henry IV* he realized he had too much material for one five-act drama; the short scene 4 in act 4, which introduces Archbishop Scroop's rebellion, exists primarily to motivate a sequel.

Although Shakespeare may have had too much material for one *Henry IV* play, he did not have quite enough for two, and *2 Henry IV* tends to replay much of *1 Henry IV* in a different tone. The ludic exuberance of the first part is absent. Falstaff becomes an isolated character, his comedy channeled into dialogue with the audience rather than with the heir to the throne. The tavern trick in *2 Henry IV* (which occurs at exactly the same place as the trick in Part 1: act 2, scene 4) could not be more different in ambience from its precursor. Hal seems overcome with ennui, the trick fizzles out, and Falstaff's excuse (an unimaginative and bathetic eightfold repetition "no abuse") functions to convince the prince of the knight's

"Henry IV, Parts One and Two? What's wrong with Elizabeth 1st?"

Plate 4 Elizabeth I's indignation is only possible in a contemporary cartoon: in the sixteenth century it was forbidden to portray the reigning monarch on stage. Had Shakespeare written an Elizabeth I play, he would have found himself in jail. Ben Jonson was imprisoned for his share in *Eastward Ho!* (1605) because the inclusion of a character with a Scottish accent was deemed disrespectful to James I.

worthlessness rather than to provoke hilarious outrage. Eastcheap is not only less carnivalesque than in Part 1 but less benign: the prostitute, Doll Tearsheet, is arrested for her role in a murder (*2HIV* 5.4.6).

A rival green world springs up. The Gloucestershire recruits display a concern for humanity (Leggatt 1988: 103): Mouldy's anxiety for his mother who "has nobody to do any thing about her when I am gone, and she is old, and cannot help herself" (3.2.230–2) exposes the selfish utilitarianism of Falstaff ("I have led my ragamuffins where they are pepper'd"; *1HIV* 5.3.35–6). The agricultural milieu of Justice Shallow is a world where the temporal rhythms of the natural world are observed – "shall we sow the hade [unploughed] land with wheat?" (*2HIV* 5.1.14–15). It is a world where men accept the passing of time: contrast Shallow's philosophical "Death is certain" (*2HIV* 3.2.40) with Falstaff's "Do not speak like a death's head, do not bid me remember mine end" (*2HIV* 2.4.234–5). Even the rural recruits approach mortality with dignity rather than denial; Feeble's "a man can die but once, we owe God a death ["debt" and "death" are homonyms in Elizabethan English], . . . he that dies this year is quit for the next" (3.2.234–8) cannot fail to remind us of Falstaff's opposite stance.

In the battle of Shrewsbury which concludes Part 1, Falstaff protests that although he owes God a debt/death, "'tis not due yet, I would be loath to pay him before his day" (*1HIV* 5.1.127–8). The world of comedy is the world of credit. Part 1 is about evasion and deferral: Falstaff's tavern bills are paid by Hal (1.2.47–56), and he owes Mistress Quickly for twelve linen shirts at "eight shillings an ell" (*1HIV* 3.3.71–2). But in the altered ambience of Part 2, debts have to be paid. Justice Shallow requests repayment of the thousand pounds Falstaff owes him, and Hal "redeems" time when men least think he will.

Time, money, and people are linked in the *Henry* plays through economic tropes, for everything is commodified in Hal's early modern world. By fleeting the time carelessly in Eastcheap, then throwing off such "loose behavior," Hal pays a "debt [he] never promised" (*1HIV* 1.2.208, 209). He casts Percy as a financial agent: "Percy is but my factor, good my lord, / To engross up glorious deeds on my behalf; / And I will call him to so strict account / That he shall render every glory up, / . . . Or I will tear the reckoning from his heart" (*1HIV* 3.2.147–52). Note the fiscal attitude to man and deeds: *factor, engross, account, render, reckoning.* And let us not romanticize Justice Shallow, whose generosity to Falstaff is not entirely altruistic: "A friend i'th'court is better than a penny in purse" (*2HIV* 5.1.30–1). In Henrician England, humans are financial investments.

Even amateurs know that success on the stock market depends on cashing in one's investment at the right moment. Timing is crucial. Timing is Hal's strong suit, as Exeter tells us in *Henry V*: "Now he weighs time / Even to the utmost grain" (*HV* 2.3.137–8). In *1 Henry IV* Hal is flanked by two extreme figures, Falstaff and Hotspur, and the thematic competition that is waged is not political or moral but temporal: the contrast in the characters' attitudes to time functions as a synecdoche for their attitudes to politics and ethics. Falstaff is slothful, disrespectful of time; he frustrates order and duty and history (Frye 1986: 77). His first words in the play at 1.2.1 – "Now, Hal, what time of day is it, lad?" (presumably Hal has just woken him up) – are appropriately rebuked: "What a devil has *thou* to do with the time of the day? unless hours were cups of sack, and minutes capons, and clocks the tongues of bawds, and dials the signs of leaping-houses, and the blessed sun himself a fair hot wench in flame-color'd taffata" (1.2.6–10). Falstaff's markers of time are alcohol, food, and prostitutes. It is typical, if ironic, that when Falstaff hears of Hal's accession at the end of *2 Henry IV*, he borrows horses and gallops through the night to attend the coronation. Unfortunately, time cannot be redeemed in this way; a night's gallop cannot compensate for a life in which time is improperly measured.

Hotspur's attitude to time is conveyed in his nickname. He is impetuous in attitude, rhetoric, and combat. In 1.3 he does not let his uncle Worcester finish his sentences (Worcester actually exits the scene in frustration); he rebuffs the romantic pleas of his wife in 2.3 because he can think only of mounting his horse; he fights (and is killed) at Shrewsbury because he ignores the advice to wait for reinforcements. In the BBC film version of the lyrical scene in Glendower's Castle, where Mortimer's wife sings a song in Welsh, Hotspur lies with his head in his wife's lap, as the dialogue instructs him, but a telling camera close-up captures the impatient tapping of his fingers. Mortimer's uxorious lingering underlines Hotspur's energetic impatience: "Come, come, Lord Mortimer, you are as slow / As hot Lord Percy is on fire to go" (*1HIV* 3.1.263–4).

Over two plays Hal hones his temporal skills in preparation for leadership. In *1 Henry IV* he kills his hasty rival, Hotspur; in *2 Henry IV* he rejects the tardy tutor of his riots, Falstaff. In *Henry V* he emerges as a king who knows not just how to act, but when to act. Like Henry IV, the new monarch "knows at what time to promise, when to pay" (*1HIV* 4.3.52–3).

If good timing is a requirement of the successful investor, it is also a skill of the good actor (Leggatt 1988: 89). Like Richard III, Hal is an actor. Whereas Richard plays the villain, Hal plays the prodigal. When he ascends the throne, he betrays an initial trepidation, as would any actor on assuming his first major role, assuring the court that he is not as confident as they assume: "This new and gorgeous garment, majesty, / Sits not so easy on me as you think" (*2HIV* 5.2.44–5). The clothing image is significant. Kingship is not a quality but a costume (Macbeth, murderer and usurper, is constantly presented as someone who is wearing clothes that are too big for him).

If a good actor needs perfect timing, he also requires a good wardrobe. This is not true in the world of twenty-first-century theater, a world where the Shenandoah Shakespeare Express can present Hamlet in baseball boots and black rehearsal clothing, or where Brechtian and poststructuralist productions can deliberately puncture realism, presenting theater as metatheater; but in the sixteenth- and seventeenth-century theater costume was king. Philip Henslowe, the entrepreneur who built the Rose Theatre and managed some of the companies who played in it, kept an account book, known (misleadingly) as *Henslowe's Diary*. From this *Diary* we know that Henslowe regularly paid more for a single costume for a play than he had paid the author(s) for the play itself. A dramatist might earn £6–£10 for a play (handsome remuneration when we consider that in 1600 a Stratford schoolmaster could earn £10 per annum). In November 1596 Henslowe paid 40s (£2) for copper lace for a play; the next day he paid a further 25s (£1.25) for more lace for the same play (Foakes and Rickert 1991: 49). Such sums are typical. Small wonder, then, that Elizabethans liked to borrow or rent theatrical costumes for special occasions, a practice invoked in Jonson's *Alchemist*: "Thou must borrow / A Spanish suit. Hast thou no credit with the players?" (4.7.67–8). Theater costumes were the most expensive investments a theater company made.[8]

Not just an investment, costume was also character. Hamlet's "inky cloak," Shylock's gabardine, Petruccio's marital dishabille, Parolles's scarves: clothing functioned as a shorthand for identity. In the instances above, the identity is variously emotional (Hamlet's mourning), racial (Shylock's Jewishness), ideological (Petruccio's attempt to disrupt the link between inner and outer), and social (Parolles's pretensions). At the end of *Twelfth Night* much is made of the fact that Viola's "maiden weeds" (lodged offstage with "a captain in this town") will confirm her identity as a female. Dressed as Cesario she remains Cesario; not until she is rehabited will she be regendered, "Orsino's mistress, and his fancy's queen" (5.1.388). This might seem one more example of the superficial attitudes that typify the main characters in *Twelfth Night* (where Viola is the only character to marry someone she knows and wants), and it contrasts with Feste's attitude ("I wear not motley in my brain"; 1.5.57), and with Shakespeare's attitude to clothing generally: Hamlet protests that there is more to his grief than costume, Shylock that a Jew has eyes and ears, Petruccio that the jay is not

---

[8]   For an excellent analysis of early modern expenditure on clothing, both inside and outside the theater, see Jones and Stallybrass (2000: chaps. 1 and 7).

more precious than the lark because his feathers are more beautiful. In *Merry Wives* the two suitors who identify Anne Page "by her garments" (5.5.195–6) are disappointed (they marry boys). But the equation of Viola's identity with her clothing is not discordant in terms of Elizabethan society: on one occasion a customer refused to pay a brothel on the grounds that he had experienced the prostitute's dress before (Varholy n.p.). Sexual variety and sartorial variety were synonymous. Apparel oft proclaims the man (or woman).

Henry V knows this. Referring to his new royal robes, he says "I will deeply put the fashion on / And wear it in my heart" (*2HIV* 5.2.52–3). This is a strikingly anticomedic sentiment, and it decisively severs the *Henry IV* plays' links with comedy. In comedy, costume is a means to an end; that end is either plot (as when Viola is able to serve Orsino as a page) or identity (as when Rosalind's disguise permits her to explore masculine characteristics). But costume is always abandoned, and the expanded self reclaimed. Henry V not only embraces but internalizes costume, and by extension, role. From now on, Hal is lost to us, as to himself: public and private fuse in the man-monarch Henry V.

Henry V offers us not a unified hero but a series of roles played by Henry. The opening scene presents the statesman, pursuing justice and responding to French humiliation; one cannot forget the dramatic nonchalance of Olivier's Henry as he tossed his crown on to the finial of his throne, the coordinated adroitness that even today (illogically) inspires political confidence and wins the Health Club vote in American elections. In act 2 Henry acts the betrayed friend, and stages a morality play to unmask the traitors on the quayside at Southampton (Henry has a flair for the dramatic dénouement, exposing the rebels as he rejected Falstaff: in public). Act 3 shows Henry in Tamburlaine-cum-Rambo mode, threatening the governor and citizens of Harfleur with atrocities – rape, infanticide, geronticide – and an army that is allegedly beyond his control. In act 4 Henry plays the common man; he talks with his soldiers incognito, maintaining that the king is no different from his subjects: "his ceremonies laid by, in his nakedness he appears but a man" (4.1.104–5). The wooing scene of act 5 presents a constellation of starring roles: the negotiator who drives a hard bargain (5.2.345–7); the soldier, capable only of leaping into saddles; the poetically challenged wooer; the Petrarchan romantic; the inept language student; the imperialist who overrides the customs of the nation he has just conquered.

Some of these roles are self-evidently poses which serve important political ends. We know that Henry's army is sick and cannot perform what it threatens at Harfleur; rhetorical posturing thus achieves conquest without bloodshed. But on other occasions separating the actor from the essence is more difficult. Henry's wooing, in performance so often a delightful scene of romantic comedy, is undercut by his earlier rejection of Katherine (the Chorus explains the accompanying French territory was insufficient).[9] In his soliloquy in *1 Henry IV* Hal explained the advantage of this tactic of concealment and subsequent revelation: "That when he please again to *be himself,* / Being wanted, he may be more wond'red at" (1.2.200–1). Three plays later we realize that we do not know what it means for Henry to "be himself." He has become a stereotype of the overzealous actor: one who is never out of role. Henry wears motley (or rather majesty) in his brain.

That other committed actor-politician, Richard of Gloucester, allowed us glimpses of his inner self through contradictions in soliloquy, rhetorical sleight of hand, and even poignant confession of embryonically Dantean quality ("And I – like one lost in a thorny wood, / That rents the thorns, and is rent with the thorns, / Seeking a way, and straying from the way, / Not knowing how to find the open air, / But toiling desperately to find it out – / Torment myself"; *3HVI* 3.2.174–9). In *Richard III* his wife, Anne, reveals one aspect of this torment: Richard suffers from bad dreams. In act 5 we actually experience one of these dreams as his conscience, and the ghosts of his victims, torment him. Thus, the gap between actor (Richard the human being) and role (Richard the monster) is constantly visible to the audience.

This is not the case in *Henry V*. The one scene in the play where we glimpse Henry's interiority – on the eve of Agincourt, where he meditates on kingship, prays, and reveals his anxiety about the "fault / [His] father made in compassing the crown" (4.1.293–4) – also encourages our skepticism. Henry walks round the English camp to commune with his conscience ("I and my bosom must debate awhile"; 4.1.31), only to end up in debate with John Bates about the difference between the king's feelings and those of the common man. Henry insists that the two are the same because

---

[9]   In the ESC production (1987–9), Katherine's hostility to Henry and to the marriage was shown in her resistance to, and resentment at, compulsory English lessons. When the marriage was concluded through conquest in act 5, her brother, the Dauphin, left the scene in disgust, knocking over his chair in hasty exit.

the king *is* a common man. We recall, however, that Henry has borrowed Sir Thomas Erpingham's cloak for his walkabout. Even the common man requires a costume; even the common man is a role (Hopper n.p.).

The question *Henry V* poses is whether all identity is simply role playing, or whether Henry's predicament is peculiar to public figures. Does appearing on the world stage privilege the public identity at the expense of the private person? The question can best be explored through an examination of names. We saw in chapter 1 that the personal name was firmly attached to the private self ("Katherine" as opposed to "Kate" in *The Shrew*). At the end of *2 Henry IV* Henry V assumes his public regal role – a tense moment which requires the rejection of his former private self and the companions associated with it. Like *The Shrew*'s Katherine, Henry V performs a public role in defiance of the onstage audience's expectations, and, also like Katherine, he realizes that public order requires the adoption of a public persona. But whereas Katherine becomes binominal, able to assume and doff "Kate" and "Katherine" (and their corresponding behaviors) as circumstances require, a coronation is a one-way process. Having been renamed King Henry V, the king cannot revert to the titles Prince or Hal, or to the Eastcheap persona that accompanied them. For a ruler, taking a place in public life means forfeiting the private life unequivocally and for ever.

Coriolanus (1608); Julius Caesar (1599)

The combination of politics and acting ability receives even more detailed scrutiny in two of Shakespeare's Roman plays, *Julius Caesar* (written in the same year as *Henry V*) and *Coriolanus* (1608). The plot of *Julius Caesar* depicts the rebels' assassination of Caesar, their reasons for the assassination, and the political consequences thereof. As Ralph Berry points out (1981: 328), in the world of *Caesar* the actor has become frozen in his role, not a man but a statue: Caesar "doth bestride the narrow world / Like a Colossus" (1.2.135–6). Caesar is not the only ossified figure in the play, but he is the most problematic, for this republican world is suspicious of rulers who are elevated to statuesque deities. Cassius says he "had as lief not be as live to be / In awe of such a thing as I myself" (1.2.95–6). Exploiting the faultline between man and role, Cassius reminds us of Caesar's deficient corporeality. Not only is he subject to illness but he is a poor athlete, unable to swim the turbulent Tiber; "and this man / Is now become a god" (1.2.115–16), Cassius says with scorn.

In the Rome of *Coriolanus*, Caius Martius (later named Coriolanus in honor of his conquest of Corioles) is admired and elevated as Rome's military hero. He supplies in health and stamina all that Caesar lacks. In battle he advances alone when his army retreats. In victory he is so covered in blood that he is recognizable only by his voice. The proud bearer of twenty-seven battle scars ("every gash was an enemy's grave"; 2.1.155–6), he is a conqueror identified with destruction: "before him he carries noise, and behind him he leaves tears" (2.1.158–9). Unfortunately, the qualities that serve him so well in battle – obstinacy, determination – translate to the field of politics as pride and arrogance. Unable to woo voters with mildness and humility ("it is a part / That I shall blush in acting"; 2.2.144–5), Coriolanus alienates the plebeians, is banished and, ultimately, destroyed. Acting, it seems, is a political survival skill; lack of it, in this instance, proves fatal.

Shakespeare's Rome is not a world of political parties but of factions. Both *Julius Caesar* and *Coriolanus* use this far-from-neutral term. Brutus admits the conspirators to his orchard in *Julius Caesar*: "Let 'em enter. / They are the faction" (2.1.76–7); a stage direction in *Coriolanus* reads "Enter three or four conspirators of Aufidius' faction" (5.6.8SD). Later, a telling choice of vocabulary illustrates the political maneuverings of the factions in each play. Brutus, debating in soliloquy his decision to murder Caesar, ruminates on the relation between power and tyranny. He acknowledges that the assassination is merely prophylactic, a form of political preventive medicine: "so Caesar may [change his nature]; / Then lest he may, prevent" (2.1.27–8). Because there are no current grounds for assassination, the PR angle needs to be carefully presented:

> And since the quarrel
> Will bear no color for the thing he is,
> Fashion it thus: that what he is, augmented,
> Would run to these and these extremities (2.1.29–31)

"Will bear no color": the assassination is not justified by Caesar's behavior. "Fashion it thus": present it this way to the public.

A decade later (in Shakespeare's career) and four centuries earlier (in Roman history) something remarkably similar is happening in *Coriolanus*. Coriolanus's new ally, Tullus Aufidius, kills Coriolanus for the same reason that motivates the earlier conspirators: jealousy. Here is John Nettles's assessment of *Julius Caesar*: "Cassius wants Caesar dead because, quite simply, he envies him his glory...It has all to do with hate and little to do with reason" (Nettles 1998: 181). Similar emotions are to the fore in *Coriolanus*. Aufidius is "dark'ned" by comparison with Coriolanus (4.7.5); "therefore shall he die, / And I'll renew me in his fall," he concludes (5.6.47–8). After the deed is done, Aufidius speaks like Brutus before him:

> My lords, when you shall know (as in this rage,
> Provok'd by him, you cannot) the great danger
> Which this man's life did owe you, you'll rejoice
> That he is thus cut off (5.6.135–8)

The sincerity of this public assurance is undermined by the private statement which precedes it: "my *pretext* to strike at him *admits / A good construction*" (5.6.19). In other words: "the quarrel will bear no color for the thing he is" so "fashion it thus." There is only one word to describe such speeches: policy.

The worlds of *Julius Caesar* and *Coriolanus* are worlds of political campaigning, and when politicians go campaigning, we know we cannot trust everything they say. In these two plays every speech and character has to be scrutinized: does the character mean what he says? What does he stand to gain from presenting facts or events in this way? Let us assess each play separately.

Coriolanus (1608)

Coriolanus is a soldier. His mother, Volumnia, lives vicariously through his successes and is politically ambitious for her son. After his conquest of Corioles, Coriolanus is persuaded to run for office. The play insistently reminds us of the Machiavellian world of policy. Volumnia invokes the noun "policy" twice when trying to persuade Coriolanus to don the gown of humility, present his wounds to the people and beg for votes:

> I have heard you say
> Honor and policy, like unsever'd friends,
> I' th' war do grow together; grant that, and tell me
> In peace what each of them by th'other lose
> That they combine not there.

She repeats her argument immediately:

> If it be honor in your wars to seem
> The same you are not, which, for your best ends,
> You adopt your policy, how is it less or worse
> That it shall hold companionship in peace
> With honor, as in war, since that to both
> It stands in like request? (3.2.41–51)

Volumnia is asking Coriolanus to "seem / The same you are not" – to appear humble. But the policy she proposes is not just tactical: it requires Coriolanus to act something he is not and therefore it strikes at the heart of his identity. This poses no problems for Richard III or Henry IV or Hal/Henry V. But unlike them, Coriolanus is not an actor; in Shakespeare's world this means he is unqualified to be a successful politician.

That Coriolanus is at heart a soldier is taken for granted by the play's dramatis personae and by a large number of critics and directors. The poster for the RSC London production in 1995 featured a bloody Toby Stephens with the heading "Natural Born Killer." The question of what is nature and what is nurture will shortly be investigated by Shakespeare in the *Tempest*, but it has visible roots in *Coriolanus*. We are told that Coriolanus "has been bred i' th' wars / Since 'a could draw a sword" (3.1.318–19), and Volumnia claims the credit: "When yet he was but tender-bodied . . . I . . . was pleas'd to let him seek danger where he was like to find fame. To a cruel war I sent him" (1.3.5–14). She explains that if she had a dozen sons she would rather lose eleven in war than have one die idly in peace. Coriolanus's father-substitute, Menenius, and his mother, Volumnia, relish Coriolanus's military achievements: they envisage blood and danger, and compete in counting his scars. Thus, Coriolanus becomes a fighting machine, an "engine," a "thing," a "sword," a "dragon," a "dog" (5.4.19; 5.4.14; 1.6.76; 5.4.13; 4.5.51). Had he wished otherwise, one suspects that he would have had little chance. (My students entertained me one Christmas with a series of Shakespeare sketches. *Coriolanus at the Careers Office* depicted the young Caius Martius explaining to the careers adviser that he wanted to work for Greenpeace.)

Note the vocabulary to describe Coriolanus: animals and inanimate objects. His identity is professional (a sword), mechanical (an engine), inhuman (a thing, a dragon), unsocialized (alone, lonely). His very name, a crucial marker of identity in Shakespeare, becomes eclipsed by his agnomen, with its links to city, destruction, and public triumph; it is, as the general Cominius tells him when he bestows it, a "sign of what you are," not a reward for "what you have done" (1.9.26–7; cf. Leggatt 1988: 193). Cominius offers this explanation to mollify the limelight-shy hero; but what is, in Roman terms, a professional compliment (identity derived externally from city) is, in Shakespearean terms, a personal disaster. Identity cannot be thus outwardly derived, cannot be a reflection.

Coriolanus's identity as a silent and social creature, moved to tears by his family's presence, is found belatedly in act 5, scene 3, a scene to which we shall return. Acts 2 and 3, however, present the idea of a mild Coriolanus as a strategic act requiring exemplary performance skills. He has to perform Rome's electioneering equivalent of kissing babies for the cameras: to be elected consul, he must wear the "napless vesture of humility" (2.1.234), display his wounds in public, and ask "kindly" for votes (2.3.75). This he does, briefly and awkwardly. Unlike Henry V, however, he cannot wear his garments in his heart: "May I change these garments? . . . That I'll straight do; and, *knowing myself again*, / Repair to th' senate-house" (2.3.146–8). Almost immediately he alienates the plebeians, who rescind their votes. Coriolanus accusingly questions his mother:

> Why did you wish me milder? Would you have me
> False to my nature? Rather say, I play
> The man I am (3.2.14–16)

The resonant verb "play," however, shows the problematic interface, *à la* Henry V, of essence and performance. Who is Coriolanus?

Coriolanus is different things to different people, partly because we are in a political world where people have tactical functions rather than personal identities. At the end of the play Aufidius's public "pretext" presents Coriolanus as a flatterer ("he watered his new plants with dews of flattery, / Seducing so my friends"; 5.6.22–3), an aspect of Coriolanus so unlikely, and so flatly contradicted by act 2, scene 3, where he cannot ask "kindly" for votes, that even the third conspirator balks (Vickers 1977: 261). But this suits Aufidius's current needs, just as it earlier suited him to see Coriolanus as a noble challenge (1.2.34–6), a serious enemy (1.2.12; 1.8.2–4), a loved friend (4.5.113–18), a revered ally (4.5.194–202). Politics is "th'interpretation of the time" (4.7.50); and interpretation depends on presentation. Coriolanus is multiply presented, and it becomes clear that although he has many roles, he is not acting: he is acted upon (Vickers 1976: 40).

The patricians see Coriolanus as a military machine because Rome needs to see him this way (Vickers 1977: 247). The imagery is exaggerated in order to magnify the threat. Even when they have been rejected by Coriolanus, individual patricians still use his name as the *sine qua non* of military destruction. Thus Cominius: "he does sit in gold, his eye / Red as 'twould burn Rome" (5.1.63–4). Here is Menenius's similar hyperbole: "This Martius is grown from man to dragon: he has wings, he's more than a creeping thing . . . The tartness of his face sours ripe grapes. When he walks, he moves like an engine, and the ground shrinks before his treading. He is able to pierce a corslet with his eye, talks like a knell, and his hum is a battery" (5.4.12–21). Faced with such exaggerated images, the tribune Sicinius questions whether Menenius "report him truly" and is assured "I paint him in the character" (5.4.25–6). The patricians' character painting remains constant in peace and war, because in both situations Coriolanus serves as their agent to threaten enemies (Volscians or plebeians).

Others' "character" of Coriolanus necessarily differs from that of the patricians. To the tribunes he is proud and ambitious, so that even his acceptance of second-in-command in war is a self-seeking strategy: "Fame, at the which he aims, / . . . cannot / Better be held nor more attain'd than by / A place below the first; for what miscarries / Shall be the general's fault" (1.1.263–7). The tribunes need to present Coriolanus as self-interested, of course, because they are trying to inflame the plebeians against him. Coriolanus's attitude in the first two acts constantly challenges the validity of the tribunes' view. Warfare reveals Coriolanus's patriotism rather than any desire for glory, and his reluctance to accept public praise and political reward seems genuine ("I had rather be their servant in my way / Than sway with them in theirs"; 2.1.203–4) rather than the theatrical charade it so clearly is in *Julius Caesar* when Caesar refuses a crown "he would fain have had" (*JC* 1.3.239–40). Although the plebeians' behavior is influenced by the tribunes, they do not have a herd mentality (Berry 1988: 149). Thus, the 1st Citizen's characterization of Coriolanus as "chief enemy to the people" is countered by the 2nd Citizen's judicious question, "Consider you what services he has done for his country?" (1.1.7–8, 30). The BBC film captures the tone of this scene perfectly: it is serious and *sotto voce*, a debate not a riot. Riots are about a unified viewpoint; *Coriolanus* is about multiple perspectives.

The perspectives continue to multiply. To Volumnia the Coriolanus who disobeys her instructions is proud (3.2.126); to Coriolanus his military achievements fulfill Volumnia's ambition rather than his own ("My mother, you wot well / My hazards still have been your solace"; 4.1.27–8). Menenius's lengthy fable of the belly distracts the citizens from the insurrection elsewhere in the city (Voss 1998: 155) and conveniently sidesteps the plebeians' grievances. An allegorical answer about distribution does not address a complaint about starvation. As Leggatt puts it: "to the citizens' claim that they are starving, Menenius replies in effect that they . . . just don't realize they're being fed" (Leggatt 1988: 197). The 1st Citizen comments that Menenius's fable "was an answer." This is not meant as a compliment, for the fable is neither an appropriate nor a helpful answer as far as the plebeians are concerned. But that was never its point, as Menenius acknowledges at the outset: "it serves my purpose" (1.1.91). This patrician's purpose is not the plebeians'; one party's purpose is not another's.

As we have seen, the interested parties in the play (plebeians, patricians, Volscians, Roman matriarch) are linked by their focus on presentation. Successful PR presentations depend on performance, and to perform successfully characters must be directed, rehearsed, prompted (Vickers 1977: 244, 246). The tribunes coach the plebeians in 2.3, directing them in the rejection of Coriolanus's consulship. Note the imperatives: "Enforce his pride" (2.3.219); "Lay / A fault on us, your tribunes" (2.3.226–7); "Say you chose him / More after our commandment" (2.3.229–30); "Lay the fault on us" (2.3.234); "Say we read lectures to you" (2.3.235); "Say you ne'er had done't / (Harp on that still) but by our putting on" (2.3.251–2).

Meanwhile, on the other side, the patricians direct Coriolanus. Volumnia choreographs gestures, blocks movement, and provides props. Her directorial command is clearly indicated by her use of the demonstrative pronoun "this" and her double use of the adverb "thus." She is attentive to the visual needs of the groundlings, and she offers the actor alternatives:

> Go to them, with this bonnet in thy hand,
> And thus far having stretch'd it (here be with them),
> Thy knee bussing the stones (for in such business
> Action is eloquence, and the eyes of th'ignorant
> More learned than the ears), waving thy head,
> Which often thus correcting thy stout heart,
> Now humble as the ripest mulberry
> That will not hold the handling: or say to them,
> Thou art their soldier, and, being bred in broils,
> Hast not the soft way. (3.2.73–82)

Coriolanus acknowledges the difficulty of the role ("You have put me now to such a part which never / I shall discharge to th' life"; 3.2.105–6), and

Cominius assures Coriolanus of his services as a prompter. The keyword note for the role – "mildly" – is stressed four times in the scene's last four lines.

We return immediately to the tribunes and their last-minute rehearsal of details from dialogue to sound effects:

> when they hear me say, "It shall be so . . .
> then let them,
> If I say fine, cry "Fine!"; if death, cry "Death!" . . .
> And when such time they have begun to cry,
> Let them not cease, but with a din confus'd
> Enforce the present execution. (3.3.13–21)

Coriolanus's acting (in)ability inevitably loses out to the staged mutiny. Coriolanus is banished, whereupon we see that even the directors of this political pageant are actors: having got what they want, the tribunes now assume a milder stance: "Let us seem humbler after it is done / Than when it was a-doing" (4.2.4–5; Leggatt 1988: 200). In this play everyone is acting, in order to act upon Coriolanus.

Coriolanus subliminally realizes that his function is to serve others' purposes. When he offers himself to Aufidius in act 4 he instructs him, "make my misery serve thy turn" (4.5.88). Serving others' turn has been his role throughout life, from his early dedication to military activity to satisfy his mother's agenda to his current political uses for Romans and Volscians alike. The images of cannibalism which color the play are localized, lexical expressions of the theme of political feeding off others. And once again, their perspective varies according to the speaker. Aufidius's Volscian servants, like the Roman plebeians, see the world as do the fishermen in *Pericles* (written at the same time as *Coriolanus*), as an arena in which the big fish eat up the little ones (*Pericles* 2.1.28–9; cf. *Coriolanus* 1.1.85 and 4.5.188–9). In Aufidius's mouth, however, the image of cannibalism becomes one of phoenix-like self-recreation: "I'll renew me in his fall" (5.6.48). The different images are not those of cynics and poets but of losers and winners (at the post-victory press conference, "phoenix" makes a better impression than "cannibal"). Hal uses the Eastcheap crowd; in *Julius Caesar* Antony uses Lepidus: "though we lay these honors on this man / To ease ourselves of divers sland'rous loads, / He shall but bear them as the ass bears gold, / . . . And having brought our treasure where we will, / Then take we down his load, and turn him off (*JC* 4.1.19–25); *everyone* uses Coriolanus.

There is one exception: Virgilia. Her lack of manipulation is shown most obviously in her silence, for if presentation is tied to rhetorical persuasion (and all the characters, as we have seen, are notable for their linguistic manipulation), Virgilia is notable for her silence. "My gracious silence" is how Coriolanus greets her in 2.1.175, and in 5.3 she speaks a mere four lines to her mother-in-law's one hundred. Volumnia generally receives the critical credit for returning Coriolanus's loyalties to Rome, but the stage directions embedded in her dialogue suggest that Coriolanus responds to Virgilia's silence rather than to Volumnia's oration. (Shakespeare typically encodes crucial stage directions in dialogue [Slater 1982: 1–2].) Volumnia's frequent imperatives to her family – son, daughter-in-law, grandson – to speak (5.3.148, 153, 155, 156) indicate her repeated (failed) attempts to provoke a reaction (and for Volumnia, ever the Roman, reaction equals rhetoric). Coriolanus's attention, it seems, is elsewhere – with the woman who "comes foremost" (5.3.22), the silent, weeping figure whose tears Volumnia views as ineffective ("He cares not for your weeping"; line 156).

Words have been Coriolanus's downfall for five acts. As he himself acknowledges in act 2, "When blows have made me stay, I fled from words" (2.2.72). Throughout the play he is caught in the crossfire of verbal manipulation, and language consistently provokes him to impetuous (over)reactions: "Shall?" (3.1.87, 90); "traitor?" (3.3.67; 5.6.86); "boy?" (5.6.103, 112, 116). Now he responds to silence, and he responds *in* silence: "Like a dull actor now / I have forgot my part, and I am out [at a loss for words]" (5.3.40–1). This is the ultimate in stripping away of identity: Coriolanus is reduced to a prelinguistic being. But given the manipulative use of language in this play, silence cannot be other than a good thing. Words and theater in this play have not held the mirror up to nature; they have distorted it. Thus, the only optimistic conclusion is a speechless one: the rest is silence.

Julius Caesar (1599)

Silence is never an option in *Julius Caesar*, Shakespeare's most rhetorical play: persuasion, of oneself or of others, is its dominant mode. The stress on rhetoric, on public image, on performance, means that, as in *Coriolanus*, the entire play becomes an exercise in interpretation, for the characters as for us. "Men may construe things after their fashion, / Clean from the purpose of the things themselves," says Cicero in act 1 (1.3.34–5); in act 5 the same note is sounded fatally: "Alas, thou hast misconstrued every thing," Titinius accuses Cassius (5.3.84). What the characters construe and misconstrue, we must deconstrue, a challenging exercise given that the characters are never honest even with themselves. Rhetoric all too easily becomes rhetorical sleight of hand.

Rome has two problems – characters' propensity for misinterpretation, and their concern with self-image. The common denominator is acting. In act 5 Lucilius tells Antony that when he finds Brutus, dead or alive, Brutus "will be found like Brutus, like himself" (5.4.25); we realize with a shock that we do not know what "like himself" means in this play.[10] The adverb "like" should disconcert us further, for even as it asserts equivalence it reinforces difference (which is, after all, how similes work). We recall an earlier example in the play. On the eve of his assassination Caesar invites the conspirators to drink wine with him "like friends" (2.2.127).[11] Brutus's sorrowful aside, "That every like is not the same" (2.2.128; i.e., "being like friends is not the same as being friends"; Daniell 1998: 227, 2.2.127n.), could serve as an aphorism for the entire play. The same semantic slippage occurs in *Hamlet*, written the year after *Julius Caesar*. The prince questions Marcellus about the appearance of the Ghost: "Is it not like the King?" "As thou art to thyself" is the reply (1.1.58–9). Intended to reassure, Marcellus's response actually disconcerts for, as Stephen Greenblatt notes, "Marcellus is not 'like' himself; he *is* himself" (Greenblatt 2001: 211). Greenblatt's confident assertion of confluence could never be made of *Julius Caesar*.

In *Julius Caesar* acting is the *modus operandi*. Caesar refuses the crown in the marketplace in a theatrical pageant of humility to which the crowd responds with clapping and hissing "as they use to do the players in the theater" (1.2.260–1). Casca's bluntness is but an act (1.2.300–2). Brutus enjoins the conspirators: "Let not our looks put on our purposes, / But bear

---

[10]   Cf. Pindarus's assertion that Cassius "will appear / Such as he is" (4.2.11–12).

[11]   In Shakespeare's vision of politics, friends are either fakes ("*like* friends") or, as Leggatt points out in *2 Henry IV* (1988: 81), creatures whose power to hurt has been neutralized: "my friends, which thou must make thy friends, / Have but their stings and teeth newly ta'en out" (*2HIV* 4.5.204–5). When Macbeth becomes king, he immediately becomes suspicious of his supporters. Derek Jacobi reminisces: "Even the final 'Come, friends' [in 1.3] seemed to have a double edge: 'Come, . . .' – and what am I to call them? Are they friends? Yes, everyone is a friend at the moment. What *am* I worrying about?" (Jacobi 1998: 196).

it as our Roman actors do, / With untir'd spirits and formal constancy" (2.1.225–7).

What all Romans do – act with "untir'd spirits and formal constancy" – is presented as a problem of literally Colossal proportions in regard to Caesar who bestrides the narrow world (1.2.135–6). Cassius reminds us that beneath the formal role is a man: human, frail, flawed. Caesar is deaf in one ear; he suffers from epilepsy; he succumbs to illness.

Cassius describes a fever Caesar suffered in Spain: he shook, his lips lost their color and his eyes their sparkle; he was dehydrated; he groaned and begged for water. None of this is other than one would expect from someone experiencing a high temperature, but Cassius subtly gives Caesar's symptoms a moral inflexion. "His coward lips did from their color fly," he says (1.2.122), adding an inappropriate adjective to a poetic anthropomorphization.[12] Caesar cries for water "as a sick girl" (1.2.128); by associating him with the feminine, Cassius marks him as unfit to rule. Cassius's scorn for these infirmities, including Caesar's inability to cross the Tiber, is undisguised: "it doth amaze me / A man of such a feeble temper should / So get the start of the majestic world / And bear the palm alone" (1.2.128–31).[13] Occasional illness, and failure to qualify for the swimming team, have never precluded a career in politics, but in a city concerned with appearance, Cassius exposes the discrepancy between public image and private man.

In Rome identity is not what you are but how you appear. And how you appear is unhealthily determined by how others see you. Reflection in this play refers to mirrors, glasses, eyes – surfaces that present an image – not to meditation or introspection. (The Latin root *re-flectere* means to bend back.[14]) Cassius tells Brutus:

> And since you know you cannot see yourself
> So well as by reflection, I, your glass,

[12]   One might note, *en passant*, how often politicians have inappropriate recourse to this emotive adjective. George W. Bush's use of the adverbial form "cowardly" on September 11, 2001 is but the most recent example. Referring to the tragedy caused by terrorism in New York City, Bush promised to find and punish those who perpetrated "this cowardly deed." Whatever the men were who flew the planes into the World Trade Center (immoral, evil, for example), they were not cowards.

[13]   The swimming match is Shakespeare's addition to his source material, Plutarch's *Lives of the Noble Grecians and Romans*.

[14]   Shakespeare stresses the noun's etymology in *Macbeth* when the sergeant talks of the sun's "reflection" – its turning back at the vernal equinox (1.1.25).

Will modestly discover to yourself
That of yourself which you yet know not of. (1.2.67–70)

Although Brutus knows (initially at least) the difference between "that of [him]self which [he] yet know[s] not of" and "that which is not in me" (1.2.65), he becomes influenced by the reflecting surfaces of the conspirators: "every one doth wish / You had but that opinion of yourself / Which every noble Roman bears of you" (2.1.91–3).

Characters in this play not only look to others for their identity but perform constant identity checks by measuring themselves against Romans past and present. Looking back to an ideal (Aeneas) or an ancestor (Lucius Junius Brutus), or performing a compare-and-contrast exercise with their contemporaries ("if I were Brutus now and he were Cassius"; 1.3.314; "were I Brutus, / And Brutus Antony"; 3.2.226–7), the characters locate their identity in the city and its citizens rather than in the self (Berry 1981: 328; Velz 1968: 150–3). Brutus calls himself a "son of Rome" (1.2.173); Ligarius addresses Brutus as "Soul of Rome" (2.1.321). Hence the play's elision of public and private, for the urban precedes the internal; the self is subsumed by, and dedicated to, the civic. In this play the family is political and retrospective: ancestors rather than parents (Berry 1988: 145). With such non-Shakespearean values – i.e., identity as externally rather than internally derived – the future is inevitably sterile: Calpurnia is barren, Mark Antony "pricks" his nephew for death. Social relations in *Julius Caesar* degenerate into puerile competition. Cassius and Brutus engage in schoolboy arguments of the "no I didn't," "yes you did" variety (see 4.3.30–4, 55–62, 82–4). Politics is a competitive sport (Leggatt 1988: 149, 198–9).

Brutus and Antony, political opponents, compete in the most Roman (and still the most important) of political arenas: rhetoric. If one wants to succeed in the public sport of politics, one needs to know how to use language to win friends and influence people.

The constituents of effective public speaking have not changed since Aristotle formulated the rules of classical rhetoric in the fourth century BCE. They are in evidence in advertising, in party political broadcasts, in any media presentation that seeks to persuade. Brutus begins his address to the crowd in the forum scene with a tricolonic apostrophe (an address with three balanced parts): "Romans, countrymen, and lovers" (3.2.13). Max Atkinson's analysis of political "claptrap" (the rhetorical techniques which guarantee audience applause) shows that audiences are regularly moved to clap after a list of three (Atkinson 1984: 56–73[15]). These lists are effective whether in shorthand slogan form (*veni, vidi, vici; liberté, egalité, fraternité; ein Volk, ein Reich, ein Führer*) or in longer form: "never in the field of human conflict has so much been owed by so many to so few"; "a Mars a day helps you work, rest, and play." In recent times, Earl Spencer's funeral oration for the Princess of Wales provides a memorable example: "I stand before you today, the representative of a family in grief, in a country in mourning, before a world in shock." Many Shakespeare characters know the dramatic effect of lists of three. Malvolio bursts upon the midnight revelers in *Twelfth Night* with "Have you no wit, manners, nor honesty? . . . . Is there no respect of place, persons, nor time in you?" (2.3.87, 91–2), and the Bastard in *King John* muses "Mad world, mad kings, mad composition!" (2.1.561).

Triadic formulae in rhetoric provide a condensed version of a traditional narrative structure dating from mythology's three Fates or Paris and the three goddesses; this structure dominates our early life in nursery tales such as the Three Little Pigs or Goldilocks and the Three Bears; it continues in adulthood in narrative jokes such as "An Englishman, an Irishman, and a Scotsman . . . " and in literature with Lear's three daughters and Portia's three caskets. The list of three works in rhetoric as it does in narrative: we are primed to expect (and hence to respond to) the climactic third item (Atkinson 1984: 58).

Antony later repeats Brutus's opening triad more effectively through the simple device of asyndeton (missing out connective conjunctions): "Friends, Romans, countrymen" (3.2.73). If one wonders why Antony's address, rather than Brutus's, has become immortalized to the point of cliché, asyndeton is only part of the explanation. Antony's triad of terms has an incremental rhythm moving from the monosyllabic "Friends" to the bisyllabic "Romans" to the trisyllabic "countrymen." This sequence escalates and energizes, unlike the bathetic cadence of Brutus's "Romans, countrymen, and lovers."

Brutus follows his opening with epanalepsis (the repetition of words at the beginning and end of clauses or sentences): "*hear* me for my cause, and be silent, that you may *hear*. *Believe* me for mine honor, and have respect to mine honor, that you may *believe*" (3.2.13–16). He is a master of con-

---

[15]   I am indebted to an RSC theater program for *Julius Caesar* (1991) which brought Atkinson's book to my attention and highlighted its relevance to the forum speeches.

trast: "Not that I lov'd Caesar less, but that I lov'd Rome more" (3.2.21–2). Rhetorical questions, perennially effective in political speeches, abound, again in an incrementally triple formation; they are reinforced by anaphora (repetition of the same word or sequence – "who is here so . . . " – at the beginning of successive clauses), which alternates with epistrophe (repetition of the same word – "offended" – at the end of successive clauses).

> Who is here so base that would be a bondman? If any, speak, for him have I offended. Who is here so rude that would not be a Roman? If any, speak, for him have I offended. Who is here so vile that will not love his country? If any, speak, for him have I offended. (3.2.29–34)

The effect is aurally hypnotic, luring listeners to attend.

Antony outdoes Brutus, however. He begins his oration with a contrast: "I come to bury Caesar, not to praise him" (3.2.74). Contrast is a staple of modern political speeches. "U-turn if you want to – the lady's not for turning," proclaimed a defiant Mrs. Thatcher, coupling contrast with polyptoton (repeating a word in a different form). John F. Kennedy's "Ask not what your country can do for you – ask what you can do for your country" is an even more memorable formation in which the contrast is expressed in an elegant parison (an equal balance in the components of a sentence). Among Shakespearean examples, Hamlet's "To be or not to be" is a famously succinct contrast.

Antony's opening contrast is also cunningly apophatic (apophasis is when one promotes a subject by denying that one will talk about it). He later uses a variant of this, autoclesis (introducing something in the negative to whet the audience's appetite), when he calls attention to Caesar's will "which, pardon me, I do not mean to read" (3.2.131). The introduction of Caesar's will illustrates another no-fail technique in public speaking, one which has nothing to do with classical rhetoric and therefore no technical term to define it: the use of props.

Antony's instincts in this direction have already been manifest. He enters the scene with the ultimate in props, the body of Caesar, which he proceeds to use for empathetic effect. He anthropomorphizes the vascular system ("the blood of Caesar . . . rushing out of doors to be resolv'd / If Brutus so unkindly knock'd"; 178–80), heightens emotional response by improbably identifying the wounds made by specific conspirators, and in a flight of sentimental fancy (which carefully reminds the crowd of Caesar's achievements), claims to recall the first time Caesar wore the mantle which his corpse now bears: " 'Twas on a summer's evening, in his tent, / That day he overcame the Nervii" (3.2.172–3). Despite his specific disavowal of rhetorical skills, Antony is clearly not the "plain blunt man" he claims to be (line 218). Note his use of tapinosis (repetition of a word to debase it, as in "honorable" man); of antistoichon (balanced opposition of ideas): "I speak not to disprove what Brutus spoke, / But here I am to speak what I do know" (3.2.100–1, here joined with polyptoton, parison, and contrast); of hyperbaton (reversal of word order for rhetorical effect, as in "then burst his mighty heart"; 3.2.186). His speech provides a convenient handbook of key rhetorical terms.[16]

One does not need to be a rhetorician to appreciate Antony's oratory, but an Elizabethan audience, whose education system was based entirely on rhetoric, would immediately recognize the rhetorical devices he employs. The university curriculum was organized round rhetoric: exercises asked students to defend the difficult and the indefensible (Helen of Troy or Brutus, for instance) as a test of their debating ability, and exams took the form of public debates (the practice lingers in today's *viva voce* PhD defense).

Despite their brilliant construction, neither character's speech seems particularly sincere. Brian Vickers notes Brutus's "totally emotionless attitude"; and the fact that he speaks verse before and after his funeral oration (which is in prose) suggests that the oration "is a prepared speech, penned and learned in a vacuum, oblivious to the audience's response" (Vickers 1968: 243; cf. Goddard 1951: I, 322). John Nettles, acting Brutus for the RSC in 1995, found the speech "too short, even perfunctory, really to fulfill its purpose . . . ; it appears not a little arrogant in its brevity and lack of substance" (Nettles 1998: 184). In the 1955 film of *Julius Caesar* Marlon Brando's Antony turned from the crowd in emotion, pausing to collect himself as the dialogue instructs; this staged effect was caught by the camera in a close-up of Antony's satisfied smile. Antony is probably genuinely emotional but he is also a professional performer.[17] His loyalty to Caesar lasts only until 4.1 where we see him editing Caesar's will.

[16] For a useful and succinct introduction to classical rhetoric see Dixon (1971). Vickers's *The Artistry of Shakespeare's Prose* (1968) provides a detailed analysis of rhetoric in Shakespearean drama.

[17] David Daniell glosses Antony's pause as follows: "Genuine emotion allows him at the same time to test reaction: he is skilful enough to know that the break in his speech will be to his advantage" (Daniell 1998: 258, 3.2.108n.).

Both funeral orations are highly patterned, and are designed as public relations exercises, the first to calm foment, the second to create it. Both are acts, performed by politicians. Only the second is successful. That Brutus's rhetorical ratiocination is ineffective is seen by the 3rd Plebeian's response: "Let *him* be Caesar" (3.2.51). Awarding Brutus the office whose abolition he has just defended misses the ideological point. Antony survives act 3, and survives the play, partly because of political *savoir-faire* (contrast Brutus who naively and disastrously overrules sound tactical advice from Cassius) and partly because of rhetorical skill. Although the play (anticipating his role in *Antony and Cleopatra*) characterizes Antony as a reveler, a lover of plays and music who is given to "sports, to wildness, and much company" (2.1.188–9; 1.2.203–4), it also depicts him as a competitor and a winner. In the rhetorical competition waged (staged) between Brutus and Antony in the forum, Antony emerges as a professional politician in every way. He can act, and he can speak; consequently he can survive.

2   Surviving Politics

"[Rulers] maintain their position only by considerable exertion. They make the journey as if they had wings; their problems start when they alight" (Machiavelli 1977: 53)

Introduction

Survival in politics and success in politics are not synonymous. The former is undramatic (endurance always is) partly because it is unteleological; or rather, it becomes an end in itself. Drama is about trajectory, upwards or downwards; survival is about maintaining altitude. *Henry V* chronicles the politician's rise to the top and leaves Henry at the pinnacle of success, conquering a country and a princess. *Julius Caesar*, on the other hand, illustrates the difficulties of maintaining one's place at the top. Caesar no longer achieves (his triumphs are antecedent to the play); he simply is. And being, in public life as in plays, is far less interesting than doing.

Henry V and *Julius Caesar* were written sequentially (1598–9) and, despite their different historical settings, form a dramatic diptych. For Shakespeare, Henry V and Julius Caesar were related icons. One of his earliest plays, *1 Henry VI*, links the two heroes when the Duke of Bedford addresses the corpse of Henry V with the most complimentary comparison he can find: "A far more glorious star thy soul will make / Than Julius Caesar" (*1HVI* 1.1.55–6). *Julius Caesar* is the second part of *Henry V*. It answers the question audiences and readers pose at conclusions to plays, novels, and television series: what happens next? What happens next in *Julius Caesar* is not continued heroism but a suspicious public, envious political rivals, and physical vulnerability.

The epilogue to *Henry V* continues to extol Henry's military achievements in hyperbolic terms ("This star of England. Fortune made his sword"; Epilogue. 6), glossing quickly over the bathetic sequel in which Henry VI's multiple advisers "lost France, and made his England bleed" (Epilogue. 12). Even if we register this anticlimax, it is a benign political summary in comparison to the antiromantic historical details: Henry died two years after winning the battle of Agincourt, unglamorously afflicted with dysentery. Just three miles away, Katherine of France was, unusually, not called to his bedside; this, and her earlier pronouncement that she would rather marry a French soldier than an English king (Seward 1987: 147), indicates the emotional tenor of the short marriage. Whereas weddings hold promise, marriage equals reality. This is why several of Shakespeare's history plays end, like his comedies, with imminent nuptials and an optimistic future.[18] Triumph, romantic or military, is a hard act to follow. Even continued triumph can become tedious, as Tamburlaine's relentless conquests in Marlowe's *2 Tamburlaine* show (they lack the verve and excitement of *1 Tamburlaine*). Continued triumph is, in a sense, decline, because it fails to expand. It is maintenance rather than improvement; it is mere survival. And survival is the beginning of the end.

If *Henry IV* and *Henry V* chronicle the growth of a political career, and *Julius Caesar* illustrates the difficulty of maintaining that career, *Richard II*

---

[18]   Henry VI marries Margaret of Anjou (*1 Henry VI*); Richmond marries Elizabeth (*Richard III*); Henry V marries Katherine (*Henry V*). All the comedies (with three exceptions) conclude with a wedding or the promise of one: weddings were the destination of comedy, as we saw in chapter 2. Burgundy acknowledges this traditional generic ingredient of comedy when Talbot receives an invitation from the Countess of Auvergne in *1 Henry VI*: "Nay, then I see our wars / Will turn unto a peaceful comic sport, / When ladies crave to be encount'red with" (*1HVI* 2.2.44–6). When Shakespeare introduces an early wedding into a comedy, as he does in *Taming of the Shrew, Merchant of Venice*, and *All's Well* (which feature weddings in acts 3 and 2), the road to act 5 is rocky. The same applies if a history play introduces a wedding in the middle acts, as happens in *King John* when Lewis and Blanche marry in act 2. Virginia Vaughan analyzes our "thwarted" expectations as "the peace it [the wedding] is intended to foster never arrives" (1984: 417).

depicts political decline. Richard neither achieves nor stays still. John of Gaunt believes that "the setting sun, and music at the close, / As the last taste of sweets is sweetest last" (*RII* 2.1.12–13), but whatever aesthetic appeal the "dying fall" (as Orsino calls it) may possess, it has no political value. Apemantus in *Timon of Athens*, more realistic than Gaunt, knows that "men shut their doors against a setting sun" (1.2.145). And the setting of Richard's sun is not gradual, like Gaunt's peaceful sunset, but precipitate and spectacular like that of the son of Apollo: "Down, down I come, like glist'ring Phaëton" (3.3.178).

Richard II (1595)

Richard II begins his play with the blood of a kinsman on his hands: it was widely believed that Richard was responsible for the murder of his uncle, Thomas of Woodstock, and that Mowbray, accused by Bullingbrook in act 1, was acting on Richard's orders. Richard deals with Bullingbrook's accusation of Mowbray by arranging a trial by combat, only to interrupt the joust and banish both Dukes. When Bullingbrook returns in the middle of the play, he forces Richard to abdicate.

Richard II is Shakespeare's most histrionic king. Richard (self-)dramatizes; he is the master of grand gesture and extravagant language. When he interrupts the lists between Mowbray and Bullingbrook in act 1, scene 3, he sentences the competitors to banishment. A shrewder politician might have delivered this decree in private before jousting began, but Richard's goal is not expedience but effect. He halts the lists dramatically, with an actor's sense of timing.

In 4.1 he turns his abdication into a reverse coronation, signaling the inverted nature of the ceremony with anaphorically ritual incantation:

> With mine own tears I wash away my balm,
> With mine own hands I give away my crown,
> With mine own tongue deny my sacred state,
> With mine own breath release all duteous oaths. (4.1.207–10)

Although the usurping Bullingbrook is politically in control, it is Richard who drives the scene. In the ESC production in 1987–9, Michael Pennington's Richard "played with Bolingbroke as a cat with a mouse. The crown was dangled like a carrot, it was held high, gently offered, snatched away, the anguish of the virgin, refusing yet knowing ultimately the prize would have to be given away, determined to tease and frustrate, delaying the moment as long as possible" (Bogdanov cited in Shewring 1996: 113). Playing the role for the BBC television production in 1978, Derek Jacobi detected Richard's "actor's instinct" in the abdication scene: "If I've got to go, I'm going in style" (Alexander 1978: 26).

Richard's language is as exaggerated as his gestures. He claims his sighs "shall lodge [dislodge] the summer corn, / And make a dearth in this revolting land" (3.3.162–3). All his major speeches are about himself. When Richard instructs his wife, "Tell thou the lamentable tale of me" (5.1.44), we are reminded of the emotional self-focus of Sidney's Astrophil: "Pity the tale of me" (Evans 1977: 20). Richard's narcissistic speech and action unite when he calls for the ultimate emblem of vanity, a looking-glass (like Mark Antony in *Julius Caesar*, he knows the theatrical value of a prop). Frank Kermode believes that "in a sense [Richard] is always calling for a mirror" because of his "habit of studying himself from the outside" (Kermode 2000: 43). Richard is not unique in this (as we saw, characters in *Julius Caesar* refer to themselves in the third person and respond to images of reflection), but he is unusual, as Howard and Rackin observe, in turning the mirror, an image of "feminine vanity," into "the means of theatrical empowerment for it demands that all eyes in the playhouse, including Richard's own, will be fixed on Richard's face" (Howard and Rackin 1997: 155). When Richard dashes the mirror against the ground, smashing it into "an hundred shivers," he makes an emblematic point ("how soon my sorrow hath destroy'd my face"; 4.1.289, 91), but he also ensures that he triumphantly upstages Bullingbrook. As at Coventry, he has an eye for theatrical climax.

Theatrical ability and inability is a leitmotiv of the political plays but *Richard II* differs in that the king is not an actor: he is merely a performer. The distinction hinges on the performer's concentration on externals, on exhibition, on entertainment. Ceremony is divorced from meaning. Richard is so busy appearing regal that he fails to act royally.

The historical Richard was very much concerned with appearance. He was the first king to care for fashion and was renowned for conspicuous consumption (£2,000 on a single outfit – in the fourteenth century!). His first wife, Anne of Bohemia, was a fashion innovator. She introduced the practice of women riding side-saddle, and popularized shoes with toes so long that they eventually had to be supported by silver chains or silk laces suspended from the knee. (The costume designer for the BBC television production wisely eschewed this historical accuracy on the grounds that it "would have been too expensive, would have got in the actors' way and wouldn't show much on television anyway"; Alexander 1978: 21.) Richard invented the pocket handkerchief. His obsession with appearance extended to deferential genuflection by his courtiers. He devised a narcissistic power game: when he entered the presence chamber, whoever caught his eye, irrespective of rank, had to kneel immediately (*Eulogium Historiarum*, cited in Zitner 1974: 250–1).[19]

The historical Richard may have been concerned with fashion but Shakespeare's Richard lacks skill in *self*-fashioning. He has one (inherited) identity: king. Subscribing to the medieval theory of the divine right of kings, he sees himself as God's anointed deputy on earth: "Not all the water in the rough rude sea / Can wash the balm off from an anointed king" (3.2.54–5). In this he differs from Richard III and Henry V. The difference is partly one of birth. Hal is the first inheritor of a usurped title. Richard III systematically murders his way to the throne, disposing of those ahead of him in the queue. But Richard II was the twelfth in an unbroken line of hereditary monarchs from William the Conqueror; he inherited the throne at the age of ten, and in Shakespeare's play there is no gap between man and role. This becomes a problem when another man wants the role; there is no other ontological space for Richard to occupy. Richard has no middle ground between kingship and annihilation: "I am unking'd by Bullingbrook, / And straight am nothing" (5.5.37–8). (By contrast, we are in no doubt that Henry VI could be quite happy in a monastery.)

In this context an apparently otiose conversation between the Duke and Duchess of York in 5.2 assumes significance. Aumerle's entry is heralded by the Duchess's observation, "Here comes my son Aumerle" (5.2.41). York corrects his wife: "Aumerle that was, / But that is lost for being Richard's friend; / And, madam, you must call him Rutland now" (5.2.41–3). Because of his alleged involvement in Gloucester's murder, Aumerle had been stripped of his status as Duke of Aumerle but had retained his title Earl of Rutland. The Duchess ignores such agnomenic niceties, and greets her son with an identity independent of title: "Welcome, my son!" (5.2.46). York's corrective speech about Rutland's title is thus sandwiched between two lines which grant his child a permanent filial identity.

It is easy to become sidetracked by the subsequent farce of the Yorks' two confrontation episodes in act 5 (parents and son; parents, son, and

---

[19] For Ian McKellen's portrayal of Richard (for the Prospect Theatre Company in 1968) as a man "expecting an automatic response to his presence . . . waiting for the conditioned response," see Shewring (1996: 86–7).

king), but we should not forget the import of the initial discussion: the ability to exist as an individual, to retain an identity, when title is removed. This is an ability which Richard lacks. When Exton presents Henry with Richard's coffin in the last lines of the play, he identifies the former king simply and toponymously as "Richard of Burdeaux" (5.6.33). If Richard had been able to see himself in such human terms, his course would have been very different.

This "if" is an ahistorical wish, however, for as a medieval king, one ruling by divine right and primogeniture, Richard's political identity is rooted in a religious identity. The common man is not an option. It is only when regicides and usurpers (and their sons) ascend the throne (Henry IV, Henry V, Henry VI, Richard III) that the common man can enter the picture.

Richard is therefore trapped by the trappings of kingship. He mistakes ceremony for the thing itself. This accounts for his theatrical tendencies: he responds artistically to events, to the performance rather than to the substance. When Bullingbrook offers a lengthy, passionate speech about justice, Richard's one-line reaction is not judicial but aesthetic (Barkan 1978: 8): "How high a pitch his resolution soars!" (1.1.109). Bullingbrook, as we see in the later *Henry IV* plays, knows all about the value of appearance. In raising the issue of Woodstock's murder, Bullingbrook resorts, as is proper, to court ritual and ceremony. He still observes due form and linguistic proportion when he is banished: "Then let us take a ceremonious leave / And loving farewell of our several friends" (1.3.50–1). But whereas Richard has only two modes (he observes ceremony or violates it), Bullingbrook knows how to manipulate it. He pays lip-service to outward form.

The most extended example of this is in act 5, scene 3, where he grants Aumerle a pardon at line 35 (a pardon granted incidentally for political rather than spiritual reasons: "to win thy after-love I pardon thee"). The scene continues for a further hundred lines as Henry presides judicially over a ceremony-cum-charade whose outcome has already been decided; but Henry humors the Yorks by observing outward ceremony.

Earlier in the play we had observed Henry's linguistic legerdemain (legerdelangue?). He gains a toehold in England, and crucial supporters, by claiming he comes "but for mine own" (3.3.196). He wins over York with sophistry: "As I was banish'd, I was banish'd Herford, / But as I come, I come for Lancaster" (2.3.113–15). Critics point out that in the deposition scene he never uses the word "depose," preferring the more diplomatically euphemistic "resign" (4.1.190, 200). It is Richard who introduces the vocabulary and concept of deposition, allowing Bullingbrook to react as if the thought of kingship had just occurred to him: "In God's name I'll ascend the regal throne" (4.1.113). This is disingenuous given that Bullingbrook had earlier launched an electioneering campaign. Richard notes "his courtship to the common people, / How he did seem to dive into their hearts / With humble and familiar courtesy, / What reverence he did throw away on slaves, / . . . Off goes his bonnet to an oyster-wench" (1.4.24–7, 31). From the start Bullingbrook knows how to exploit ceremony, manipulate language, and woo the crowd.

The rivalry between Richard and Bullingbrook is that of two actors:

> As in a theatre the eyes of men,
> After a well-graced actor leaves the stage,
> Are idly bent on him that enters next,
> Thinking his prattle to be tedious,
> Even so, or with much more contempt, men's eyes
> Did scowl on gentle Richard (5.2.23–8)

This theatrical rivalry was embodied in John Barton's production for the RSC in 1973–4, where Richard Pasco and Ian Richardson alternated the roles of Richard and Bullingbrook; they were allocated their roles in a prefatory dumbshow by "Shakespeare." Barton's primary interest, like Shakespeare's, was in theatrical role play rather than rivalry. If Richard II is trapped by his role, so too is the actor. "The actor is himself a prisoner, the prisoner of his author and his director. He cannot change a line of what he has to say. He is governed by outside forces whose existence is independent of himself" (Hobson cited in Shewring 1996: 123).[20] Inevitably Bullingbrook is the winner, politically and theatrically. He has many roles and linguistic registers, Richard only one.

Richard is undone, literally, and the play becomes a study of reversal and annihilation. Negative prefixes appear with remarkable frequency. The Duchess of Gloucester's residence is characterized by "unfurnish'd walls, / Unpeopled offices, untrodden stones" (1.2.68–9). Gaunt wishes to "undeaf" Richard's ear, others to "uncurse" or "unsay" or "undeck" or

---

[20] Shewring (1996: 122–37) provides a detailed description of this production.

"undo." Richard is "unhappied" by his flatterers and he tries to "unkiss" his wedding vows.[21] The Orwellian neologisms resonate most eerily in the double use of "unking'd" at 4.1.220 and 5.5.37. "God save King Henry, unking'd Richard says" (4.1.220). The past participle functions adjectivally as a title; Richard can find identity only in negation.

In prison Richard realizes "I am unking'd by Bullingbrook, / And straight am nothing" (5.5.37–8). This forceful terminative line is immediately qualified by uncertainty: "But *what e'er I be*, / Nor I, nor any man that but man is, / With nothing shall be pleas'd, till he be eas'd / With being nothing" (5.5.38–41). Leaving his identity in suspension, Richard introduces the consolations typically associated with Greek tragedy: count no man happy until he dies. But this is to move from identity to emotional state. The sentence does not provide a transition and Richard's identity is left unresolved. The fleeting reclamation of royalty seventy lines later when he tells his murderer that he has "with the King's blood stain'd the King's own land" (5.5.110) is unconvincing. This kind of assertion without support takes us back to the opening world of ceremony devoid of substance.

Richard II is a play about signs: ceremony (lists, coronations), emblems (scales, buckets in a well, the crown, a looking-glass), and language. All three areas are characterized by duality. Because Richard reduces ceremony to mere show, it is split into substance and performance. Emblems are double: the twin pans of the scale, the two buckets in the well, the crown with two claimants, the mirror which reflects. Language, too, becomes twofold for, as Leggatt points out (1988: 74–5, 59), absolute terms such as kingship become relative, homonyms tantalize ("Ay, no, no ay"; 4.1.201), and ambiguity is frequent ("'This other Eden' . . . 'Other' in what sense?"). Not content with negating verbs through prefixes to create a stark conceptual opposite (as in "unkiss"), the play creates unexpected reflexive verbs: Bullingbrook "repeals himself" (2.2.49); Richard will "undo myself" (4.1.203). The terms jar solecistically. Language, like ceremonies and emblems, is disruptable and transferable. And in a play whose central stage image is a crown held by two men, kingship becomes not a religious or ethical concept but another linguistic sign, to which more than one meaning (or man) may lay claim.

Shakespeare extends the play's duality to audience response by refusing to come down on one political side. He presents us with a five-act opinion

---

[21]   2.1.16; 3.2.137; 4.1.9; 4.1.250; 4.1.203; 3.1.10; 5.1.74.

poll, a dramatic equivalent of the scales image used by the gardener in which "their fortunes both are weigh'd" (3.4.84). Thus, Richard is the rightful king (plus one point); Bullingbrook usurps the throne (minus one point). Bullingbrook is an efficient politician (plus one point); Richard is whimsical, vain, and, by abdicating, a traitor to himself (minus two points). There may be a theatrical victor (Richard), and a political winner (Bullingbrook), but critics point out that there is no clear moral victor. Bullingbrook survives, and spends *Henry IV* consolidating his position.

Although Richard does not survive the play, it is England who is the real loser.[22] No other Shakespeare play stresses the words "blood" and "earth" as often as does *Richard II*, and the terms are linked through two early stories in Genesis: expulsion from Eden, and Cain's shedding of Abel's blood. In the middle of the deposition the Bishop of Carlisle prophesies in terms straight from the Geneva Bible, "the blood of English shall manure the ground, / And future ages groan for this foul act" (4.1.137–8). He concludes the scene in a similar tone: "the children yet unborn / Shall feel this day as sharp to them as thorn" (4.1.322–3). Genesis haunts the play explicitly, as in Gaunt's description of England as an "other Eden," or the Queen's view of the gardener as a second Adam ("old Adam's likeness"; 3.4.73), but the Genetic vocabulary throughout is implicitly insistent: blood, exile, banishment, wander, serpent, adder, snakes, garden, painful childbirth, inheritance, fertility, language, linguistic deceit (Maveety 1973). England is a paradisiacal garden, and the shedding of sibling blood has consequences for generations to come, as the Wars of the Roses will show.

Shakespeare moderates Bullingbrook's triumph with a Biblical image. The new king banishes Exton, the murderer of Richard II: "With Cain go wander thorough shades of night" (5.6.43). Since Cain's crime was murder of a brother, the allusion more aptly denotes Bullingbrook who has just shed the blood of a kinsman. The play ends where it began with Bullingbrook repeating Richard's crime, with an image of Bullingbrook-as-Cain completing the opening image of Richard-as-Abel, with Bullingbrook banishing Exton as Richard had banished his murder instrument, Mowbray.[23]

---

[22] In fact, in a rare moment of philosophical ratiocination, Richard's attitude to loss sounds remarkably like that in the poem "One Art" by Elizabeth Bishop. "Say, is my kingdom lost? Why, 'twas my care, / And what loss is it to be rid of care?" (*RII* 3.2.95–6). Cf. Bishop: "The art of losing isn't hard to master; / . . . / I lost two cities, lovely ones. And, vaster, / Some realms I owned, two rivers, a continent. I miss them, but it wasn't a disaster" (1, 13–14).

[23] For this circular Attic structure see chapter 1, "Introduction."

This trochilic structure places Bullingbrook's triumph in a larger, somber frame: the politician survives but the country has sufferings in store.

Macbeth (1606)

Scotland suffers in *Macbeth*. No sooner has Macbeth assumed the throne (a throne he acquires by murdering its occupant) than references to the country's afflictions appear: "our suffering country" (3.6.48); "bleed, bleed, poor country!" (4.3.31); "alas, poor country, / Almost afraid to know itself!" (4.3.164–5). The anthropomorphization continues in act 5 with images of Scotland as a sick patient in need of a doctor, diagnosis, and herbal medicine (5.2.27; 5.3.50–6).

Whether *Macbeth* is the tragedy of a nation or an individual has long been debated. Holinshed's *Chronicles* provided the source for "the Scottish play," just as they did for the English histories. Yet in 1623, when *Macbeth* was printed in the first collected edition of Shakespeare's plays, it appeared not in the section of Histories but in Tragedies. One assumes geography rather than genre was the motivating factor in this decision: both *Richard II* and *Richard III* were labeled tragedies on the title page of their first editions yet appear in the Folio under Histories. To Heminge and Condell, the Englishmen who prepared the Folio, history meant the history of England.

And yet the landscape of *Macbeth* is not merely geographic. To England, Ireland, and Scotland are added Heaven and Hell. The vastness of this moral landscape is counterbalanced by a close-up of Macbeth's mind as it negotiates the psychological space between a crime and its consequences. Scotland suffers and recovers; Macbeth never does.

Macbeth is one of Shakespeare's shortest plays, a drama of extraordinary concision and compression. The play omits the "before" and "after": we only hear about Macbeth's previous successes, reinforced through the adjectives "noble" and "valiant," just as we only hear about his later despotism (the word "tyrant" occurs fifteen times in the last acts). Instead the play dramatizes the act in-between – murder – which it divides into three parts: the plan; the performance; the personal consequences.

The common denominator of these three parts is fear. Thinking about Duncan's murder causes fear: it "doth unfix my hair / And make my seated heart knock at my ribs" (1.3.135–6). Murdering Duncan causes fear: "I am afraid to think what I have done; / Look on't again I dare not" (2.2.48–9). Thereafter Macbeth is constantly fearful: "our fears in Banquo / Stick deep" (3.1.48–9); he eats meals "in fear" and sleeps "in the affliction of these terrible dreams / That shake us nightly" (3.2.17, 18–19); he is "cabin'd, cribb'd, confin'd, bound in / To saucy doubts and fears" (3.4.23–4); his nerves tremble (3.4.101–3). When in act 5 he hears the offstage cry of women, he says "I have almost forgot the taste of fears" (5.5.9). The adverb is important: *almost*. In Aristotelian theory a hero is supposed to commit a crime and then suffer; through suffering he learns. Macbeth, unusually, suffers before he commits evil. Surely no criminal has ever derived less joy from the fruits of his crime.

Julius Caesar denies fear – "I rather tell thee what is to be fear'd / Than what I fear" (1.2.211–12) – although his disavowal surely reveals the fear he so insistently denies. Personal emotions do not suit public Roman figures: "for always I am Caesar" (1.2.212). Macbeth, on the other hand, speaks of fear in every scene (Jacobi 1998: 197). "A soldier, and afeard?" we might ask incredulously with Lady Macbeth (5.1.37). Her binary summarizes in interrogative form her lengthier, earlier scorn when she accuses her husband of cowardice (1.7.39–45). But cowardice has never been part of Macbeth's military make-up. The first scene describes him as a Scottish Coriolanus: his weapon smoked "with bloody execution," he "carv'd out his passage [cut his way through the enemy]," and "unseam'd" Macdonwald "from the nave to th' chops" (1.2.18, 19, 22). This last image is not just one of professional efficiency but of relish. Macbeth is a killer; coward and he be many miles asunder.

But killing in civilian life is very different from killing on the battlefield, and neither Macbeth nor his lady realizes this until it is too late. Shakespearean tragedy often concerns individuals who are miscast in the part they are required to play. Brutus in *Julius Caesar* is the most obvious example: a noble private citizen who is called upon to commit an ignoble act for the public good. Hamlet, an introspective meditative student, is cast in the role of active revenger. And Macbeth, who murders for a living and loses no sleep over it, finds that killing a king causes nightmares.

Whereas Macbeth the soldier created "strange images of death" by creating corpses (1.3.97), Macbeth the regicide creates "strange images of death" in his mind. He sees a dagger and the ghost of Banquo; he imagines bloody detail – "never shake / Thy gory locks at me" (3.4.49–50); he is obsessed with key words – "I could not say 'Amen,' /. . . / . . . wherefore could not I pronounce 'Amen'? /. . . / 'Amen' / Stuck in my throat" (2.2.26, 28–30) – and hysterically repeats imagined curses:

Methought I heard a voice cry, "Sleep no more!
Macbeth does murther sleep"– . . .
Still it cried, "Sleep no more!" to all the house;
"Glamis hath murther'd sleep, and therefore Cawdor
Shall sleep no more – Macbeth shall sleep no more." (2.2.32–3, 38–40)

Lady Macbeth's response shows the different world she inhabits. "Who was it that thus cried?" she asks uncomprehendingly (2.2.41). Her tone is that of an adult addressing an overcreative child whose story she cannot understand because it comes from an imagination she cannot share. Lady Macbeth, here as elsewhere, is pragmatic: wash, go to your bedroom, put on your nightgown (2.2.43, 63–8).

Macbeth's tragedy is partly one of imagination: his heat oppressèd brain sees images of disturbing beauty (Duncan's "silver skin lac'd with his golden blood"; 2.3.112) as well as images of horror ("twenty mortal murthers" [wounds]; 3.5.80). He suffers, as he himself acknowledges, from "the torture of the mind" (3.2.21). But if imagination undoes Macbeth politically, it also redeems him theatrically. No mere regicide, Macbeth is also a poet. In act 5, he analyzes and articulates emotional states, and expresses his sufferings and thanatopic reflections in elegiac metaphors. He meditates on old age ("the sear, the yellow leaf"; 5.3.23), on the agonies of memory (5.3.40–5), on "the taste of fears" (5.5.9; note the tangibility: fear is not just emotional but sensual), on time, where a temporal abstract is reified, tomorrows are endowed with "pace" (5.5.19–20).

In expressing himself thus, Macbeth differs enormously from that other regicide, Claudius, whose situation, as critics point out, is otherwise analogous to Macbeth's. Both fight against Norway; both are murderers and usurpers; both are unable to say "Amen"; both commit further crimes to enhance their security. But whereas Claudius's speeches are businesslike (he features in the section on "Crisis Management" in Augustine and Adelman's *Shakespeare in Charge: The Bard's Guide to Leading and Succeeding on the Business Stage*), Macbeth's are metaphoric. John Turner may detect something pornographic in Macbeth's description of Duncan's corpse (Holderness, Potter, and Turner 1988: 140), but the dwelling on body parts (Duncan's skin, blood, gashes), like the later vision of Banquo's twenty gashes and bloody locks, bespeaks a mind haunted rather than excited by the visual. This is incipient trauma, not obscenity.

There are some indications that Macbeth realizes his propensity to imagine, and that his reluctant regicide may stem from foreknowledge of its after-effects. His perpetual fear stems not just from conscience ("he's here in double trust") or admiration ("this Duncan / Hath borne his faculties so meek") or theology ("the deep damnation of his taking-off") or political pragmatism ("He hath honor'd me of late, and I have bought / Golden opinions from all sorts of people, / Which would be worn now in their newest gloss, / Not cast aside so soon") but from self-knowledge. Macbeth cannot face Duncan. Macbeth is conspicuously absent from act 1, scene 6, in which Lady Macbeth alone, as hostess, has to welcome Duncan to the Macbeths' castle at Inverness. In scene 7 he absents himself from the banquet; his wife, conscious of the breach of etiquette, comes to find him ("why have you left the chamber?"; 1.7.29).[24] He cannot look at Duncan's corpse or think about his murder: "I am afraid to think what I have done; / Look on't again I dare not" (2.2.48–9). It is these lines which I think G. K. Hunter must have in mind when he says Macbeth fears "the image of himself committing the evil deed, rather than the evil deed itself" (1975: 10).

A few lines later Macbeth broaches the subject of identity: "To know my deed, 'twere best not know myself" (2.2.70). The line is difficult, but the general sense – that Macbeth's "self" is not that of a murderer – is clear. Macbeth is neither evil (Hecate calls him a "wayward son"; 3.5.11) nor egregiously ambitious (the litotes of Lady Macbeth's character summary is revealing: "Art not without ambition"; 1.5.19). Nor is his course determined by witchcraft, for the limitation of the witches' power (like that of Marlowe's Mephistopheles) is made clear. As Harold Bloom says, witchcraft cannot change things but imagination can (Bloom 1999: 516). The play is both a tragedy of imagination and a tragedy of self-knowledge, and the two are linked: Macbeth knows his mind's capacity for impressions. In response to the doctrine that Macbeth "should have known better," Graham Bradshaw retorts "He did know better: that is exactly what worries his wife" (Bradshaw 1987: 226). Macbeth's act against nature (so often stressed in the play) is actually against his own nature (Bloom 1999: 521). In strikingly un-Aristotelian fashion, Macbeth's crime is "not an error of judgement, it is an error of will" (Helen Gardner cited in Braunmuller 1997: 42).

---

[24] In the 1999 RSC production, Anthony Sher and Harriet Walter were in evening dress, and the scene was accompanied by the offstage clinking of cutlery and glasses, and the noise of guests talking and laughing. The formal dress underlined the significance of the occasion and the seriousness of the host's absence.

The will is first supplied and then encouraged by Lady Macbeth. Despite her knowledge of her husband as one "too full o' th' milk of human kindness" (1.5.17), she never foresees the effect murder will have on him. (Her fate is ironic, a compulsively physical flashback as her imagination goes belatedly into overdrive replaying the night of the crime.) She does not imagine the hysteria, the continued fear, the further crimes, the murder of children, or the isolation, as he embarks on a life of crime independent of her.

The emotional isolation caused by the regicide begins even before the crime is committed. In act 1 the very thought of the crime separates Macbeth from Duncan (in the social events he avoids in 1.6 and 1.7). In act 2 he separates himself from Banquo, closing down a conversation about the witches with the mendacious "I think not of them" (2.1.21), and he becomes isolated from himself ("to know my deed, 'twere best not know myself"; 2.2.70). In act 3 he is separated from his wife: productions regularly play the line "we will keep ourself / Till supper-time *alone*" (3.1.42–3) as marital rejection, made more emphatically hurtful by a pause before "alone." Later we see his separation from the Scottish nobles, as he plants spies in their houses: "there's not a one of them but in his house / I keep a servant fee'd" (3.5.130–1). By act 5 Macbeth is separated even from his own supporters, who fly to Malcolm's side (5.3.1–8). This isolation is typical of Shakespearean tragedy. Tragedy tends toward emotional and physical separation whereas comedy moves toward social inclusion. Malcolm's first act as king therefore concludes the play on a nationally optimistic note: he restores Scotland's fragmented social fabric, "calling home our exil'd friends abroad" (5.9.32).

If murder disrupts Macbeth's social integration, it also disrupts time. Time is always a problem in Shakespearean tragedy. For Hamlet, the time is out of joint. For Romeo and Juliet, timing is regularly disastrous (the tardy mail service, the accelerated wedding to Paris, Romeo's impulsive suicide).[25] The Macbeths seek "the future in the instant." The play is characterized by frantic speed. Macbeth rides hastily to Inverness, the

---

[25]   Baz Luhrmann's film *Romeo & Juliet* subtly stresses the play's accidents of timing. Friar Lawrence's letter, delivered by the courier firm "Post Post Haste," is left at the trailer-park when Romeo is absent; the wind blows it away in Hardyesque fashion. In the vault scene in 5.3 a camera close-up shows Juliet's eyelids fluttering as she begins to wake from her drugged sleep, just a second too late to prevent Romeo's suicide.

messenger arrives breathless, Duncan courses hard at his heels. Macbeth wishes Banquo's horses "swift and sure of foot" (3.1.37), the third murderer greets the dusk lyrically with "Now spurs the lated traveler apace / To gain the timely inn" (3.3.6–7), and Macbeth's speeches contain images of spurring, riding, and leaping. Once launched on a life of crime, Macbeth acts speedily and decisively to eliminate Banquo, kill Fleance, visit the witches. However, these kinetic images and hasty actions are countered by an emotional freeze-frame as the Macbeths become imprisoned in affective stasis. Macbeth feels perpetual fear, Lady Macbeth continually washes her hands, the smell of blood lingers (5.1.50), the couple repeat and repeat lines (Kermode 2000: 208n.). "When will this fearful slumber have an end?" Titus's question can be aptly posed of *Macbeth*, which portrays a nightmarish world of emotional iteration. With Macbeth's bloody images and his wife's flashbacks, the couple remain on a temporal treadmill.

Macbeth wants a clean end to a finite action: "If it were done, when 'tis done [if it were over once it is committed] . . . / . . . If the assassination / Could trammel up the consequence, and catch / With his surcease, success; that but this blow / Might be the be-all and the end-all . . . / We'ld jump the life to come" (1.7.1–5, 7). The subjunctive protasis (the first clause in a conditional sentence) in line 1 indicates Macbeth's lack of confidence in the proposition, and the play bears out his skepticism by fastening on the emotional horror of a perpetual present. Instead of going from the "blow" to the "end-all" he, like the play, is locked in the interim, the period between beginning and ending, between "assassination" and "surcease" (Kermode 2000: 203–11). Macbeth's desire for action, conclusion, then business as usual seems naive (although it is achieved in Holinshed's *Chronicles*, which portray Macbeth's prosperous and judicious ten years as king of Scotland). For Shakespeare's Macbeth, the regicide which has a clear beginning has no end.

We often lament the lack of imagination in our public leaders, or we lament the inappropriateness of such imagination as they do possess (the conquest and world domination of Tamburlaine, Hitler, Saddam Hussein). Imagination in this context denotes not just vision but humanity. Macbeth never loses his humanity because he never loses his ability to imagine. Unfortunately, the imagination that could make him a sympathetic leader disqualifies him from a successful career in crime; and his emotional failure as a criminal makes political survival as a king impossible.

3   The Personal versus the Political

"Art not without ambition, but without
The illness that should attend it" (*Macbeth* 1.5.19–20)

Richard II (1595); *1* and *2 Henry IV* (1596–7; 1597–8); *Henry V* (1598–9)

Entering the political arena often entails giving up something in private life, in the early modern period as in the twenty-first century. Adjustments of personality are made, modifications of the balance between public and private, personal sacrifices. In this section I want to return briefly to the plays of the second tetralogy: *Richard II*, *1 Henry IV*, *2 Henry IV*, and *Henry V*.

It used to be customary to view *Henry V* as a play about a hero, England's greatest warrior-king, the glorious conqueror of Agincourt. It was less usual to see *Henry V* as a play about a monster, yet this is the term used by William Hazlitt, hinted at by W. B. Yeats, and investigated by Harold Bloom.[26] Hazlitt modifies his designation oxymoronically: Henry is not just a monster but a "very amiable monster." Hazlitt's adjectival qualification seems to anticipate Norman Rabkin's bipolar view of Henry, as a "ducks and rabbits" hero – referring to the way in which the brain registers two opposing images but cannot see them simultaneously. For Bloom, however, the adjectival qualification promotes not opposition and contradiction but duality and simultaneity: a great king is "necessarily something of a coun-terfeit" and Henry V is "an admirable politician" by whom we are "rather chilled" (Bloom 1999: 323). In 1987 Antony Hammond put it more bluntly: "Henry is a great hero, and a cold, conniving bastard." The contradictions "jostle uncomfortably" and force us to think "not perhaps always comfort-ably, or comfortingly, about what it is that being a hero actually means" (Hammond 1987: 144).

The contradictions are introduced in the *Henry IV* plays. These plays cement the transition from the chivalric, ritual, and medieval world of *Richard II* to the *realpolitik* of *Henry V*. "Good manners be your speed" says

---

[26]   Hazlitt and Yeats are cited in Bloom (1999: 319–20).

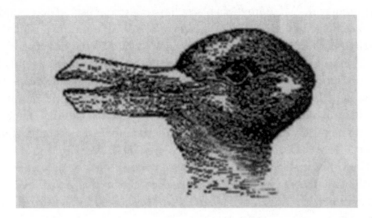

Plate 5 Norman Rabkin first associated the way the brain sees this rabbit/duck image with the way viewers see Henry V. Just as the image can be a rabbit and a duck but not both simultaneously, so Henry can be a glorious epic hero and a distasteful politician – but not together. In the play, the Chorus tells us about the former Henry but the action shows us the latter.

Hotspur (half-heartedly? sarcastically?) to his good-natured brother-in-law Mortimer in *1 Henry IV* (3.1.188). It is not good manners but *bad* manners that bring soldiers success, as Prince John demonstrates at Gaultree Forest in *2 Henry IV*. Having enticed the rebels to parley, he agrees that both sides shall dismiss their armies prior to negotiations. Although the rebel army disbands eagerly, the royal army awaits its instructions from Prince John's mouth. With this military security, Prince John immediately arrests the rebel leaders "of high treason" (4.2.107). The rebel Mowbray protests: "Is this proceeding just and honourable" (4.2.110). It is, of course, neither; but it is politically shrewd and pragmatic. Prince John avoids bloodshed and restores order.

Prince John thus provides an example of what we are to see later in his brother, Henry V: actions of questionable morality but incontestable policy. Henry uses morally dubious methods (befriending and rejecting Eastcheap, mendaciously threatening Harfleur with atrocities, killing "the poys and the luggage") for practical ends.

These frequent, isolated incidents combine to form a political philosophy, a philosophy expounded in a comic, and deceptively otiose, discussion in *Henry V* 4.7. In this scene the Welsh captain Fluellen offers a series of parallels between Alexander the Great and Henry V. Both come from places beginning with "M." Both these places have rivers and fish: "There is a river in Macedon, and there is also moreover a river at Monmouth . . . and there is salmons in both" (4.7.26–8, 31). Alexander killed his best friend and Henry rejected Falstaff. The English captain, Gower, objects to this last parallel, reminding us that Henry rejected his friend not while drunk (like Alexander) but in sober judgment. The reintroduction of Falstaff at this late stage is odd. On the eve of a politically crucial battle, designed to cement a morally dubious invasion, we are reminded of a morally dubious event in Henry's history.

The conversation is kept comic by Fluellen's earnestness, his solecistic speech, and his regional pronunciation. He refers to the Macedonian hero as Alexander the Big, or, as his percussive Welsh has it, Alexander the Pig:

> Is not "pig" great? The pig, or the great, or the mighty, or the huge, or the magnanimous, are all one reckonings, save the phrase is a little variations. (4.7.15–18)

Alexander the "Great," Shakespeare implies, became Alexander the "Big" because he was also Alexander the "Pig."

It is the adoption of pig-like qualities which makes Henry such a successful military leader, and which identifies him as an early modern politician rather than a medieval monarch. The contrast was well made in the ESC production of *1 Henry IV* (1987–9) when Hal defeats Hotspur at the battle of Shrewsbury. Hotspur is a medieval warrior, motivated by honor. In the ESC battle sequence Hal lost his sword, affording Hotspur an easy opportunity to kill him; instead Hotspur paused and chivalrously returned Hal's sword, allowing the combat to proceed on equal terms. The positions were reversed just a few moments later, giving Hal the advantage, whereupon he seized the opportunity and stabbed Hotspur decisively. Good manners be your speed? Not in the early modern world.

This pig/big binary differentiates the early modern politics of the *Henry* plays from the divine kingship of *Richard II*. The transition from one world to another is signaled in two contiguous scenes at the end of *Richard II*. In act 5, scene 3, the scene in which the Duchess of York begs forgiveness for her treasonous son Aumerle, Henry IV freely offers pardon: "I pardon him as God shall pardon me" (5.3.131). The Duchess is cautiously jubilant and requests that Henry repeat the magic word: "Speak it again, / Twice saying 'pardon' doth not pardon twain [divide], / But makes one pardon strong"

(5.3.133–5). Henry obliges: "With all my heart / I pardon him" (5.3.135–6). The next scene presents Sir Pierce Exton trying to interpret the new king's wishes: "Didst thou not mark the King, what words he spake? / 'Have I no friend will rid me of this living fear?' ... / *He spake it twice,* / And *urg'd it twice* together" (5.4.1–2, 4–5). In one scene Henry twice offers mercy, in the next he twice urges murder. Murder and mercy, pig and big, are symbiotic components of the new regime. By the time we reach *Henry V*, "pig" seems uppermost in the monarch. (Lady Macbeth's criticism of Macbeth – "Art not without ambition, but without / The illness that should attend it" – could never be said of Henry.) Readers and audiences understandably have a hard time forgiving Henry for his rejection of Falstaff, or for his failure to react to Bardolph's death. Recent stage productions, and Branagh's film, hang Bardolph on stage, allowing Henry to flinch and show regret as he makes a determined effort to suppress the personal in the interests of the political. Such stagings remind us that Henry's pig-like behavior is necessary, not natural.

The tension between the personal and the political is also seen in the domestic scenes in the second tetralogy: the scenes with Hotspur and his wife, Kate, the rebel Mortimer and his Welsh wife, Henry and Katherine of France. With marriage Mortimer has lost his martial alacrity, as his father-in-law points out at *1 Henry IV* 3.1.263–4. In *Alarm to England* (1578) Barnaby Rich, an ex-soldier, views love as incompatible with success in war: "if all the lovers that are in the world were made in one whole army, there is neither emperor nor monarch but would be amazed to see such a company of Bedlam fools" (sig. H2v). Bardolph has less military credibility than Rich but he adopts the same military attitude when, in *2 Henry IV*, he reproves Shallow for his innocent domestic enquiry about Falstaff's wife: "Sir, pardon, a soldier is better accommodated than with a wife" (3.2.66–7). Personal life and military success are incompatible. After describing at length the characteristics of lovers, Rich advises them to "set aside all such trifling affairs, and vain follies, ... and rather to endeavour themselves to such exercises which have gained Hercules, Achilles, Thesus, Caius, Martius, Epaminondas, Themistocles, Alexander, Pyrrhus, Hannibal, Scipio, Pompey, Caesar, with diverse others, such immortal glory as neither the envious rage of cruel death may blemish, neither the furious force of fortune's fickle wheel may diminish, neither the tract of devouring time shall ever be able to remove from memory" (sig. H4v). Hotspur and Henry V follow Rich's advice, becoming historical legends through military prowess. But to participate in history is to deny oneself the fullness of personal life as obtained by Mortimer, a character who will never attain top billing in the history books.

The contrast between Mortimer's relationship with his wife (depicted in a scene of tears, kisses, and song) and those of Hotspur and Henry with their partners is marked. The domestic picture revealed in Lady Percy's long speech in *1 Henry IV* (2.3.37–64) is dispiriting. Martial thoughts not only dominate Hotspur's working hours, frustrating communication between the couple, but disturb his slumbers. Lady Percy is neglected, exiled from Hotspur's bed. What motivates Hotspur is war and he does not scruple to conceal this from his wife: "I love thee not, / I care not for thee, Kate. This is no world / To play with mammets and to tilt with lips" (2.3.90–2). Although his tone may be teasing, it is difficult to deny that, in personal terms, the Mortimers' marriage is superior to that of the Percies. This point was made forcefully in the final frame of 3.1 in the BBC film where Lady Mortimer glanced at a tearful Lady Percy with a look of quiet triumph.

Henry V's relation with his Kate is no more romantic. The *Henry* plays are, as we have seen, full of images of financial transaction, and Katherine is simply a pawn in an international game of exchange. In the ESC production the actress who played Doll Tearsheet reappeared as Princess Katherine. The point made by casting was unmistakable: both these women were for sale; the only difference was the price. Henry tells Burgundy "you must *buy* that peace" (5.2.70) and Katherine, Henry's "capital demand" (5.2.96), is part of the negotiation; she has been rejected once already when her accompaniment was only "some petty and unprofitable duke-doms" (3.Chorus.31). Lance Wilcox points out that Henry's discourse has depended heavily on images of rape throughout the play, and if Henry's French language simile in act 5 is anything to go by, his view of marriage is far from romantic – "like a new-married wife about her husband's neck, hardly to be shook off" (5.2.179–81). Furthermore, matrimony serves only military ends: "Shall not thou and I, . . . compound a boy, half French, half English, that shall go to Constantinople and take the Turk by the beard?" (5.2.206–9). Like his father before him, who "was thinking of civil wars when he got me" (5.2.225–6), or Hotspur, who tells his wife she is "perfect in lying down" (*1HIV* 3.1.226), Henry sees woman as fulfilling a political rather than a personal need. The man who rejects Falstaff has no difficulty treating his bride-to-be with the same politically expedient lack of senti-ment. "I love thee cruelly" is a necessary paradox, like Alexander the pig and big. Mortimer sacrifices his military prowess for love; Hotspur and

Henry do not. (Othello, who tries to unite both, fails to achieve success in either.)

Throughout the second tetralogy Shakespeare explores the high personal cost of political life. With kingship comes polished perturbation and golden care. The crown is accompanied by unquiet rest: "How many thousand of my poorest subjects / Are at this hour asleep!" (*2HIV* 3.1.4–5). It is accompanied by mistrust: "He shall think that thou, which knowest the way / To plant unrightful kings, wilt know again" (*RII* 5.1.62–3). It leads to misinterpretation and ambivalence, as Bullingbrook finds out when Exton murders Richard. (King John also feels Bullingbrook's predicament: "It is the curse of kings to be attended / By slaves that take their humours for a warrant / To break within the bloody house of life, / And on the winking of authority / To understand a law"; *KJ* 4.2.208–12). Above all, kingship is accompanied by personal sacrifice – Henry IV forfeits his health, his son domestic felicity. These points apply equally to rebel leadership, for Hotspur's position is accompanied by mistrust, lack of sleep, and marital rupture. The romantic scenes are therefore important for, in plays which deal with the dichotomy between political and private life, the anagrammatic duality of marital and martial has particular resonance. Unlike the pig/big binary, where opposites coexist, marital bliss and martial fame are incompatible. Mortimer forfeits a political career; for better or for worse, Hotspur and Henry V enter the history books.

4

Public Life:
Shakespeare and Social Structures

"The past is a foreign country: they do things differently there" (Hartley 1972: 9)

Introduction

The problem with the Renaissance past is that, although it happened a long time ago, it didn't happen sufficiently long ago. Thus, it is both distant and proximate, foreign and familiar.

Difficulties arise when we encounter the misleadingly familiar. This problem occurs most obviously with Elizabethan words which are identical to contemporary words but have entirely different meanings. For example, to the Elizabethans "incontinent" was an adverb meaning "quickly" and an adjective meaning "unchaste." (An unchaste person lacked self-restraint, and this leads to today's narrower meaning of "unable to retain natural evacuations"; *OED* a.3.) When Rosalind describes the love-at-first-sight experienced by Celia and Oliver, she explains that they "made a pair of stairs to marriage, which they will climb incontinent [immediately], or else be incontinent [unchaste] before marriage" (*AYLI* 5.2.37–9). In such instances editors protect us from misunderstanding with footnote annotation. But what happens when meaning is not lexical and local but cultural and osmotic? Let me take two examples, one from literary genre and one from religion.

All of Shakespeare's plays were adapted from other literary works: for example, Roman dramatists (Plautus's *Menaechmi* for *Comedy of Errors*), Italian narrative poetry (Boccaccio's *Decameron* for *All's Well that Ends Well*), English romance (Sidney's *Arcadia* for the Gloucester plot of *King Lear*).[1] Sometimes Shakespeare's sources were

---

[1] There are three exceptions – *Midsummer Night's Dream, Merry Wives,* and *Tempest* – for which we have no specific sources, which may simply mean that we have not yet identified them; the plays are clearly indebted in general ways to literary legend (Theseus in *Midsummer Night's Dream*) and contemporary events (the founding of the Virginia colony in America for *Tempest*, the garter ceremony for *Merry Wives*), and more specific indebtednesses may yet emerge.

themselves taken from other sources. The Bianca subplot in *Taming of the Shrew* comes from George Gascoigne's play, *Supposes*, which was itself a translation of a play by Ariosto, *I Suppositi.*

Translation, like adaptation, was not an inferior literary form. Christopher Marlowe translated Ovid and Lucan. Mary Sidney, the sister of England's most accomplished courtier and poet, Sir Philip Sidney, was, like her brother, a poet and translator. Translation was a dominant literary genre in a way that is hard for us to appreciate now where we tend to think of translation as synonymous with "not original." In 1985, when *Liaisons Dangereuses* opened in the West End, Christopher Hampton, who had translated and adapted Laclos's epistolary novel for the stage, was interviewed by the *Guardian* newspaper. The question he was most often asked, Hampton said, was "are you doing any original work these days or is it just the translations?" This kind of attitude comes from a post-Romantic perspective; but translation, like adaptation, is a creative and complex carrying across cultures as the noun's etymology attests – *trans-latio.*

I take translation as one example of the different kinds of literary creation in the Renaissance period but there are many equally prolific forms: history books, sermons, reports of trials, conduct books, private and devotional journals, almanacs, popular ballads, political speeches, commonplace books, misogynist pamphlets. It may not be what we think of as literature on the school syllabus, but it is part of what is nowadays called "intertext" – what used to be called, more prosaically, background. Background is now foreground, and context is a text in its own right. A culture is defined by what it reads and writes, and Elizabethans didn't just sit around reading Spenserian epic any more than we privilege Tom Paulin over *Private Eye* or *People* magazine. Reading genres we tend not to think of as literature helps us contextualize and familiarize the Renaissance past.

But we must also contextualize and *de*familiarize the Renaissance. The official religion of twenty-first-century England is Protestantism; Elizabethan England was a Protestant country. However, there is a world of difference. Unlike us, everyone living in the late sixteenth century had a Catholic grandparent (and possibly parent), and they didn't know what we know, that their Protestant queen would reign for nearly half a century. When Elizabeth ascended the throne in 1558, England had experienced twenty years of religious turmoil. In 1533 Henry VIII was excommunicated by the pope; the next year he made himself Head of the Church in England, whereupon England became a Protestant country. When Henry died in 1547, he was succeeded by his sickly ten-year-old son, Edward VI, who ruled as a Protestant until his early death in 1553. Edward's half-sister, Mary I, returned the country to Catholicism, but died in 1558, aged forty-two. For all anyone knew, Elizabeth's reign, like those of Edward VI and Mary I, might be just another five-year period, leaving uncertainty in its wake; or she might marry a Catholic (she certainly contemplated doing so, or appeared to contemplate doing so), who could exert religious influence. We talk of Elizabeth's reign as the Protestant succession, but those who lived during it did not view the country's Protestantism as secure; as late as 1590 the childless Elizabeth had not named her successor.

Religious change and uncertainty affected an area not generally invoked in this context: language. We credit post-structuralism with the rupture between word and meaning, but such linguistic crisis was a particularly pertinent issue in the Reformation. As Robert Weimann points out, in a Roman Catholic world signifier and signified, symbol and meaning, could not be prized apart; interpretation was a given, a constant. In a Reformation world, a world whose exegetical coordinates had been disrupted, all meaning, and the means of meaning (word, image, icon), had to be investigated anew (Weimann 1996: 55–6, 65). Shakespeare's plays are haunted by the disjunction between word and thing, or name and person, as in *All's Well that Ends Well* where Helena is the name of wife but not the thing. George Bernard Shaw's celebrated observation about England and America being two countries separated by a common language can be transferred to religion, for both sixteenth- and twenty-first-century England are two periods separated by a common religion. We must be as attentive to deceptive congruence as to obvious difference.

In this chapter I want to look at the ways Elizabethan society viewed three topics: money, women, and language.

1   Money

Introduction

In the Sermon on the Mount, Jesus teaches Christians how to pray (Matthew 6:9–13). The Lord's Prayer which he offers addresses God as father, honors His name, prays for His kingdom and for bread, and asks for forgiveness. The object of forgiveness varies depending on the translation. *The Book of Common Prayer* (1549, revised 1550, 1559, 1561) has "forgive us our trespasses as we forgive those who trespass against us," whereas the King James version (1611) reads "Forgive us our debts as we forgive our debtors." Given that "debts" was an Aramaic euphemism for sin, the two versions say the same thing. But the fiscal vocabulary in the King James version – the version still in use in Scotland, which has not adopted the Church of England's *Book of Common Prayer* – continues the financial imagery that permeates both Old and New Testaments. The Bible's recurrent financial imagery illustrates the ways in which feudal societies inflected monetary tropes positively: a debt was a bond, a tie, kinship, duty, obligation, not simply an overdraft. (And in the political and linguistic economy of the King James version of the Lord's Prayer, sin fractures the bond between man and God.)

Bonds, duties, and obligation form a complex two-way system, however, for debtor and debtee overlap. When Duncan suggests that he sojourn with the Macbeths in Inverness "and bind us further to you" (1.4.43), the verb is Janus-like: it means both "obligate ourself to you" (Duncan as recipient of hospitality, Duncan as debtor) and "reward you with friendship" (Macbeth as recipient, Macbeth as debtor). After the banquet Duncan sends a diamond to Lady Macbeth "by the name of most kind hostess," i.e., as thanks for her hospitality (2.1.16). The gift works (or is designed to work) not to conclude a transaction (Duncan's Bed and Breakfast – Lady Macbeth's diamond) but to continue one (Duncan as king – Lady Macbeth as loyal subject). In feudal relations there is no surcease, success, end-all. One obligation leads to another: a diamond is forever. The diamond which the King of Navarre sends the French princess in the romantic economy of *Love's Labour's Lost* is no more a gesture of unconditional generosity than is Duncan's, as the princess's metaphor of enclosure reveals: "A lady *wall'd about* with diamonds!" (*LLL* 5.2.3).[2]

Gifts, then, are rarely donations; they are symbolic payments. Elizabeth's court was founded on an elaborate system of gift-exchange. Suitors, sovereigns, courtiers, foreign ambassadors, and visitors offered and received gifts, all of which had political purposes: they served to flatter, reward, appease, preempt, court, position, patronize. (The Dauphin in *Henry V* offers a carefully calculated insult when he sends the new English king a tun of tennis balls.) Jewels, decorations, embroidery, accessories, and original compositions such as poems, calligraphically copied works, and translations were sent from courtier to queen. The eleven-year-old Princess Elizabeth sent Catherine Parr a gift that combined translation, decorative penmanship, and embroidery – "her own translation of a work by Marguerite of Navarre, *The Glass of the Sinful Soul*, in a cover she had embroidered with blue and silver threads with clusters of purple flowers" (Bassnett 1988: 21). As queen, Elizabeth gave courtiers and visitors gifts which ranged in value appropriate to the recipient's rank. Although gift-giving occurred all year, New Year's celebrations provided a general opportunity for exchange.

Feudal societies relied on gifts to bind, to foster loyalty, to cement trust, to develop relationships. The *OED* definitions of gift (II.1 and II.2) do not indicate the word's nuances to feudalism: "something . . . voluntarily transferred to another without the expectation of receipt of an equivalent . . . Not quite a bribe." But a return *was* expected. Timon of Athens describes how "rich men deal gifts, / Expecting in return twenty for one" (4.3.509–10). His two thousand per cent is a cynical exaggeration but the

---

[2] For an excellent discussion of gifts in *Love's Labour's Lost* see Burnett (1993).

principle of increase (what he describes as "usuring kindness"; line 509) is not. Gifts are a form of currency which buys loyal subjects. Given that Shakespeare's father was a glover, and that gloves were one of the most popular gift items, Shakespeare must have been well aware of the court's gift-exchange operations. Shakespeare's political language is thus frequently fiscal.

But financial imagery has early modern implications beyond the merely monetary. "Owe" also meant "own" or "possess." Antipholus of Ephesus is barred from "the house I owe" in *Comedy of Errors* 3.1.42; in *Midsummer Night's Dream* Puck anoints Lysander's eyes with "all the power this charm doth owe" (2.2.79); Lear asks Cordelia's suitors to accept his dowerless daughter "with those infirmities she owes" (1.1.202). Sometimes the two meanings collide or coalesce. Bassanio tells Antonio "I owe you much, and like a willful youth, / That which I owe is lost" (*MV* 1.1.146–7), where the second use of the verb carries both senses. When Shakespeare's monarchs or citizens talk about owing lives to king or state, they introduce, in one verb, two senses: reciprocal obligation. Thus Katherine in *The Shrew*, describing that emblem of the state in miniature – the relation between husband and wife – stresses reciprocity. Asked to articulate "what duty they [women] do owe their lords and husbands," she begins not by describing a wife's duty but by outlining the labors of the husband. Financial vocabulary follows: the husband "craves no other tribute at thy hands / But love, fair looks, and true obedience – / Too little payment for so great a debt. / Such duty as the subject owes the prince, / Even such a woman oweth to her husband" (5.2.131, 152–6). Similarly when Hector asks "What nearer debt in all humanity / Than wife is to the husband?" (*T&C* 2.2.175–6), "debt" refers expansively to "bond," not just to "dues." Financial vocabulary in Shakespeare does not simply denote financial structures.

Macbeth (1606)

Macbeth is much concerned with "such duty as the subject owes the prince" and vice versa; like Katherine in *The Shrew*, the play uses fiscal conceits to express social bonds. King Duncan, a tactical forebear of Queen Elizabeth, uses gifts as emotional currency to cement loyalty. A Scottish noble, Angus, tells Macbeth that he is sent "To give thee from our royal master thanks, / Only to herald thee into his sight, / Not pay thee" (1.3.101–3). Gratitude and reward are separate: royal thanks are simply a prelude to later payment.

(Nor is promotion to Thane of Cawdor the later payment, for it is specifically billed as but "an earnest of a greater honour"; 1.3.104). The king's division of gratitude into two entities, verbal and material, is reinforced in the next scene when Duncan fears that his "thanks and payment" are insufficient.

Macbeth replies ceremoniously: "The service and the loyalty I owe, / In doing it, pays itself" (1.4.22–3). Debt and payment fuse, as they do in *All's Well* where Helena's duty to the King is constituted as payment: "My duty then shall pay me for my pains" (2.1.125).[3] Duncan, however, hints at further rewards: "I have begun to plant thee, and will labor / To make thee full of growing" (1.4.28–9).[4] As in Elizabeth's court, the monarch benefits from his generosity, as Banquo's response to the same promise acknowledges: "There if I grow, / The harvest is your own" (1.4.32–3). This cycle of giving and receiving, of endowing and deriving benefit, permeates the play's language as antitheses become mutually constitutive ("fair is foul"; 1.1.11) and courtly paradoxes abound: "The rest [leisure] is labor, which is not us'd for you" Macbeth tells Duncan (1.4.44), and Lady Macbeth later explains that "what is theirs, in compt" can be audited and returned to the king (1.6.25–8). Thus, royal gratitude is doubled (thanks and reward) and benefit is mutual.

The conversations about gratitude and financial reward in act 1 follow speeches about disloyalty (the Thane of Cawdor's treason in 1.2 and his reported death in 1.4). How, the play asks, can one encourage loyalty? Gratitude, it seems, is not enough; one must also buy it (Bradshaw 1987: 248). Duncan promotes his son to Prince of Cumberland but also offers "signs of nobleness" to "all deservers" (1.4.41–2), a gesture which Ralph Berry characterizes as "buying off future disaffection, cash down" (1988: 119). Malcolm behaves equally shrewdly at the end of the play, creating Scotland's first earls. This is an act of accounting, not a donation: "We shall not spend a large expense of time / Before we reckon with your several loves, / And make us even with you. My thanes and kinsmen, / Henceforth be earls" (5.9.26–9). (Today's Honours List, like Malcolm's, dispenses rewards not honorifics.) Duncan feels the need to provide continual reas-

---

[3] Cf. the later interlude in *Macbeth* where the witches entertain Macbeth "that this great king may kindly say / Our duties did his welcome pay" (4.1.131–2).

[4] Bradshaw suggests (1987: 249) that, to the Elizabethan mind, this could only mean a monopoly, a title, a post, further promotion; hence Macbeth has cause to be surprised at the sudden elevation of Malcolm.

surance to his hosts, telling Lady Macbeth not just that he loves Macbeth "highly" but also that he intends to "continue our graces towards him" (1.6.29–30). There is a nervous edge here, perhaps because, for a social structure dependent on loyalty, "there is a great deal of disloyalty around" (Berry 1988: 119); but it is also an alternative way of making assurance double sure. Duncan speaks and acts like a saint; but he also speaks and acts like a businessman (Bradshaw 1987: 249). Elizabethans and Jacobeans would find nothing unusual in this. It is how nature herself operates: "she determines / Herself the glory of a creditor, / Both thanks and use [interest]" (*MM* 1.1.38–40). In other words, nature lends life and expects humans to make something of it, to repay her with interest (see below, *Timon of Athens*, for further discussion of nature as a usurer).

Life itself, like the social structures in which it is rooted, is about indebtedness. Life is leased and must be repaid. Using documentary images, Macbeth describes his urge to "*cancel* and *tear to pieces* that great *bond* / Which keeps me pale" (3.2.49–50); this bond is, of course, Banquo's lease on life. In *2 Henry VI* starvation prevents Jack Cade staying in hiding, even if he were offered "a lease of my life for a thousand years" (4.10.5–6). In *Cymbeline* Posthumus prays for death: "If you will take this audit, take this life, / And cancel these cold bonds" (5.4.27–8). Posthumus here puns on bonds as prison fetters as well as lease of life. The most frequent pun to express life's contractual nature is the homonym debt/death. "Thou owest God a death," Hal tells Falstaff; "'Tis not due yet, I would be loath to pay him before his day," the coward responds (*1HIV* 5.1.126–8). "He that dies pays all debts," pronounces Stephano in *Tempest* (3.2.131). Mardian reports Cleopatra's (fake) death to Antony: "Death of one person can be paid but once, / And that she has discharg'd" (*A&C* 4.14.27–8). Killed in battle, young Siward "has paid a soldier's debt" (*Macbeth* 5.9.5).

Macbeth, like Falstaff, wishes to evade premature death, hoping to live "the lease of nature, pay his breath / To time and mortal custom" (4.1.99–100). (Macbeth is here oblivious to irony: one cannot respect time's lease on one's own life while violating it in that of one's king.) Macbeth's regicide interrupts the circuit of exchange that is the gift. It interrupts the social bonds of kinsman, subject, and host; it violates the temporal cycle of lending and repaying; it cuts off biological movement as children are killed. Thus Macbeth's attempt to gain and retain tyrannical power, to crown his rapid upwards trajectory with a period of political stasis, is an attempt to cut off movement – and hence an attack on the basis of Scottish (and early modern English) society.

The issue of debt returns us to the question of time in *Macbeth*. Macbeth's desire for a lease of life and normal mortality ("mortal custom") is doomed from the moment he forces the future in the instant. Unfortunately, time cannot be repaid (as that comic misuser of time, Falstaff, realizes at the end of *2 Henry IV*). Some debts are not symbiotic; some debts, once incurred, will always remain outstanding.

Merchant of Venice (1596–7)

Merchant of Venice is a play about money. This is hardly surprising given both the setting (Venice was the banking center of early modern Europe) and the trade of the principal characters (Antonio, the eponymous merchant, and Shylock are moneylenders). But the focus on finance is not confined to these professionals: all the characters are concerned with money, whether through lack or abundance, and it affects their lexicon, their attitudes, and their actions. Lines like Portia's declaration to Bassanio, "Since you are dear bought, I will love you dear" (3.2.313), offended Alexander Pope's Augustan sensibilities (financial imagery violates decorum); when he edited the play, he relegated the line to the foot of the page, the textual dustbin for passages he deemed "unShakespearean." But if one were to follow this subjective editorial principle to the letter, *all* of *Merchant of Venice* would appear at the foot of the page. There is no avoiding the play's financial focus, as we saw in chapter 2 ("Love and Hazard").

Merchant of Venice is a deeply uncomedic comedy, and the disturbing tone is partly linked to the characters' financial focus. It is easy to romanticize Shylock's daughter, Jessica, and present her as a victim, as did Trevor Nunn's production at the National Theatre in 1999–2000. But we must not overlook her outrageous robbery of her father: a diamond worth 2,000 ducats, "other precious, precious jewels" (3.1.87), a turquoise ring, of presumably known sentimental value (a courtship gift to Shylock from his wife), and two sealed bags of ducats. Nor does Jessica attend to the value of money. She exchanges the ring for a monkey, and spends eighty ducats in one night in Genoa. (In the 1978 RSC production, Tubal, acting as private eye in pursuit of the runaway Jessica, presented Shylock with his bill of expenses from the Genoa Hilton, which is presumably where Jessica stayed too.)

An Italian ducat was worth approximately five shillings (25 pence) in the first decade of the seventeenth century; thus Jessica steals a diamond worth £500, as well as jewelry and cash. It is notoriously difficult to make useful comparisons of monetary value across the centuries, but some Shakespearean parallels might be helpful. In *Merry Wives of Windsor* Anne Page laments the fact that the inept Slender's substantial annual income of £300 makes him an appealing suitor in her parents' eyes; she herself is desired for her inheritance of £700; Master Froth, a "gentleman" in *Measure for Measure*, has £80 a year; the Bastard in *King John* is deprived of "fair five hundred pound a year" (*KJ* 1.1.69). In 1597 Shakespeare bought New Place in Stratford, an impressive piece of real estate, for £60. In 1600 the annual wage of one Stratford schoolmaster was £10. When Shakespeare died in 1616 he left £300 to his daughter Judith. Whichever way one calculates it, Jessica's theft is more than adequate to her needs for a very long time.

The play presents various means of acquiring and disposing of money. Bassanio borrows money, marries it, and reclothes his entourage with it. Portia inherits it. As one critic points out, Portia, like many rich people, only talks of money, and then cavalierly, when she wishes to dispose of it: "Pay him six thousand and deface the bond; / Double six thousand, and then treble that" (3.2.299–300). Jessica and Lorenzo steal money; they also spend it. This could be healthy (money is for spending), but a diamond for a monkey seems irresponsible. Shylock makes money by lending it at high interest rates and seems not to spend it. He consoles himself for Launcelot Gobbo's departure by thinking of what he'll save on food bills. (His idiolect in the play – short, repeated phrases in preference to complete sentences – provides the linguistic equivalent of his fiscal parsimony.) Antonio trades money in silks and spices, lends it, has cash-flow problems, borrows it, and charges emotional interest on it. "To you, Antonio, / I owe the most in money and in love," acknowledges Bassanio (1.1.130–1); "All debts are clear'd between you and I, if I might but see you at my death," writes Antonio (3.2.318–20). Thus the play presents a range of incomes and attitudes.

Merchant of Venice stresses the need for money to function symbiotically and symbolically, as it does in the later *Macbeth*, as an emblem of society, kinship, of human ties. Portia uses financial imagery in matrimonial terms when she itemizes herself and gives the sum to Bassanio (3.2). But what the characters achieve in the romantic sphere in this play, they fail to achieve in social relations. The play is notable for the number of characters excluded from the ending. Antonio is isolated, as he was at the beginning; Shylock is destroyed; the Gobbos et al. have no part in the world of Belmont (Christopher Luscombe, who played Launcelot Gobbo in the 1993 RSC production, describes his portrayal of the servant as "an outsider . . . in this ruthless, macho world" [1998: 24]); Jessica may have a husband but she has lost a father (productions sometimes conclude with a melancholy Jessica alone on stage). The last scene is unusually private and antisocial. It is also indifferent to preceding events: the characters indulge in bawdy jokes, oblivious to the fact that they have just destroyed a man. The final impression is one of individuals rather than society, and of flawed individuals at that. As Portia acknowledges in act 1, "If to do were as easy as to know what were good to do, chapels had been churches, and poor men's cottages princes' palaces" (1.2.12–14).

There is something remarkably Thatcherite in this concluding vision of individuals rather than community. Individuals pursue money, society fragments. The play is anxious, as Elizabethans may have been, about the side-effects of incipient capitalism, increasing commercialism, and burgeoning consumerism. Despite agricultural upheavals such as enclosures, which benefited the few rather than the many, inflation, and harvest failures which caused suffering for all, the last decades of Elizabeth's reign enjoyed peaks of prosperity. The defeat of the Spanish Armada in 1588 provided immediate plunder as well as reparations from Spain. Courtiers-turned-explorers like Drake and Raleigh traversed the globe and returned with gold, jewels, and precious metals. London continued to develop as a center of culture and commerce, an English Venice. But delight in wealth is always accompanied by suspicions about its destructive potential, as we see every time lottery winners declare that money won't change them.

The sixteenth century had known wealth and prosperity before the 1580s. But, as critics and economists alike point out, having money or inheriting money is very different from trading in money. Money in *Merchant of Venice* leads to division. Shylock separates the commercial and the social (he will trade with Christians but not dine with them, obviously for religious dietary reasons), as does Antonio, who offensively talks about Shylock in the third person despite Shylock's presence ("is he yet possess'd / How much ye would?" he asks Bassanio in 1.3.64–5). Launcelot Gobbo deserts his master; Jessica steals from her father. Gloucester's vision of a world in which "love cools, friendship falls off, brothers divide . . . and the bond crack'd 'twixt son and father" (*Lear* 1.2.106–9) has its roots in *Merchant of Venice*. Money does not make the world go round; it may do quite the opposite.

Romeo and Juliet (1595); *Merry Wives of Windsor* (1597–8);
Timon of Athens (1605)

Money is the root of all evil in *Romeo and Juliet* and *Timon of Athens. Romeo and Juliet* was written shortly before *Merchant of Venice*, and its subtle criticism of money and commodification paves the way for the extended treatment in the comedy to follow. When Romeo purchases poison from the Mantuan apothecary he says

> There is thy gold, worse poison to men's souls,
> Doing more murther in this loathsome world,
> Than these poor compounds that thou mayest not sell.
> I sell thee poison, thou hast sold me none. (5.1.80–3)

His speech concludes a dialogue which began with poverty. The apothecary reluctantly agrees to break the law by selling fatal drugs:

> *Apothecary:*   My poverty, but not my will, consents.
> *Romeo:*   I pay thy poverty, and not thy will. (5.1.75–6)

This sequence of poverty/money/gold-as-poison could have come from the pen of a Marxist philosopher rather than that of a lyric poet. It is the culmination of imagery which begins in act 1 when Romeo laments that Rosaline will not "ope her lap to saint-seducing gold" (1.1.214), a sentiment inappropriate to a Petrarchan lover whose role is to worship not to seduce. In the same act the Nurse tells Romeo that Juliet's future husband shall "have the chinks" (1.5.117). Baz Luhrmann's film brings out the financial importance of the feuding families with the Capulets' CCTV system, patrolling Alsatians and security guards, to say nothing of both families' business prominence in skyscraper advertisements and news bulletins.

The romantic love of Romeo and Juliet impedes the Capulets' desire to enhance their new money by marrying their daughter to title and lineage (4.5.71–2). Act 5's gold monuments, which the grieving parents propose to erect as memorials to their dead teenagers, indicate that Verona's mercantile values have not been altered by tragedy: as Northrop Frye scathingly observes, "nothing like a couple of gold statues to bring two dead lovers back to life" (1986: 31). Michael Bogdanov's RSC production in 1986 extended the hollowness of the play's ending. After Escalus's concluding speech, the Capulet and Montague patriarchs shook hands for the television news, a staged show of reconciliation that was hastily dropped when the cameras stopped rolling. The gold tombs were clearly competitive symbols of stature rather than genuine tributes.

Merry Wives is the only Shakespeare comedy to be set in England. It is a recognizably middle-class bourgeois England: Windsor is associated not with the court but with landowners (Ford and Page), rich foreign tradesmen (the French Dr. Caius), and paying guests and horse rental at the Garter Inn. Impecunious courtiers like Fenton and Falstaff are suspected and excluded; the Pages prefer a foreigner with money (Caius) or a fool with a great chamber (Slender) as suitors to their daughter. The French and the Welsh, conventional targets of derision or butts of comedy on the Elizabethan stage, are happily assimilated in Windsor life because of their financial contributions.

But money leads to hypocrisy. As go-between for both Caius and Fenton, Mistress Quickly receives payment from two masters. Ford accuses Falstaff of cozening him of money despite having himself offered it as incentive for Falstaff to seduce Mistress Ford: "if money go before, all ways do lie open" (2.2.168–9). Windsor society has not yet worked out its ethical attitudes in a consumer society.

Shakespeare's most scathing attack on money is reserved for *Timon of Athens*. Gold is worthless ("I cannot eat it," says Timon; 4.3.101); it is harmful (4.3.291); it corrupts, motivates, and perverts:

> This yellow slave
> Will knit and break religions, bless th'accurs'd,
> Make the hoar leprosy ador'd, place thieves,
> And give them title, knee, and approbation
> With senators on the bench. This is it
> That makes the wappen'd widow wed again;
> She, whom the spittle house and ulcerous sores
> Would cast the gorge at, this embalms and spices
> To th'April day again. (4.3.34–42)

This speech fueled Marx's thoughts on money in *Capital*, thoughts which, as Kenneth Muir reveals, were first expressed at length in the unfinished and unpublished *Political Economy and Philosophy* (1844). In this essay, written just after he had read *Timon*, when he was on the verge of converting to communism, Marx muses on Timon's speech as follows:

> I am what I possess. I am the owner of money, and my power is as great
> as the power of my money. The qualities of money – the owner's qualities
> and essential powers – are mine. What I am, and what I can do, are not
> determined by my individuality. (Marx in Muir 1977: 71)

"I am what I possess"? This is the tail wagging the dog. It is a strikingly
unShakespearean concept, unthinkable from the author of the plays discussed in chapter 1, where selfhood is endogenous.

The structure of *Timon* is bipartite. In the first half Timon has wealth,
friends, and loves everybody; in the second half he is penniless, friendless,
and hates mankind. His earlier philanthropy is as extreme as his later
misanthropy, and he becomes a type rather than a character: "I am
Misanthropos, and hate mankind" (4.3.54).

The question of value permeates both parts (Pope was as offended by
mercantile language in *Timon* as he was in *Merchant of Venice*; he omitted
the gift-exchange sentiment of 4.3.508–10, for example). Timon is unusual
for a Shakespearean hero in being defined by his having: he is, as Marx
realized, what he possesses. (But cf. King John, who is king only because
he possesses the crown.) Shakespeare denies us any antecedent information, such as how Timon gained his wealth. Timon has no family, no profession, no history. He simply is; and what he is is rich. His friends,
soi-disant, are flatterers, and although we might see Timon as unjustly
treated by rapacious Athenians, there is a sense in which he is as culpable
as they. The Cynic philosopher Apemantus observes, "He that loves to be
flatter'd is worthy o' th' flatterer" (1.1.226–7).

Although he himself may not realize this, Timon's generosity is not
entirely disinterested: he buys friendship, or the appearance of friendship.
His instinctive fiscal vocabulary, which unites finance and ceremony,
indicates his Athenian values. "You have added worth unto't and lustre" he
tells a masquer (1.2.149); "I am wealthy in my friends" he tells his guests
(2.2.184). But complimentary financial metaphors cannot be entirely
innocent in this play in which everyone is motivated by gain. As Timon,
at his nadir, points out, greed is the universe's operating principle:

> The sea's a thief, whose liquid surge resolves
> The moon into salt tears; the earth's a thief,
> That feeds and breeds by a composture stol'n
> From gen'ral excrement; each thing's a thief.
> The laws, your curb and whip, in their rough power
> Has uncheck'd theft. (4.3.439–44)

Timon's initial generosity may be fiscally foolish – I am thinking not just of the elaborate dinner parties and extravagant gifts but of his refusal to accept repayment of a debt when it is offered him – but it is also double-edged. His munificence is seen in the first scene when Timon intervenes in a dispute between his servant Lucilius and a rich old Athenian. The old Athenian complains that the romance between his daughter and Lucilius is inappropriate because of the couple's social disparity: "my estate deserves an heir more rais'd / Than one which holds a trencher" (1.1.119–20). He explains that his daughter's wealth is a dowry of three talents, with the entire estate to follow after his death. Timon provides his servant with matching wealth: "Give him [Lucilius] thy daughter; / What you bestow, in him I'll counterpoise, / And make him weigh with her" (1.1.144–6). It is a generous gesture; the King of France does as much in the attempted fairy-tale of *All's Well that Ends Well* when he supplies Helena with rank. But in the world of Athens, Timon's gesture looks dangerously like commodification. Philip Brockbank characterizes this episode as "Timon's complicity in the polite harlotry of Athens when for three talents he buys for his servant the 'love' of a richly endowed bride" (Brockbank 1989a: 24).

It is often thought that Marx was hostile to money. In fact, he is hostile to commodification, the way in which money turns people into goods and goods into transactions. Money is "the universal whore – the universal bawd of men and peoples" (Marx in Muir 1977: 72). In *Merchant of Venice* Bassanio rejects not gold *per se* but gold's power "as an instrument of hypocrisy and false appearances" (Brockbank 1989a: 14). Money on its own is harmless, as Timon realizes when he discovers treasure hidden in the woods: "here it sleeps, and does no hired harm" (4.3.291). Once it is employed, however, the situation alters. In act 1, Timon employs money as does the rest of Athens, for gain – in his case, increase of friends, respect, and popularity.

In Elizabethan banking, "increase," like its near-synonyms "use" and "excess," had a technical meaning: the interest charged on a loan. The three words are often used ambiguously or punningly in Renaissance drama. "Methoughts you said you neither lend nor borrow / Upon advantage," Shylock queries; "I do never use it," replies Antonio, meaning both "I do not practice usury" and "it is not my habit" (*MV* 1.3.69–70). The nouns are also often used metaphorically to refer to emotional increase. "O love, be moderate, allay thy ecstasy, / In measure rain thy joy, scant this *excess*," says Portia (*MV* 3.2.111–12). Juliet declares "They are but beggars that can count their worth, / But my true love is grown to such *excess* / I cannot sum up sum of half my wealth" (*R&J* 2.6.32–4). The sonnets are permeated by images of usury, as the poet persuades the young man to beget children: "How much more praise deserv'd thy beauty's *use*, / If thou couldst answer, 'This fair child of mine / Shall sum my count'" (Sonnet 2); "Profitless usurer, why dost thou *use* / So great a sum of sums, yet canst not live?" (Sonnet 4); "beauty's waste hath in the world an end, / And kept *unused*, the user so destroys it" (Sonnet 9).

Although usury referred technically only to moneylending – to banking – by Shakespeare's time it had come to mean the lending of money at extortionate rates of interest, a practice associated with the Jews. It is unlikely that Shakespeare knew many Jews. Although Edward I had expelled them from England in the thirteenth century, their gradual return was permitted if they practiced Christianity. They were concentrated in one area (the street to which they had given their name in the middle ages, Old Jewry), where they functioned, as they did elsewhere in Europe, as moneylenders. It is impossible for us, in a post-Holocaust age, to dissociate Shylock from his race and religion, but to the Elizabethans his Jewishness probably marked him professionally rather than racially: he was a banker, his Jewish gaberdine was a pinstripe suit, and his haunt was the City. The taunts leveled at him in *Merchant of Venice* are frequently anti-usury taunts, functioning as do today's lawyer jokes. ("Why do sharks not eat lawyers?" – "Professional courtesy.") It is noticeable that Shylock's idiolect – in which he forms plurals with "s," as in "my moneys and my usances" (1.3.108), "we would have moneys" (1.3.116), "moneys is your suit" (1.3.119) – is shared by the Athenian usurer in *Timon*: "Importune him for my moneys" (2.1.16).

The Elizabethan attitude to usury was ambiguous. Classical and Biblical texts made it clear that money, being barren, could not breed. Henry Smith preached a sermon on usury, published in 1591, noting that "when God had finished his creation, he said unto man and unto beasts and unto fishes, 'Increase and multiply,' but he never said unto money, 'Increase and multiply,' because it is a dead thing which hath no seed, and therefore is not fit to ingender" (Smith 1591: 15). In the New Testament Christ enjoined Christians to lend, hoping for nothing in return (Luke 6:35). Nonetheless, Elizabethans acknowledged that there will always be human beings who need to borrow money, and others who will lend it to them; their compromise was to fix a ceiling on interest rates. The 1571 usury statute set the limit at 10 percent (Shapiro 1996: 98), and individuals who charged more than this were liable to prosecution. Shakespeare's father was twice in trouble for charging interest of 20 percent and 25 percent on loans of £100 (Shapiro 1996: 256, n.35). Attitudes to usurers were contemptuous, and usurers were frequently characterized as the devil. Overbury's "Character" of the usurer is headed "A devilish usurer"; Shylock is regularly associated with the devil; and Luther preaches that there is "no worse enemy of mankind on earth, next to the Devil himself, than the covetous man and the usurer, for he wishes to become God over all men" (Pearlman 1972: 218, n.2).

Timon's Athens is not simply founded on money; it is based on usury, and usury sits at the heart of government: the Senate. The odd, and strangely unintegrated, scene in which Alcibiades, an Athenian captain, petitions the Senate unsuccessfully for mercy for a transgressive but loyal soldier concludes with the banished Alcibiades accusing the Senate: "Banish me? / Banish your dotage, banish usury, / That makes the Senate ugly!" (3.5.97–9). Alone on stage, he expands: "I have kept back their foes, / While they have told [counted] their money, and let out / Their coin upon large interest – I myself / Rich only in large hurts" (3.5.105–8). Athens's public policy of usury, like Timon's private policy of generosity, is unhealthy. Both are "faults for which society and its victim share the guilt" (Kermode in Evans 1974: 1444). Timon's attitude to sex and prostitution grows out of the play's attitude to usury, for bodies and money are linked by trade. "'Twas never merry world since of two usuries the merriest was put down, and the worser allow'd by order of law," says Pompey, the bawd in *Measure for Measure* (3.2.5–7). The merriest usury is sex.

Money in Shakespeare is frequently associated with sex. Shylock boasts of his ability to make money breed (*MV* 1.3.96); in *Twelfth Night* Feste tries to coax a second coin from Cesario: "Would not a pair of these have bred, sir?" (3.1.49); in *Winter's Tale* one of Autolycus's tabloid-headline ballads associates offspring specifically with usury ("How a usurer's wife was brought to bed of twenty money-bags at a burthen" (4.4.262–4); and in *Timon of Athens* Apemantus characterizes usurers' men as "bawds between gold and want" (2.2.60). At one level the equation is simple: courtesans lend their body at interest. But on another level it is more complex, for the "merriest usury" is not just prostitution but sex in general. This larger equation is part of the system which views life as a lease of nature (see the discussion of *Macbeth* in this chapter, above); the repayment for nature's debt, the "increase," is children (Pearlman 1972: 217–18). Humans produce offspring; money generates offspring; hence the association of sex and usury. By this reasoning Shylock's balanced lament for the loss of his daughter and his ducats – "O my ducats! O my daughter!" (2.8.15), balanced chiastically two lines later, "my ducats, and my daughter" – is logical. He has lost two different but associated types of progeny (Pearlman 1972: 223).

In act 4 Timon is visited by two whores, Phrynia and Timandra. Timon tells them to spread syphilis. He inveighs against married women (they are hypocrites), virgins (they are traitors), babies (they are bastards); he hopes that soldiers, lawyers, and priests will be afflicted by venereal disease. Although Shakespeare elsewhere uses fiscal language to indicate love (as we saw in chapter 2, "Love and Hazard"), in *Timon of Athens* love is commodified. It exists only as professional sex; the play's only female characters are whores who confess "we'll do any thing for gold" (4.3.150).

Timon's Athens is like Titus's Rome: "the commonwealth of Athens is become a forest of beasts" (*Timon* 4.3.347–8); "Rome is but a wilderness of tigers" (*Titus* 3.1.54). As in *Titus*, images of cannibalism indicate society's self-serving appetite: "What a number of men eats Timon, and he sees 'em not" (1.2.39–40). Such images of consumption literalize the ambience of consumer society. Shakespeare's world was a fledgling capitalist world, in which a new moneyed class was assuming position and authority. *Timon* shows this world at its potential worst. It is a world in which, as Marx saw, money destroys social bonds and sabotages the concept of the individual ("I am what I possess"). "If money is the link which binds me to human life, to society, to nature and to other men . . . is it not also the universal means of separation?" (Marx in Muir 1977: 72).

2   Women and Politics

"what's a play without a woman in it?" (Kyd, *Spanish Tragedy* 4.1.97)

Introduction

In 1558, the year that Elizabeth I came to the throne, John Knox published a pamphlet, *The First Blast of the Trumpet against the Monstrous Regiment of Women*. The pamphlet's traditionally misogynist content is expressed in the strongest terms: "it is more than a monster in nature that a woman shall reign and have empire above man" (pp. 3–4). To the Elizabethans "monstrous" was not just a hyperbolic adjective of disapproval. Physically, it denoted size: "the sheriff with a most monstrous watch is at the door" (*1HIV* 2.4.482–3); Coriolanus modestly resists hearing his achievements inflated, his "nothings monster'd" (*Coriolanus* 2.2.77). Morally, it signified the deviant and unnatural, so that Knox's expansion, "a monster *in nature*," is something of a tautology. In *Richard III* Edward IV's wife is "that monstrous witch" (3.4.70). Hamlet finds it "monstrous" that a player can be passionate about a fiction (*Hamlet* 2.2.551). Knox's "more than a monster in nature" is thus a serious complaint: God's in his Heaven but all's not right with the world – a woman's on the throne.

Although this section on women and politics fits as logically in chapter 3 ("Political Life") as here under "Social Structures," I include it in this chapter because I wish to focus not on specific strategies for, and tropes of, government, as in chapter 3, but on the larger issues of societal structures and attitudes.

In early modern England, women and politics were incompatible. Born in 1533, Elizabeth was twenty-five when she ascended the throne. From the start of her reign, it was assumed that Elizabeth's spinster rulership would be temporary, an assumption Elizabeth encouraged by entertaining marriage suitors and negotiating matrimonial and political alliances for twenty years (long after any likelihood of her bearing children – the political reason for her to marry – had vanished). She went as far as having marriage articles drawn up between herself and the Duke of Anjou in 1570, and as late as 1579 she was considering marriage to the Duke of Alençon.

Even as Elizabeth capitalized on her status as the most eligible royal virgin in Europe, she presented herself as one already wedded to her people. Furthermore, in her speeches she regularly refers to herself as both masculine and feminine: thus the country need not fear a female ruler, because she is both king and queen. Her address to her troops at Tilbury after the defeat of the Spanish Armada in 1588 stresses that inside her female body is "the heart and stomach of a King." In a speech to the Commons in 1601 she describes herself as a "Prince," refers to her "kingly bounties," and talks of the burdens of being "a King and wear[ing] a crown" (Bassnett 1988: 73–4, 76). It is this skillful manipulation of the masculine and the feminine that contemporary political analysts see as contributing to Mrs. Thatcher's political success in the twentieth century: photographs of Thatcher at the kitchen sink coexisted with pronouncements like "A General doesn't leave the field of battle just as it's reaching a climax" (see Atkinson 1984: 111–21 for an analysis of Thatcher's development).

The nicknames given to Mrs. Thatcher by cabinet colleagues and international media – Attila the Hen, the Iron Lady, the Leaderene, the Bossette – indicate public unease at a woman in the male world of politics (Atkinson 1984: 115). The epithets offer soundbite versions of the descriptions of an earlier political Margaret, Margaret of Anjou, in *3 Henry VI* who is a "she-wolf," a "tiger's heart wrapp'd in a woman's hide" (1.4.111, 137). Shakespeare's Margaret is an anomaly: a woman in politics.

It is usual to see *Richard III* as a play which depicts the growth of a monster, physical and political, as Richard of Gloucester develops from the clan warrior of *3 Henry VI* to become the fratricide, regicide, and double infanticide of *Richard III*. This attitude is not confined to critics; characters in the play refer to Richard as a bottled spider, a lump of foul deformity, a poisonous bunch-back'd toad, an elvish-mark'd, abortive roasting hog, the son of hell, a dog, a foul devil, a hedgehog. But the monstrous in the first tetralogy is focused initially on the female. Margaret, introduced in *1 Henry VI*, is in every way aberrant. Like Richard, she is described in animal terms. She leads armies; she plans tactics and makes policy; she dismisses her husband, King Henry VI, from the field of battle. She is like those other monstrous political women in the *Henry VI* plays, Joan of Arc (Part 1) whose unnaturalness is signaled in acts as diverse as rejecting her father and trafficking with spirits, and Eleanor of Gloucester (Part 2) whose political ambitions for her husband lead her to employ a conjuror (Howard and Rackin 1997: 45–6, 76–7). A decade later Shakespeare will again depict the unnaturalness of a politically ambitious female in diabolic terms: Lady Macbeth calls on spirits to unsex her.[5] The first tetralogy thus focuses on teratology, on the development of monsters. It begins and ends with political animals, female and male.[6]

Elsewhere in the Shakespeare canon female warriors, confined to rhetorical gesture and wishful-thinking, are feisty rather than threatening. Glendower explains his daughter's reluctance to part with her husband: "She'll be a soldier too, she'll to the wars" (*1HIV* 3.1.193). Given Desde-

---

[5]   In the Creation Theatre Company production in Oxford (2002), Lady Macbeth used the velvet ribbon with which her husband's letter to her had been tied to make a conjurer's circle on the ground; she stepped hesitantly into the circle to invoke the spirits, crossing the boundary from empty rhetoric to deliberate diabolism.

[6]   However, the human beneath the monster is poignantly visible: Margaret's disappointment in Henry VI, her grief at Suffolk's death, her fiercely maternal protection of her son's dynastic rights; Richard's rejection by his mother, his grief at his father's death, his physical otherness.

mona's insistence on accompanying her husband to the war-zone of Cyprus, the grammatical ambiguity of "She wish'd / That heaven had made her such a man" (*Othello* 1.3.163–4) may be resolved in favor of the accusative (rather than the dative) "her." In *Much Ado About Nothing,* Beatrice wishes she were a man so she could be vengefully violent to Claudio: "O God, that I were a man! I would eat his heart in the market-place" (4.1.306–7). At the level of language, female military ambition seems comic exaggeration, and its threat is contained.

In the mature Roman tragedies, however, women have considerable power in public life (Volumnia creates Coriolanus in her own bloodthirsty image; Cleopatra rules Egypt) and men try to escape their influence. "I must from this enchanting queen break off," says Antony (ruefully? determinedly?) in *Antony and Cleopatra* (1.2.128). But Antony's position is not analogous to Coriolanus's attempt to liberate himself from his mother, because it is complicated by sex. And sex and politics make poor bedfellows.

Antony and Cleopatra (1606)

"I have a technical objection to making sexual infatuation a tragic theme. Experience proves that it is only effective in the comic spirit" (Shaw 1967: 30)

Antony and Cleopatra is often considered a tragedy of love. The evidence for this is slight, confined (I believe) to the title, where the double billing encourages one to approach the play as a rerun of *Romeo and Juliet* with maturer protagonists. But the hallmarks of romantic tragedy, as established by *Romeo and Juliet,* are absent. With the possible exception of one four-line dialogue in 1.1, Antony and Cleopatra exchange no lyrical lines; there is no examination of their interior consciousness; they do not soliloquize; they are alone together on only one occasion (3.13), and on that occasion they fight. Even in a play as blatantly ironic and detached as *Troilus and Cressida,* Shakespeare grants his lovers privacy and poetic confession. Antony and Cleopatra, figures on the world stage, always appear in public. Consequently it is hard to know the depth or sincerity of the emotion they label "love."

Bernard Shaw is unequivocal in his identification of the protagonists' motivating emotion: "sexual infatuation." It is true that Cleopatra fantasizes sexually about Antony when he is absent in Rome ("O happy horse, to bear the weight of Antony!"; 1.5.21), and that Enobarbus observes her sexuality ("The holy priests / Bless her when she is riggish [aroused]"; 2.2.238–9) and alludes to her capacity for climax ("She hath such a celerity [speed] in dying [achieving orgasm]"; 1.2.144). But the encounters which Antony and Cleopatra themselves remember are remarkable for their nonsexuality. They walk the city streets in the evening and "note / The qualities of people" (1.1.53–4); they go fishing; they swap clothes; they indulge in idleness; they stay up late ("mock the midnight bell"; 3.13.184); they eat, drink, and converse. They talk of pleasure and of living for the moment, but the pleasures portrayed seem domestic and innocent rather than hedonistic and reprehensible. If it be love indeed, the word has different associations from the heat it carries in *Romeo and Juliet* or even in *Troilus and Cressida*. (One thinks of Juliet's impatience as she anticipates her wedding night, or Troilus's sensuous soliloquy about lily beds.) It is an enduring irritation of the English language that we have only one noun to cover a range of loves (cf. Goddard 1951: II, 192, and Parker 2000: 6); the love depicted in *Antony and Cleopatra* seems not grand passion but connubial contentment.

Of course, the domestic ease is not connubial but extramarital; and there's the rub (Makaryk 1996: 111–15). The play begins with Antony married to Fulvia; when it ends he is married to Octavia. That Cleopatra is not indifferent to these Roman marriages is clear. Her first conversation with Antony opens with sarcastic remarks about Fulvia: "Fulvia perchance is angry"; "Where's Fulvia's process? – Caesar's I would say"; "shrill-tongu'd Fulvia scolds" (1.1.20, 28, 32). She begins her next conversation with Antony in 1.3 with reductive references to Fulvia: "What, says the married woman you may go? / Would she had never given you leave to come!" (1.3.20–1). The ensuing lines have a barbed edge, indicating Cleopatra's anxiety that her exaggerated denial may be true: "Let her not say 'tis I that keep you here, / I have no power upon you; hers you are" (1.3.22–3). The end of the play shows her harping on the same string when, in Antony's dying moments, Cleopatra compares herself with Octavia: "Your wife Octavia, with her modest eyes / And still conclusion, shall acquire no honor / Demuring upon me" (i.e., because the distance between the monument and the ground prevents Cleopatra kissing Antony, she is now as demure as Octavia; 4.15.27–9). Bloom rightly identifies Cleopatra's "taste and timing" here as "dubious" (1999: 571). In the next act, Cleopatra views her suicide as heralding marriage: "Husband, I come! / Now to that name my courage prove my title!" (5.2.287–8). Thus, at the heart of the play lies not a physical relationship (sex) but the absence of a legal one (marriage).

This nonrelationship is poignantly conveyed in a nonconversation in 1.3. Recalled to Rome by civil war and Fulvia's death, Antony comes to say goodbye to Cleopatra. She provocatively accuses him of insincerity, whereupon he becomes exasperated ("You'll heat my blood; no more," 1.3.80) and businesslike ("I'll leave you lady"; 1.3.86). Chastened, Cleopatra stops playacting (Makaryk 1996: 115), and the tone of the scene changes abruptly with her hesitant attempt to introduce a new topic:

> Courteous lord, one word:
> Sir, you and I must part, but that's not it;
> Sir, you and I have lov'd, but there's not it;
> That you know well. Something it is I would –
> O, my oblivion is a very Antony,
> And I am all forgotten. (1.3.86–91)

She abandons the subject and we never find out what she intended to ask, although the sentimental tone continues with her vulnerable confession that "my becomings kill me when they do not / Eye well to you [even my virtues pain me if they do not please you]" (1.3.96–7). It is a rare moment of emotional pain and honesty. The content of the absent conversation is therefore worth pondering.

It is clear that at line 86 Cleopatra intended to ask a favor: "One word . . . Something it is I would." Robert S. Miola concludes: "Shakespeare probably has no one word in mind but merely wishes to dramatize Cleopatra's love by depicting her confusion" (1983: 126). This is unlikely both in terms of human psychology and in terms of Method acting, for the actress must decide what her character wants – and hesitates – to ask.

Critics have plausibly identified Cleopatra's desideratum as marriage (Alexander 1981: 26; MacCallum 1967: 656; Makaryk 1996: 115). The context supports this deduction. Earlier in the scene Antony tells Cleopatra of Fulvia's death but as Jane Lapotaire, who played Cleopatra in the BBC film, points out, he "never says 'Now I'll marry you' which is what any woman in a triangular situation would hope" (Alexander 1981: 26).

Coppélia Kahn observes (1997: 114) that *Antony and Cleopatra* is full of triangular relationships: Antony–Fulvia–Cleopatra; Antony subordinate to Caesar and Fulvia; Fulvia versus Caesar versus Antony; Pompey versus Antony and Caesar; Antony–Octavia–Cleopatra. But while the political triangulations can resolve into a dyad, the three-way romantic relations cannot be so easily reduced. Cleopatra, the Queen of Egypt, international sex symbol and public figure, is shown as emotionally vulnerable. Her public stature cannot prevent her from feeling threatened by Octavia's relative youth, a threat felt generally, even before Antony's marriage, in Charmian's unusual choice of oath: "Wrinkles forbid" (1.2.20). Cleopatra may talk openly of her sunburned skin, but her conversation lacks the playful confidence of Webster's Duchess of Malfi who anticipates her old age as starting a fashion for gray hair. *Antony and Cleopatra* reminds us that a powerful political female can experience qualms about the potential or incipient loss of personal power. Irena Makaryk observes that Cleopatra is not just the exotic Eastern Other but a more familiar figure: the Other Woman (1996: 111). By showing her emotional vulnerability, the play domesticates Cleopatra.

In 1.3 Cleopatra approaches Antony not with honesty but with a strata-gem: "If you find him sad, / Say I am dancing; if in mirth, report / That I am sudden sick" (1.3.3–5). Charmian cautions, "If you did love him dearly, / You do not hold the method to enforce / The like from him" (1.3.6–8). She continues, "In each thing give him way, cross him in nothing" (1.3.9) but Cleopatra dismisses the advice: "The way to lose him" (1.3.10). Cressida too has a tactic ("Men prize the thing ungain'd more than it is"; 1.2.289) but she abandons pretense when the lovers finally come together. However, playacting comprises Cleopatra's permanent mode.

We see this most obviously in Antony's death scene. Refusing to leave her monument lest she be captured, Cleopatra submits the wounded and dying Antony to the ignominy of being hauled aloft – ignominious because it enacts her earlier reference (2.5.13–15) to drawing Antony up on her fishing rod (Frye 1986: 129). Furthermore Antony is not allowed to upstage her even in his dying moments. "Let me speak," he begins; "No, let *me* speak," she responds (4.15.42, 43; Frye 1986: 129). Ever the actress, Cleopatra permits no one to steal her thunder.

Cleopatra's self-conscious theatricality keeps us at an emotional dis-tance. It is often remarked that *Antony and Cleopatra* employs distancing techniques to prevent us becoming too close to the protagonists. The stage clears every one hundred lines or so, creating emotional detachment; scenes begin and end in mid-conversation (Neill 1994: 101), denying us definitive views of characters or events; frequent framing devices force us to analyze rather than feel, as in 1.1 when the conversation between the servants Philo and Demetrius provides one perspective on Antony and Cleopatra, and the behavior of Antony and Cleopatra, who enter immediately, provides another. Cleopatra's theatrical behavior functions as another framing device: as in *Henry V*, permanent performance denies us access to the "real" character. This theatricality was taken a stage further when Mark Rylance played Cleopatra at Shakespeare's Globe in London in 1999. Rylance did not simply portray Cleopatra; he portrayed an RSC actress portraying Cleopatra. Referential rather than parodic, Rylance's performance(s) kept us doubly at arm's length.

The seventeenth century sees Shakespeare experimenting with genre. The plays which cause most headaches in generic classification (all, incidentally, classical plays: *Troilus and Cressida, Timon of Athens, Antony and Cleopatra*) are those which break the Shakespearean mold of psychological intimacy. In *Troilus and Cressida* characters argue one way but act another (Adamson 1987: 34–58) and the romance of the eponymous couple is, uniquely in Shakespeare, an affair: Cressida is the only Shakespeare heroine to lose her virginity before marriage,[7] and marriage is never spoken of as a destination by Troilus. Timon is unfamilied, and we are denied any biographical context; the second half of the play distances us further from him, as he descends into vituperative rant. Ellen Terry complained about Cleopatra's lack of psychological depth, characterizing her as "a woman with a shallow nature" (cited in Neill 1994: 80).

Antony and Cleopatra has more in common with classical epic than with Shakespearean tragedy. Epic is not psychological; epic does not present characters intimately *in camera*; epic is not about individuals *per se* but about individuals' effects on public events; epic covers vast distances and presents huge panoramas (*Antony and Cleopatra* has forty-three scenes [Neill 1994: 2] and "almost two hundred exits and entrances" [Miola 1983: 117]). *Antony and Cleopatra* is not about love (there are no love scenes) but neither is it about politics (there are no crowd scenes): Shakespeare depicts effects rather than psychological causes.

King John (1596)

It may seem odd to consider *King John* alongside *Antony and Cleopatra*: the latter is a product of Shakespeare's maturity, much celebrated critically, and frequently performed in the professional theater, whereas *King John* is an anomalous history play sandwiched between the two tetralogies of the 1590s, suffers critical neglect, and, despite a history of successful perfor-

---

[7] We may exclude Juliet in *Measure for Measure* who is betrothed; see chapter 1, section 3 ("The Self and Language").

mance, is infrequently staged. Nonetheless, there are pertinent points of contact. *Antony and Cleopatra* depicts a woman in public life; in *King John*, Elinor (mother to King John) and Constance (mother to Prince Arthur) dominate the first half of the play; the rival claimants to the throne, John and Arthur, are seen primarily in relation to their mothers. Like *Antony and Cleopatra*, *King John* has a shifting perspective as moral rugs are pulled from beneath our feet. Thus, in the first scene, King John's denial of Arthur's claim to the English throne – "our strong possession and our right for us" (1.1.39) – is immediately followed by his mother's whispered modification: "Your strong possession much more than your right" (1.1.40). The central spaces of *Antony and Cleopatra* are occupied by absence: Antony loses his identity; Antony parts from Cleopatra; Antony abandons Octavia; but for the fact that nature abhors a vacuum, the air would leave its space to gaze on Cleopatra; Enobarbus deserts. Similarly, there are gaps at the center of *King John*: the Bastard succors and rallies England not because he is the right man for the job but because there is no one else to do it (Van de Water 1960: 144); he "creates a king worthy of loyalty" just as he "creates a country capable of it" (Kastan 1983: 14). Like *Antony and Cleopatra*, *King John* has no soliloquies, for, despite the title, John is not the center (or even the hero) of his own play. These tantalizing points of contact provide our entry to the otherwise very different world of *King John*.

  If King John lacks soliloquies, his illegitimate nephew and key supporter, the Bastard, compensates. The Bastard has three soliloquies[8] and five monologues, and his commentary concludes every act except the third (Van de Water 1960: 145). This rhetorical prominence marks him as the central character in a play which resembles a debate rather than a drama. Each act of *King John* centers on a major disputation (Wixson 1981: 118). Act 1 presents a debate about the Faulconbridge inheritance: should the elder (illegitimate) son inherit the Faulconbridge estate, or the younger (legitimate) son to whom it has been willed? Act 2 stages a debate before the French city of Angiers, whose gates will open for the King of England. But who is the King of England? "Doth not the crown of England prove the King?" (2.1.273). Perhaps not: we recall Elinor's aside contrasting right and possession in 1.1. In act 3 the papal legate, Cardinal Pandulph, debates

---

[8] His speech at 2.1.455–67 is technically an aside, as he is not alone on stage, but it has the same function of choric reflection as his soliloquies. In the BBC film the Bastard spoke these lines, as he did his soliloquies, directly to the camera.

with John, trying to dissuade him from renouncing the Catholic Church. In act 4 young Prince Arthur persuades John's hitman, Hubert, not to blind him (the scene is remarkable for the boy's logical *suasio* rather than, as might be expected, panic and hysteria). In act 5, Pandulph informs the French Dauphin, Lewis, that, because of John's reconciliation with Rome, France need not attack England; Lewis's obstinacy – "I will not back" (5.2.78) – initiates a debate in which Pandulph attempts to dissuade him from war.

Within this five-act structure is a binary division. The play divides neatly – perhaps too starkly – into two distinct halves. The first half is King John's play, the second that of the Bastard, who emerges as the representative of the crown ("Now hear our English King, / For thus his royalty doth speak in me"; 5.2.128–9). In the first half we have loyal lords, dominant women, and an older generation; in the second half, the lords are traitors, the female characters diminished, and a younger generation dominant. In the first half the tone and speed are slow, detailed, explanatory; in the second half all is hasty, motives are unexplained, and action is presented as *fait accompli*. We first hear of King John's poisoning, for example, when John is dying, whereas the source play, the two-part *Troublesome Reign of King John* (1591), introduces us to the monk who is plotting the murder (Leggatt 1998: 212). The first half of *King John* is a very formal, public play; the second half is private (ibid.: 209): Constance, for example, is a grieving mother rather than a political power.

The dual structure of binary contrast and five-act debate is appropriate for a play which continually presents two ways of seeing things (note, incidentally, how important optical imagery is in this play). John's public assertion of royal right is undermined by his private acknowledgment of guilt. The wedding of Blanche of Spain to the Dauphin represents a "blessed day" to King Philip (3.1.75) but "a wicked day" to Constance (3.1.83). Richard I, known for religious crusades, is shown as engaged in a different kind of siege warfare; in vocabulary which fuses the courtly and the military, Lady Faulconbridge confesses, "By long and vehement suit I was seduc'd / To make room for him in my husband's bed" (1.1.254–5). Words assume different meanings in different contexts: the changes are rung on "truth" in act 1 (Jones 1985: 397–401), "peace" in act 2 (Leggatt 1998: 207), and on "possession" throughout the play (Woodeson 1993: 93). In denying us a stable point of view, the play reminds us that history is not factual and fixed but personal and multiple. *King John* is a play about how people see things; it is also (consequently?) a play about how one tells history. This perhaps accounts for its independent position between the two tetralogies. It has no sequel, nor does it invite one (Vaughan 1984: 407). It is interested not in historical characters or events but in how characters and events *become* historical (Braunmuller 1988; Kastan 1983).

Shakespeare's Bastard is developed from a "single sentence" in Holinshed's *Chronicles* (Howard and Rackin 1997: 128): "Philip, bastard son to King Richard . . . killed the viscount of Limoges, in revenge of his father's death" (Bullough 1962: IV, 28). In *King John*, as critics point out, Philip is given a surname, a brother, a mother, a servant (who is also given a name), and a personality. In short, he is given an identity. He is also given a dramatic function: chorus or commentator on history.

I say "dramatic" function because the Bastard has no plot function. Despite his physical and rhetorical prominence, one could remove him from the play with no detriment to the action (Van de Water 1960: 145). The Bastard is there solely to write his name in the history books, as we see in his asides in the parley before Angiers:

> *King John*:   Doth not the crown of England prove the King?
>   And if not that, I bring you witnesses,
>   Twice fifteen thousand hearts of England's breed –
> *Bastard*:   Bastards, and else.
> *King John*:   To verify our title with their lives.
> *King Philip*:   As many and as well-born bloods as those –
> *Bastard*:   Some bastards too. (2.1.273–9)

The Bastard's asides insert him, and those like him, in the historical text.

Historical texts are predictable: they are patrilineal, legitimate, noble – "hearts of England's breed" and French "well-born bloods." But historical texts are no less artfully (artificially?) constructed than more overtly creative texts (Braunmuller 1988).

In a play which contests two patrilineal inheritances – Robert Faulconbridge's of his father's estate, and King John's of the throne of England – the role of women becomes crucial (Howard and Rackin 1997). The first scene reverberates with family terms – "brother," "mother," "father" (Woodeson 1993: 94) – and the family here is literally the blood unit rather than a metaphor for the state. History has a political, public side and a personal side; but the personal becomes political when it involves Richard I siring an illegitimate son. Women may receive scant attention in the official history books, but their sexual activities and their position as mothers are of great significance in determining feudal or allodial allocation (as in the Faulconbridge episode) and historical sequence (as in the rivalry between Elinor and Constance).

The women in *King John* are powerful and prominent (Shakespeare clearly had two boy actors of enormous skill for the roles of Elinor and Constance) and it is significant that they are mothers. In the play they determine inheritance both biologically and rhetorically. Elinor and Constance compete for the position of power behind the throne (Alexander 1986: 27). Elinor makes John's decisions for him (Woodeson 1993: 92), beginning with the bold recognition of the Bastard. Shakespeare augments Constance's role. Arthur was sixteen at the time of the play's events, very much a man (Ranald 1987: 180); Shakespeare's Arthur is a young boy, dependent on his mother. Claire Bloom, who played Constance in the BBC production, points out that Constance's "complex" language indicates her intellect: "nobody uses words like her except the Cardinal" (Alexander 1986: 28). The political significance of the two royal mothers is underlined paradoxically by their abrupt and unexpected disappearance from the play (they are arbitrarily, and unhistorically, reported dead in 4.2). As several critics point out, their roles as maternal authorities are taken over by two institutional mothers who are also in conflict with each other: "the Church, our holy mother" (3.1.141), and "dear mother England" (5.2.153). As the biological gives way to the institutional, the importance of the women's maternal roles in determining behavior and allegiance could not be made clearer.

The question of succession, of female sexuality, and of bastardy were sixteenth-century themes which came to a head in the 1590s. Queen Elizabeth's mother, Anne Bullen, was known for sexual looseness. After Bullen's execution, gossip suggested that Henry VIII might not be Elizabeth's real father. (In any event, political necessity meant that Elizabeth was declared a bastard.) Although Elizabeth was known as a virgin queen, and appropriated the external signs of virginity such as wearing loose, flowing hair or holding a sieve as an accessory,[9] she was not exempt from sexual scandal. Thomas Seymour, the brother of her stepmother, Jane Seymour, was allegedly her lover when she was a teenager. Elizabeth may have been

---

[9]   The sieve was the symbol of the Vestal Virgins whose intact and impenetrable hymens were "proved" by the Vestals' ability to carry water in a sieve. For the history of this symbol see Blakemore and Jennett (2001: 713–14).

sexually harassed by him or she may just have been extraordinarily naive in physical intimacy (cf. Bassnett 1988: 25). When queen, she gave Robert Dudley a bedchamber adjoining her own.

Meanwhile, over the border in Scotland, the beautiful widowed Mary Queen of Scots married the reprobate Darnley in 1565, confided her marital misery to her secretary Rizzio, and was rumored to be pregnant by the latter. In 1566 Rizzio was murdered in front of Mary's eyes, Mary gave birth to a son, James, and fell in love with Bothwell. In 1567 Darnley was murdered, Mary called a whore by passionate crowds, deposed and imprisoned, upon which she miscarried twins (Bassnett 1988: 108–11). Escaping to England in 1568, she was executed (very much against Elizabeth's desire) in 1587. Although in 1571 the English Parliament had passed a bill barring both Mary and James from the throne of England, in the 1590s Elizabeth named James as her successor. This gesture finally reassured the nation of a Protestant succession after four decades of a reign in which Elizabeth had toyed with marriage negotiations and raised hopes of her bearing a child. Succession and female sexuality were more than usually linked in this century: as the accusations of misbehavior of Henry VIII's wives and Mary Queen of Scots illustrate, sexuality, which can secure succession, can also disrupt it. A large number of plays in the 1590s center on the question of succession and inheritance (*Richard II, Henry IV, Henry V*, for example), but, as Howard and Rackin point out, only *King John* places women at the heart of the debate (Howard and Rackin 1997: 133; Rackin 1989: 85).

Elizabeth was a highly educated woman, fluent in many languages, a poet and a translator. She was educated in a humanist tradition (one of her tutors was Roger Ascham). Renaissance humanism took an anthropocentric view of the world: if humans were at the center of God's universe, the world would be a better place if humans cultivated themselves. Humanism, as its name implies, was egalitarian: it believed in educating women. These enlightened views were eroded in the wake of the Reformation and Counter-Reformation, and developing female repression seems to have gone hand in hand with other kinds of restriction: religious intolerance and "more rigid class structuring with greater social divisiveness" (Bassnett 1988: 90).

The accession of the first Stuart monarch, James VI of Scotland and I of England, was a further setback for women. James famously remarked that if a woman had wit enough to know her husband's bed from another man's, she had wit enough; and when an accomplished woman was presented at court, James dismissed the list of her achievements with the question "Ay, but can she spin?" During his reign "women and politics" were incompatible.

Nonetheless, one of the first plays written in the new reign depicts a woman who is forced to enter the world of public affairs: Isabella in Shakespeare's *Measure for Measure.*

Measure for Measure (1603–4)

Isabella has made the strongest possible statement of her wish to avoid public life and to shun sexuality: she has entered a convent. Her order is the St. Clare's, known for "strict restraint" of the kind detailed by the nun who explains the votarist's life to the novice Isabella:

> When you have vow'd, you must not speak with men
> But in the presence of the prioress;
> Then if you speak, you must not show your face,
> Or if you show your face, you must not speak. (1.4.10–13)

Before the scene has ended, however, Isabella is forced to return to the outside world to beg the governor Angelo to pardon her brother and grant him life.

Rhetoric is one of Isabella's strong points, as we saw in chapter 1, but it is not the main reason for Claudio (her brother) and Lucio (Claudio's friend) requesting Isabella's intervention. Her body language rather than her speech is uppermost in Claudio's thoughts when he describes her political efficacy in 1.2:

> In her youth
> There is a prone and speechless dialect,
> Such as move men; beside, she hath prosperous art
> When she will play with reason and discourse,
> And well she can persuade (1.2.182–6)

First priority: she looks the part; second: she speaks well (Rutter 1988: 33). When Lucio meets Isabella, he instructs her:

> Go to Lord Angelo,
> And let him learn to know, when maidens sue,
> Men give like gods; but when they weep and kneel,

All their petitions are as freely theirs
As they themselves would owe them. (1.4.79–83)

He asks her not just to speak ("sue") but to be histrionically feminine ("weep and kneel"). Isabella, of course, only thinks of her rhetorical tactics, and when her conversation with Angelo in 2.2 concludes unsuccessfully, it is Lucio who directs her physical actions:

Give't not o'er so. To him again, entreat him,
Kneel down before him, hang upon his gown;
You are too cold. If you should need a pin,
You could not with more tame a tongue desire it. (2.2.43–6)

Isabella is not simply thrust into the political arena: her political value is seen as primarily sexual. Both (the public, the sexual) are areas she has renounced.

Our attitude to Isabella's predicament depends on a number of possible character interpretations. Claudio's imprisonment for impregnating his fiancée begs two questions: is Claudio a genuinely loving suitor who has fallen foul of a Draconian law or is he a reprobate who expects his sister to bale him out of trouble? Isabella's retreat to convent life (and her choice of the strictest order) raises several questions. Is it a temporary teenage passion? Is it an act of theological misunderstanding, a belief in salvation through severity? Is it a search for what Viennese society cannot give her: restraint? (Rutter 1988: 41). Is it an act of repression and denial? (Isabella's vocabulary is charged with nuance although she is clearly unaware of its – and her – erotic potential: "your potency" [2.2.67]; "your pleasure" [2.4.31]; "strip myself to death" [2.4.102]. These phrases are all used in conversation with Angelo; in the RSC production of 1991 the buccinatory muscles of David Suchet's Angelo twitched as he swallowed hard, trying to ignore the *doubles entendres*.)

Productions offer the gamut of interpretations of Isabella, from a strident Major Barbara through the martyred Saint Joan to the ingénue Maria von Trapp. One thinks of the refined, self-knowledgeable Isabella of Juliet Stevenson (RSC 1983), wearing a rich but subtle *fin-de-siècle* black gown; the erotic Judi Dench (RSC 1962), who led one reviewer to comment, "this is the first time I have seen Isabella in so low-cut a gown" (Williamson 1975: 163); the militant Puritan of Penelope Wilton in Jonathan Miller's production at Greenwich in 1975; or the impulsively tactile schoolgirl of Clare Skinner, oblivious to her sexual effects (RSC 1991). In her first encounter with Angelo Isabella tells him, "Go to your bosom, / Knock there, and ask your heart what it doth know / That's like my brother's fault" (2.2.136–8). Skinner's Isabella flew across the stage, bent her head on Angelo's chest, and knocked innocently on his pectorals. Angelo was taken aback at such female proximity but drank in the scent of Isabella's hair. When, after Isabella's exit, he asked in soliloquy, "What's this? What's this?" (2.2.162), his double question and the demonstrative pronoun clearly referred to the unfamiliar experience of erection.

Consistent in most interpretations of Isabella is a fear of being manipulated. "I have spirit to do any thing that appears not foul in the truth of my spirit," she tells the Friar-Duke in 3.1.205–7; the line is both a statement and a warning. "To speak so indirectly I am loath," she protests in 4.6.1. But for Isabella, entering the public world means being directed against her beliefs and instincts.

The most blatant example of manipulation occurs in 2.4, in a scene of blackmail: Angelo agrees to pardon Claudio if Isabella will have sex with Angelo. The scene is iniquitous for many reasons. In resurrecting a dormant law punishing premarital sex, Angelo has presented himself as a man dedicated to sexual purity. In propositioning Isabella, Angelo is not just propositioning a virgin but a "professional" virgin. In demanding her compliance he introduces an ethical hinterland somewhere between agreement and rape. In trading sex for justice he mocks the law. In using the verb "redeem" (2.4.53, 163) he manipulatively presents Isabella's yielding of her body as a Christ-like sacrifice. He compounds all these villainies with further blackmail. When Isabella threatens to denounce him, he retorts:

> Who will believe thee, Isabel?
> My unsoil'd name, th'austereness of my life,
> My vouch against you, and my place i' th' state,
> Will so your accusation overweigh,
> That you shall stifle in your own report,
> And smell of calumny. (2.4.154–9)

Worse is to follow. If Isabella refuses to cooperate, Angelo will not only kill Claudio but torture him: "he must not only die the death, / But thy unkindness shall his death draw out / To ling'ring sufferance . . . I'll prove a tyrant to him" (2.4.165–7, 169). Isabella's subsequent soliloquy voices the dilemma experienced by any woman sexually harassed by a respectable and respected professional superior: "Did I tell this, / Who would believe me?" (2.4.171–2).

In quick succession Isabella has been asked by men to act on their behalf. Lucio asks her to plead; Angelo asks her for sex; Claudio asks her to comply with Angelo's request ("Sweet sister, let me live. / What sin you do to save a brother's life, / Nature dispenses with the deed so far, / That it becomes a virtue"; 3.1.132–5). When the Duke-Friar appears immediately with a plot – "you may most uprighteously do a poor wrong'd lady a merited benefit; redeem your brother from the angry law; do no stain to your own gracious person; and much please the absent Duke" (3.1.199–203) – Isabella accepts his instructions. He is, after all, a Friar figure, someone whose direction she is naturally disposed to follow. But, as we saw in chapter 1, the Duke, like the others, manipulates Isabella for his own ends (Riefer 1984).

The Duke has already shown himself adept at using others: he appoints Angelo as a temporary new broom to sweep clean the moral mess his own lax rule has created. He knows the rigid Angelo will enforce the letter of the law, but he clearly has misgivings about Angelo's personal tendencies (which is why he remains in Vienna in disguise). Having used Angelo to reform the city, he now uses Isabella and Mariana to expose Angelo. The dénouement he engineers is complicated and unsavory. He has kept from Isabella the knowledge of Claudio's safety (my phrasing here downplays the emotional consequence of this plot detail: the Duke makes Isabella suffer hugely and unnecessarily). In making her now beg for Angelo's life, he puts her in the position she was in at the start of the play: pleading for a transgressor.

The usual critical argument is that Isabella needs to learn about mercy (her theological position in act 2, in which she refused to sacrifice her chastity, was as rigid as Angelo's legal position, in which he refused to modify his ruling). Begging for mercy for the man who (as she thinks) has killed her brother is an important test. Laying aside the ethical dubiety of one human being setting up a moral lesson for another, we may note that the Duke does not offer mercy to Lucio when he is given the opportunity to do so. Lucio, gossip and slanderer *par excellence*, has been a thorn in the Duke's side throughout the play, reporting to the Duke-as-Friar sexual gossip about the absent Duke. Lucio has no plot function other than to test the Duke. However, unlike Isabella, the Duke does not pass the test: "here's one in place I cannot pardon . . . / Let him be whipt and hang'd" (5.1.499, 513). The Duke then proposes marriage to Isabella. The audience's sense of *déjà vu* is enormous: Isabella's virginal profession is once again being ignored by a hypocritical ruler who does not observe the morality he expects of others (sexual restraint in Angelo's case, mercy in the Duke's). Small wonder that Shakespeare does not script a response for Isabella: her silence offers an opportunity for her, and us, to register the situation's ironies.

Vienna manipulates rather than respects women. Elbow's malapropism is, in fact, far from *mal à propos*: "my wife, sir, whom I detest before heaven and your honor" (2.1.69–70). Angelo refers to the pregnant Juliet as "the fornicatress" (David Suchet's Angelo enunciated the noun's four syllables with exquisite distaste, holding the word at the rhetorical equivalent of arm's length). Denied sexual respect, women are not granted political respect either. When Isabella enters public life, she becomes the Duke's puppet. Note the verbs used of her relation with the Friar-Duke: "directed" (4.3.136); "advis'd" (4.6.3); "rul'd" (4.6.4; Riefer 1984: 161). The men, on the other hand, resist the Duke's manipulations: Angelo refuses to pardon Claudio, Barnadine refuses to die, Lucio refuses to hold his tongue (Riefer 1984: 161). Viennese public life is nothing less than a minefield for women in this play. Isabella is viewed as a sexual rather than a religious being, and she is unable to maintain her own theological voice, as we saw in chapter 1. The convent thus represents not a denial of sex and politics but an avoidance of the situation where a woman involved in public affairs is considered only for her sexuality.

3 Language

"Words are very rascals" (*TN* 3.1.21)

Titus Andronicus (1592)

It is a convention of Petrarchan poetics (the sonnetteering tradition established by the Italian Petrarch) to objectify the beautiful woman by reducing her to a series of disembodied physical parts. The woman is lauded for her sparkling eyes, her pale skin, her blushing rosy cheeks, her crimson lips, her skillful hands (dexterous in music-making, embroidery), and, above all, her silence. It is this tradition which Shakespeare mocks in Sonnet 130 ("My mistress' eyes are nothing like the sun") and in Mercutio's parody of Romeo's lovesick inventorying in *Romeo and Juliet.*

I conjure thee by Rosaline's bright eyes,
By her high forehead and her scarlet lip,
By her fine foot, straight leg, and quivering thigh,
And the demesnes [domains] that there adjacent lie . . . (2.1.17–20)

In both these works the mockery represents good-humored acceptance of a convention so long established that it hovers between commonplace and cliché.

Titus Andronicus presents a serious attack on metaphoric convention. Marcus encounters his niece, Lavinia, in the forest, bleeding and in shock: she has been raped, has had her tongue cut out and her hands cut off. For forty-seven lines Marcus *does* nothing, choosing instead to describe the missing body parts of the mutilated Lavinia in terms of what the loss will mean to the world rather than to the amputee.

Marcus first notices Lavinia's stumps, and laments the loss of "those sweet ornaments" (her hands; 2.4.18) whose embrace was desired by kings. Lavinia's silence draws his attention to the "crimson rivers" of blood which issue from his niece's "rosed lips" (2.4.22, 24). The imagery is startling because of its context: vocabulary usually applied to female features is here applied to lack of those features. Lavinia is pale, as a beautiful woman should be, but her pallor is because of blood loss; however, in a typical Petrarchan paradox, she also has red color rising in her cheeks, and again, in this instance, it is literal. The amputation of her lily hands is lamented in relation to lost artistic skills – sewing and the playing of a musical instrument – and the loss of her tongue in relation to her musical speech. Each of Marcus's images occupies several lines.

The passage is disturbing not least because of the tradition in which dead or dying female bodies (one thinks notably of the drowned Ophelia) are described as objects of beauty. But I suspect that in *Titus Andronicus* one of Shakespeare's purposes is to question poetic traditions and the conventional metaphors which underpin them. If we use "crimson rivers," "rosed lips," and cheeks "red as Titan's face" (2.4.31) to describe healthy red cheeks and beautiful lips, what vocabulary can we employ when we encounter someone to whom these images literally apply? If we praise the desirable female body as a series of detached body parts, what language can convey the tragedy of a female body which has lost its tongue and its hands? If we use the conventional images of red and white in such a case, we inappropriately turn an object of suffering into a thing of beauty; if we employ the traditional Petrarchan objectified itemization of the body, we risk turning sympathy into parody.

Titus Andronicus deals on many levels with the inadequacy of language. What words can possibly convey Titus's grief in the face of extreme suffering? Marcus's speech questions the appropriateness of literary conventions, challenging us to find a different poetic language for describing female beauty so that, when the need arises, we will have an appropriate language for responding to human suffering.[10]

Much Ado About Nothing (1598)

At the turn of the seventeenth century, Shakespeare was greatly concerned with the instability of language and the difficulty of interpretation. In *Julius Caesar* (1599) most of the characters wrestle with interpretation and mis-interpretation: "men may construe things after their fashion, / Clean from the purpose of the things themselves" (1.3.34–5). It is men's tendency to construe things after their fashion that the comic conspirators rely on in *Twelfth Night* (1601) when the arrogant steward, Malvolio, receives a forged letter addressed ambiguously to MOAI: "M.O.A.I. This simulation is not as the former; and yet, to crush this a little, it would bow to me, for every one of these letters are in my name" (2.5.139–41). Interpretation becomes a forced and violent act: "to *crush* this a little." Yet although Malvolio's eager reaction to the injunction that he "be not afraid of greatness" (2.5.144) exposes his social presumption, the encouragement is no different from Olivia's reassurance to Sebastian (whom she believes to be the servant Cesario): "Be that thou know'st thou art, and then thou art / As great as that thou fear'st" (5.1.149–50). Both social inferiors receive the same message; but how should Malvolio know to distrust and Sebastian to believe?

In *Much Ado* characters try to read texts and bodies. "This can be no trick: the conference was sadly borne," says Benedick (2.3.220–1) in the overhearing scene, interpreting the medium as well as the message, as earlier he has interpreted even the messenger: "I should think this a gull, but that the white-bearded fellow speaks it. Knavery cannot sure hide himself in such reverence" (2.3.118–20). Later he misreads Beatrice's body – "I do spy some marks of love in her" (2.3.245–6) – and as confidently misinterprets her dinner invitation: "'Against my will I am sent to bid you

---

[10]   For expanded analysis of this topic see Fawcett (1983).

come in to dinner' – there's a double meaning in that" (2.3.257–9). But language is full of double meanings, not all of which are intended by the speaker; the reader's interpretive responsibility is therefore considerable.

If language is unreliable, the interpreter must negotiate meaning by assessing appearance. When Leonato asks Antonio if the "strange news" he promises are "good" ("news" is a plural noun in Renaissance English), Antonio replies "they have a good cover; they show well outward" (1.2.7–8). But outward show has its own problems. In the church scene Claudio calls attention to Hero's maidenly blush:

> Would you not swear,
> All you that see her, that she were a maid,
> By these exterior shows? But she is none:
> She knows the heat of a luxurious bed;
> Her blush is guiltiness, not modesty. (4.1.38–42)

The Friar draws the opposite conclusion from Hero's "exterior shows":

> I have mark'd
> A thousand blushing apparitions
> To start into her face, a thousand innocent shames
> In angel whiteness beat away those blushes . . .
>   Call me a fool,
> Trust not my reading, nor my observations, . . .
> If this sweet lady lie not guiltless here. (4.1.158–61, 164–5, 169)

The Friar is as confident in his interpretation of signs as Claudio; both use the same evidence, but clearly one is wrong.

In this context the "nothing" of the play's title begins to appear multivalent. The consonantal digraph "th" was pronounced as "t" in words such as nothing (= noting). Much ado about *noting*? Noting means observing; it means overhearing; it means musical notation; it means slandering; and it means, as today, "nothing." All five meanings resonate in *Much Ado*, but each of these meanings, and the episodes they denote, has the capacity to go in contrary directions. Claudio's noting (observation) of Hero prompts him first to love and then to loathe. He "note[s] the daughter of Signior Leonato" as "the sweetest lady that ever I look'd on," and then notes her blush as guilt (1.1.162–3). Noting (overhearing) causes deception, both comically as in Beatrice and Benedick's love, and tragically as in the window episode in which Claudio overhears Borachio address the waiting-woman,

Margaret, as her mistress, Hero (Claudio's fiancée); but overhearing also undoes deception: the watch arrest the villains because they overhear Borachio confess to Conrade. Noting (musical notation) may indicate romance: "Because you talk of wooing, I will sing" (2.3.49); but it may be reduced to sheep's guts and dogs howling (2.3.59, 79–80). Noting (slandering) Beatrice leads to emotional truth as "honest slanders" (3.1.84) reveal Beatrice's love, but slandering Hero leads to near-tragedy (her dishonor and death). Noting (nothing) may indicate a trifle (2.3.57) or it may mean the destruction of identity, as in Claudio's attempt "to reduce [Hero] . . . to 'nothingness'" (Cerasano 1992: 173). Throughout, *Much Ado* pairs and parallels words and appearances to challenge our confidence in interpretation. Beatrice is accused of "fright[ing] the word out of his right sense" (5.2.55–6). But the play shows that words have no single "right" sense. They function, as they do in *Julius Caesar*, "as the event stamps them" (*Much Ado* 1.2.7).

Words in *Much Ado* have considerable somatic power. In the comic plot, Beatrice "speaks poniards, and every word stabs" (2.1.247–8); Benedick faces her "paper bullets of the brain" (2.3.240–1). In the main plot, language also inflicts wounds: "Thy slander hath gone through and through her heart," Hero's father, Leonato, tells Claudio (5.1.68). When Borachio confesses his evildoing, Don Pedro asks Claudio, "Runs not this speech like iron through your blood?"; Claudio responds, "I have drunk poison whiles he utter'd it" (5.1.244–6). War may be over but the military vocabulary shows that for as long as we are linguistic beings the world is unsafe.

All's Well that Ends Well (1604–5)

All's Well that Ends Well abounds with fairytale motifs. A young woman heals a king whose doctors have declared him beyond help. Helena's virginity, a state which in folklore facilitates miracles, is stressed. Having cured the King, Helena then passes a test and wins a husband, combining the standard folktale motifs of The Clever Wench and Fulfillment of an Impossible Task. Fairytale's speedy providential hand helps her along: she is pregnant after only one night's sexual encounter with Bertram (this is an alteration from the source story in Boccaccio's *Decameron*, which Shakespeare knew in an English translation, William Painter's *Palace of Pleasure*). But the fairytale motifs of *All's Well* are appliquéd onto a world of unremitting realism (see chapter 2, "Love and Madness").

The unsatisfactory character of Bertram is at the center of the play's realism, and, although excuses are made for him (he is young, he is misled by Parolles), he cannot be defended easily. Parolles is not responsible for Bertram's key peccadilloes – the rejection of Helena, the cowardly adieu, the lies about Helena's death, the improvised slanders about Diana's dishonor. "Bertram makes his own mistakes; Parolles merely supports them" (Parker 1984: 104). Susan Snyder relates Bertram's inadequacy to the inadequacy of language. In what follows I am indebted to Snyder's article (1992).

Language is clearly an issue in a play whose central comic scene depicts a mock language. The braggart Parolles is captured, blindfolded, and threatened with torture by his comrades who pretend to be foreigners. Unable to communicate, Parolles (whose name means "words") declares, "I shall lose my life for want of language" (4.1.70). This scene of linguistic failure is a substitute for a scene of silence which cannot be shown onstage, the scene in which Bertram beds Diana (as he thinks): "Remain there but an hour, nor speak to me" (4.2.58). The bedtrick is itself a scene of substitution, for in it Helena replaces Diana. The play is full of such substitutions and displacements (there are at least twelve), and our attention is repeatedly drawn to them. Act 5, scene 1, for example, has no plot function. Helen reaches Marseilles, expecting to find the King, only to be told by a Gentleman that "The King's not here" (5.1.22). Snyder points out (1992: 21) that this "King-is-absent scene" epitomizes the play: the gentleman is a substitute for the King, someone who points toward him; Helena thought she was at her destination but she has further to go.

Language, like the structure of *All's Well*, is a process of deferral and substitution. Any dictionary will demonstrate this. A word is a label (a signifier) for a concept (a signified), but it is clear that for every signifier we can have several signifieds: a *crib* is a manger, a baby's bed, the lining of a mine shaft, a card discarded in cribbage, plagiarism. Each of these signifieds is expressed as a signifier; and if you seek these new signifiers in the dictionary you encounter yet more signifieds. Thus language is a process of deferral, an endless chasing after meaning; but at the center is absence. The signified's not there; it's just another set of signifiers.

This linguistic insight of the early twentieth-century Swiss structuralist Ferdinand de Saussure (1857–1913) was developed by the French psychoanalyst Jacques Lacan (1901–81). Lacan's contribution was the observation that the unconscious is structured like a language. Because humans have both a conscious mind (whose contents we are aware of) and an unconscious mind (whose contents we cannot purposefully access), and because we know that what we are conscious of is only half the story, we are driven by desire: desire for the other, for fulfillment, for supplying the absence, for completion. For Lacan, then, language is "eternally stretching *forth towards the desire for something else*" (1977: 167, cited in Snyder 1992: 27, Lacan's emphasis); and since humans are constituted in language, the pattern of desire, of deferral, of displacement and substitution, of incompleteness, absence, lack of closure is built into life.

The application of this to *All's Well* is obvious, but it was not pointed out until Snyder's brilliant article in 1992. The plot of *All's Well* is structured in Lacanian–Saussurian terms: Helena is driven by desire; Bertram is a poor substitute for that desire's fulfillment. That is the rhythm of life. In the play's sobering dénouement, when Bertram recognizes and claims Helena as his wife, she protests that she is "the name and not the thing." Label and meaning do not match up. The process of deferral – the attempt to match the name with the thing – continues into the epilogue as the actor playing the King begs the audience to register its approval through applause, creating a "happy ending" which will enable the play to match its title: all's well that ends well.

5

Real Life:

Shakespeare and Suffering

"He's truly valiant that can wisely suffer
The worst" (*Timon* 3.5.31–2)

Introduction

"About suffering they were never wrong, / The Old Masters," wrote W. H. Auden (1966: 123). The Old Masters to whom he refers are the Dutch painters but his comment applies equally to Shakespeare, whose plays depict the range of human suffering. Some of the forms of deprivation and catastrophe are more typical of the sixteenth than the twenty-first century (shipwreck, for instance), but the categories of emotional blow depicted are, regrettably, timeless: loss of parents and children; pre- and postmarital problems; unrequited love; anger and revenge; political coups; civil war, foreign invasion and civic destruction; madness; family rupture. This chapter explores some of the more familiar arenas of suffering in twelve plays: death, family tensions, anger, and the solution to anger: forgiveness.

I begin, however, with genre. Section 1, "Mingled Yarns," examines three plays in which comedy competes with reality, fairytale competes with tragedy, and the threat of suffering is not always averted.

1   Mingled Yarns

"The web of our life is of a mingled yarn, good and ill together"
(*All's Well* 4.3.71–2)

Twelfth Night (1601)

Twelfth Night is often grouped with two other comedies written about the same time – *Much Ado* (1598) and *As You Like It* (1599–1600) – and the three are known collectively as the "mature" or "happy" comedies. The adjectives are not interchangeable, however. *Twelfth Night's* Illyria may sound like Elysium but the play's world is punctuated by hardship and threatened by revenge, rain, and vulnerability.

Act 5 brings to a head emotions which permeate the play: bitterness and vengeance. The humiliated steward, Malvolio, exits with the threat "I'll be reveng'd on the whole pack of you" (5.1.378), and his wrongs are insistently presented throughout the last two acts: "Never was man thus wrong'd"; "I say there was never man thus abus'd"; "there was never man so notoriously abus'd" (4.2.28, 46–7, 87–8). Released from imprisonment, he tells the Countess Olivia, "Madam, you have done me wrong, / Notorious wrong" (5.1.328–9), and she agrees, rebuking her household: "He hath been most notoriously abus'd" (5.1.379). When Donald Sinden read *Twelfth Night* in preparation for the RSC production in 1969, he telephoned his director, John Barton: "I am afraid you may have to recast Malvolio – I find him tragic" (Sinden 1989: 43). Barton had already come to the same conclusion. In act 5 Sinden's Malvolio fell to his knees and sobbed. "There is no fight left in Malvolio . . . the degradation is too great . . . there is but one thing for Malvolio – suicide" (Sinden 1989: 66). Or if not suicide, revenge. Malvolio's name – meaning ill-will (contrast the pacifist *Benvolio* of *Romeo and Juliet*)– suggests that letting bygones be bygones is not part of his make-up. One critic anticipates a sequel: *The Revenge of Malvolio*.

If Malvolio carries out his threatened revenge, he will prove no different from the characters in the subplot, Maria, Feste, and Fabian, all of whom nurse a grudge which is released in revenge. Fabian, who appears unannounced and from nowhere to participate in the gulling of Malvolio, explains his motive: "You know he brought me out o' favor with my lady about a bear-baiting here" (2.5.7–8). Olivia's waiting-woman, Maria, also views the trick on Malvolio as "revenge" for his general vices, which she enumerates (2.3.147–53). In act 5 the clown, Feste, taunts Malvolio:

> I was one, sir, in this enterlude . . . But do you remember? "Madam, why laugh you at such a barren rascal? And you smile not, he's gagg'd." And thus the whirligig of time brings in his revenges. (5.1.372–7)

Feste here throws back in Malvolio's face the words with which Malvolio had humiliated Feste in 1.5.83–8. Clearly Feste has been harboring a grievance for five acts – but when did a Shakespeare clown ever think in such a vengeful way? Not an idle diversion, the subplot's prank becomes motivated retaliation.

Feste's vengeance can be plausibly linked to his vulnerability (the two emotions are often symbiotic). Unusually for the Shakespearean world,

Feste is a freelance fool. He resides neither at Orsino's court nor at Olivia's. When Orsino requests "that old and antique song we heard last night," we are pointedly told, "He is not here . . . that should sing it" (2.4.3, 8–9). Act 1, scene 5 opens with Maria interrogating Feste about his absence from Olivia's court. In act 3 Feste tells Viola that he lives by the church. Trevor Peacock, who played Feste in the BBC film, notes the character's economic hardness: he requests money "in practically every scene" (Alexander 1979a: 26). The RSC production of 1994 underlined Feste's lack of job security. The stage cleared at 5.1.388 and the play appeared to be over; then Feste was flung out of doors like a cat being put out for the night, followed by his belongings. He sat on his upturned case to sing the concluding song, a song about life's hardship: "for the rain it raineth every day."

Reality's unpleasantness erupts in the last act when Olivia's parasitical uncle, Sir Toby, turns on his stooge, Sir Andrew. Both knights have suffered lacerations from Sebastian's sword. Sir Andrew offers to help Sir Toby off-stage to have their head wounds dressed together. Sir Toby no longer conceals his scorn: "Will *you* help? – an ass-head and a coxcomb and a knave, a thin-fac'd knave, a gull!" (5.1.206–7). Sir Andrew's reaction is unscripted. We know he has lost £2,000 to Sir Toby, and that Sebastian has put paid to his chances of winning Olivia; in the RSC production in 2001 Sir Andrew emerged from the door of Olivia's house during Feste's final song, hat and luggage in hand, and walked across the stage, leaving for good. The comic conclusion is neither inclusive nor conclusive.

One of the play's most unsettling acts of comic resistance comes in the bipartite nature of the trick played on Malvolio which tilts the subplot from comedy to cruelty. The tricksters' plan, as explained by Maria in act 2, scene 3, is to convince Malvolio that Olivia loves him and thus to "make him an ass" (2.3.169). This is achieved, and Malvolio exposed, in act 3, scene 4. What follows is otiose. Sir Toby proposes to extend the trick by having Malvolio "in a dark room and bound . . . We may carry it thus [keep it going], for our pleasure and his penance, till our very pastime, tir'd out of breath, prompt us to have mercy on him" (3.4.135–9). But the episode ceases to afford the conspirators "pleasure," nor does it end in "mercy." The darkroom trick treads a borderline between taunting and torture. Malvolio's pain, expressed with anguished clarity, removes any comedy the scene might have possessed. Furthermore, the gulling stops not because the conspirators take pity on the steward but because the trick has become inconvenient. Sir Toby laments, "I would we were well rid of this knavery. If he may be conveniently deliver'd, I would he were, for I am now so far in offense with my niece that I cannot pursue with any safety this sport t'the upshot" (4.2.67–71). He speaks from ennui not empathy; the conspirators have overreached themselves.

If the second half of the trick is excessive, it is because *Twelfth Night* is peopled by characters who behave excessively. At one extreme we have Sir Toby's excessive revelry (in a house of mourning!); at the other extreme we have the excessive devotion of Orsino and Olivia, the former to Petrarchan adoration, the latter to mourning. One extreme exposes the other. Sir Toby's first line, "What a plague means my niece to take the death of her brother thus?" (1.3.1–2) – where "thus" in production often indicates an elaborate funeral procession or memorial rite – makes a valid point. (Productions creatively indicate the disabling nature of such egregious responses. In the Shenandoah Shakespeare Express production of 1992 Orsino had a page whose sole function was to walk backwards in front of him, bearing a portrait of Olivia for Orsino to gaze at in adoration. In the Shakespeare Theatre Company production in Washington, DC, in 1998–9 Olivia was so prostrate with grief that she had to be carried everywhere by a footman.) But Sir Toby's inebriation is as self-indulgent as Olivia's grief. Malvolio's self-love, which he indulges in practicing postures to his shadow, is as excessive as Orsino's melancholy, which he indulges with music: "give me excess of it" (1.1.2).

Excess characterizes the feast which gives the play its title: twelfth night. The feast of the epiphany (January 6) legitimized temporary riot. In Elizabeth's court and in large private households, a Lord of Misrule, appointed to oversee Christmas celebrations, organized an exuberant festive finale with masques, fancy-dress plays, music, dancing, banqueting. Hierarchy was inverted with the election of a mock king (Laroque 1991: 153), and the atmosphere resembled the revels of *Antony and Cleopatra* – "Let's have one other gaudy night. . . . / Let's mock the midnight bell" (3.13.182, 184). However, the problem with feasts that celebrate the end of feasting is their conflicted ambience: one more party and then, thank God, we can get back to work (Berry 1972: 196; 1988: 68). In *Twelfth Night* exuberance is at odds with endurance. This so-called "happy comedy" pulls in two directions.

Twelfth Night is a play about pain: the pain of loss, of love, of life. It was written at the same time as *Hamlet*, and, like *Hamlet*, begins with a character in excessive grief (see below). The darker vision of the tragedies (in which the catastrophe is caused by excess) begins to make itself felt in *Twelfth Night*.

King Lear (1605–6)

Like *Twelfth Night*, *King Lear* is a play of excess: it is as if Shakespeare thought of every painful thing that one human being could do to another. The play depicts injustice, ingratitude, misjudgment, misunderstanding, gratuitous violence. The play is an endurance test of our emotions.

It is surprising that a realistic play about suffering should begin as a fairytale. Referring to the love-test of act 1, scene 1, Coleridge wrote: "the play is based on a gross improbability. Nursery stories [fairytales] are not fit subjects for tragedy" (Bate 1992: 389). Several fairytales have plots very close to that of *Lear*. In one, the royal father stages a love-test in which his favorite daughter tells him, "I love you as much as salt." Insulted by this analogy, the king banishes the princess. After a period of absence she returns in disguise to seek employment in the palace kitchen; when a large banquet is ordered, she prepares a salt-free menu. The king realizes, belatedly, the value of his daughter's analogy, the princess reveals her identity, and father and daughter are reconciled.

Shakespeare invokes fairytale structures in *Pericles*, *Cymbeline*, and *Winter's Tale*. Pericles loses his baby daughter, Marina, who, as a teenager, is captured by pirates and sold to a brothel, but survives, virtue intact, to meet and regenerate her aged father. In *Cymbeline* the princes are stolen from their nursery in infancy, brought up in a cave, and later reunited with their father and sister. In *Winter's Tale* (whose very title leads us to expect the conventions of children's stories) the baby Perdita is abandoned, rescued, and raised by a shepherd, and reunited with her parents when she is of marriageable age. The narrative pattern of fairytales is invariable: the good character is undervalued; ignored or banished; passes a test or tests; marries the hero/heroine; and they all live happily ever after.

King Lear initially follows these rules. The good sister is manipulated by her bad sisters, misjudged by her father, rejected emotionally, is exiled. Lest we be in any doubt about the deliberate nature of this fairytale structure, Shakespeare repeats it. The subplot, unusually for Shakespeare, duplicates the main plot: the good brother is maligned by his bad brother, misjudged by his father, rejected emotionally, exiles himself. The exposition creates such a strong expectation of a conventional happy ending that the Restoration playwright Nahum Tate (1652–1715) wrote a version in which Cordelia lives and marries Edgar. Audiences loved it: Tate's version, rather than Shakespeare's, was the only version performed between 1687 and 1838 because a happy ending is what the fairytale structure conditions us to expect.

But *King Lear* is a fairytale gone wrong. As James Hirsch points out, the first act sets up expectations only to thwart them. In what follows I am indebted to Hirsch's analysis.

Expositions are crucial in drama: they "give us our bearings, . . . let us know who's who and what's what and especially whom to root for and whom against" (Hirsch 1986: 86). In *Lear* we first encounter an old man, Gloucester, speaking to a courtier, Kent, about Gloucester's illegitimate son, Edmund. Edmund is present, but Gloucester insensitively talks about him as if he were not, indulging in cavalier sexual allusion: "Though this knave came something saucily to the world before he was sent for, yet was his mother fair, there was good sport at his making, and the whoreson must be acknowledg'd" (1.1.21–4). The audience, responding to the playwright's clear signals, sympathizes with the slighted Edmund and feels critical of the insensitive Gloucester. Later in the scene our judgment is reinforced by an action replay: another elderly man behaves autocratically and treats his children ill-advisedly. Since the old men, whom we are so clearly directed to condemn, become victims, the exposition is a narrative failure – unless Shakespeare's aim was "to demonstrate the fallibility of human perceptions and judgements . . . by dramatizing our similar fallibility" (Hirsch 1986: 87). We can hardly condemn Lear for his inability to "see better" when we are guilty of the same fault.

The play, as Hirsch observes, continues this pattern of expectation and frustration. In act 5 Cordelia and Lear are reunited; then Cordelia is killed. (The injustice of this moment has outraged almost all critics of the play.) The play consistently denies us the patterns it deliberately encourages us to expect: patterns of genre, of plot, of justice. This cannot be a design fault, for in 1606 Shakespeare was a mature and experienced playwright, fully capable of correcting careless red herrings. The play overturns our belief that "the gods are just" (5.3.171), that events are predictable, and that life has order (Hirsch 1986: 90). And it does this by forcing us to experience what the characters do. There is nothing improbable (pace Coleridge) about this pattern. By frustrating our expectations, art holds the mirror up to nature in the most realistic and painful way possible.

Much Ado About Nothing (1598)

Productions of *Much Ado About Nothing* usually celebrate the play's romantic potential. One thinks of the sun-drenched Messina of Gregory Doran's

RSC production in 2002, a world of village cafés and town squares, or of Branagh's film (1993) whose opening frames' frenzied domesticity – villa spring-cleaning and the airing of bedlinen – is juxtaposed with a photo-quote from *The Magnificent Seven* as the returning soldiers gallop across the Tuscan countryside to encounter a household of women ready for romantic excitement. But the play criticizes and rejects romantic love as unrealistic, based on appearance and linguistic obfuscation.

Much Ado avoids the staples of Shakespearean romance: a green world, disguise, lyricism. Messina is neither a real world (Don John's rebellion is downplayed) nor a green world; disguise is employed for entertainment or mischief, not for self-protection and self-discovery; and the play is conducted principally in prose.

The play, like *Twelfth Night*, stresses love's pain. "For which of my good parts did you suffer love for me?" asks Beatrice playfully in act 5. "Suffer love! a good epithite! I do suffer love indeed," responds Benedick (5.2.64–7). But the exaggerated verb reminds us of the play's real suffer-ings. Beatrice and Benedick appear to have been romantically involved at some stage in the play's prehistory (2.1.278–81), and one detects in Beatrice's antimarriage wit something of the bitter defensiveness of Katherine in *The Shrew*, who denies interest in marriage to suitors who have denied interest in her (1.1.59–65). *Much Ado*'s only love song advises women to "let them [men] go . . . converting all your sounds of woe / Into hey nonny nonny" (2.3.66–9). In this world, words stab, love hurts, "men were deceivers ever" (2.3.63).

These issues are expressed seriously in the church scene in 4.1, when, having volunteered to do anything for Beatrice, Benedick declines to kill Claudio. Beatrice is prompted to exit by his refusal, telling Benedick "there is no love in you" (4.1.293–4). Her personal grievance turns to generaliza-tion: "manhood is melted into cur'sies, valor into compliment, and men are only turn'd into tongue, and trim ones too. He is now as valiant as Hercules that only tells a lie, and swears it" (4.1.319–22). Maggie Steed, who played Beatrice in the 1988 RSC production, saw in this speech "the under-side of her [Beatrice's] jokes throughout the play: about men being made of clay" (Steed 1993: 50).

And men in this play are made of clay. They are a "band of brothers," united in bachelor banter. They joke about infidelity, and indulge in sexual slang (1.1.241–2). This kind of group is usually threatened by the defec-tion of one of its members to matrimony (one thinks of the tension felt by Antonio in *Merchant of Venice* or by Mercutio in *Romeo and Juliet* when

Bassanio and Romeo turn lover); but Claudio's wooing of Hero is not disruptive, perhaps because his affection is superficial (based on Hero's inheritance and looks), perhaps because it does not alter his behavioral patterns – he still participates in what Mangan (1996: 180) calls the "blokeish camaraderie" of the bachelors. If anything, his continued mistrust of the female species, which makes him all too ready to believe in Hero's betrayal and to deny any responsibility for Hero's death (5.1.72), binds him closer to his friend and patron Don Pedro in the church scene, and neither behaves differently in the last act from the first: when we meet them in 5.1 they are seeking Benedick to divert them with his wit (Mangan 1996: 198–9). Theirs is a life lived on the surface. Their libertine jokes come from a tradition "in which women can be seen as predatory" (Mangan 1996: 183), yet their attitude fails to take account of the fact that Beatrice is as misandronist as they are misogynist: she will not marry "till God make men of some other mettle than earth. Would it not grieve a woman to be overmaster'd with a piece of valiant dust?" (2.1.59–61). Socially, she is one of the boys: when Margaret goes to seek her for the orchard trick we are told that she is in the parlor talking with Don Pedro and Claudio (3.1.1–3). As Maggie Steed observes (1993: 46), this Shakespeare heroine is "not sewing in her closet."

The division of worlds in *Much Ado* is not the conventional division of comic structure (real world/green world) but of gender: male world/female world. The masculine world is geographically disparate – Don Pedro is from Arragon, Claudio from Florence, Benedick from Padua – but it is unified by its maleness. In the slander scene in the church in act 4, Benedick detaches himself from this world, transferring his allegiance to the world of women. It is a key moment. Don Pedro, Don John, and Claudio exit at 4.1.111: "Come, let us go," says Don John and presumably the three men do so: they have no further lines. Benedick immediately inquires about Hero's well-being: "How doth the lady?" Leonato rages against his daughter but Benedick restrains him ("Sir, sir, be patient") as he reflects on events ("I am so attir'd in wonder, / I know not what to say"). He begins to gather evidence ("Lady, were you her bedfellow last night?") and to reassign blame ("If their wisdoms be misled in this, / The practice of it lives in John the Bastard"). He listens to and agrees with the Friar's plan to conceal Hero through "death" (4.1.214–30), reassuring Leonato that despite his close friendship – his "inwardness and love" – with Claudio and Don Pedro, he will help in the plan to rehabilitate Hero. The boundary lines of allegiance have been redrawn.

The bride's family and attendants exit, but Benedick chooses once again to move further from the world of men, remaining on stage to comfort Beatrice. This he does by taking Hero's part: "Surely I do believe your fair cousin is wrong'd" (4.1.259–60). His belief is based solely on female testimony, the denials of Hero and Beatrice. The significance of the entire scene is seen in the solemn three-line exchange with which it concludes:

> *Benedick*:   Think you in your soul the Count Claudio hath wrong'd Hero?
> *Beatrice*:   Yea, as sure as I have a thought or a soul.
> *Benedick*:   Enough, I am engag'd. (4.1.328–31)

A play which began with two worlds (male, female) ends with the same two worlds; however, one of the men has changed sides.

Gregory Doran's RSC production (2002) blunted this point. Benedick exited with Leonato et al. at line 254, returning only to retrieve his helmet which he had left beneath his seat; encountering the weeping Beatrice, he was forced to resume conversation. While this exit and reentrance made sense of the time scheme implied in Benedick's question, "Lady Beatrice, have you wept all this while?" (line 255), the chance conversation reduced the deliberateness and enormity of his decision to support the women's viewpoint. There was little difference between this genuinely chance encounter and the deliberate chance overhearings – and this may have been Doran's somber point, given the play's statement that loving "goes by haps" (3.1.105).

Certainly the conclusion reintroduces the theme of arbitrariness – "man is a giddy thing, and this is my conclusion" (5.4.108–9) – and one last cuckold joke is indulged: "there is no staff more reverent than one tipp'd with horn" (5.4.123–4). Reality reasserts itself.

2   Mourning

"remember me" (*Hamlet* 1.5.91)

Introduction

"Most great plays are about the two greatest obstacles to human happiness," writes Gary Taylor, provocatively: "death (of which there is always too much) and sex (of which there is never enough)" (1996: 57). The second half of Taylor's paradigm does not apply to Shakespeare (unless we substitute "love" for "sex," in which case it describes Shakespearean tragedy); but the first half aptly summarizes the entire canon. "But kings and mightiest potentates must die, / For that's the end of human misery," says Talbot in *1 Henry* VI 3.2.136–7. *Two Noble Kinsmen* recasts the same sentiment in a spatial metaphor: "This world's a city full of straying streets, / And death's the market-place where each one meets" (1.5.15–16).

It is a quintessentially Greek *topos*. Innumerable Greek tragedies end with the sobering admonition to count no man happy until he is dead, a theme articulated at the beginning of *Richard II*. "Though death be poor, it ends a mortal woe," says York (2.1.152), and Richard II reaches the same conclusion in act 5: "Nor I, nor any man that but man is, / With nothing shall be pleas'd, till he be eas'd / With being nothing" (5.5.39–41).

The felicity of death leads to the frequent Elizabethan pun on "well," which functions both as an adjective meaning "in a state of good fortune, welfare, or happiness" (*OED* a.1) and as a euphemism for "dead." When the messenger tells Cleopatra that the absent Antony is well, her feelings of reassurance turn quickly to suspicion: "we use / To say the dead are well" (*A&C* 2.5.32–3). When Rosse brings news of the slaughter of Macduff's family in Macbeth, the euphemism enables him to prevaricate:

Macduff:	How does my wife?
Rosse:	Why, well.
Macduff:	And all my children?
Rosse:	Well too.
Macduff:	The tyrant has not batter'd at their peace?
Rosse:	No, they were well at peace when I did leave 'em. (*Macbeth* 4.3.176–9)

In *Romeo and Juliet* Balthasar is quicker to reveal ill news. Romeo questions him, "How doth my Juliet? That I ask again, / For nothing can be ill if she be well." Balthasar replies: "Then she is well and nothing can be ill: / Her body sleeps in Capel's monument" (5.1.17–18).

It is often alleged that high mortality rates inured Elizabethans to death: repetition either insulated them against loss or prevented them from forming strong attachments to likely objects of early death, such as children, in the first place. Renaissance literature provides no evidence to support this view. The anguish in Ben Jonson's two poems on the deaths of his six-month-old daughter and seven-year-old son, the distraction of Kyd's Hieronimo on the murder of his son in *The Spanish Tragedy*, and the grief of Constance in *King John* on the death of her son, Arthur, are recognizable emotions from the age of the nuclear family. Nor does the reverse bereavement – a child's loss of a parent – seem any more detached. Hamlet has as much difficulty in accepting the death of his father (even before he knows of his murder) as any university student in the twenty-first century. This play provides an extended examination of death and grief, with transhistorical emotions about death embedded in a localized Reformation crisis about rituals of mourning.

Hamlet (1600–1); *Twelfth Night* (1601)

Life has 100 percent mortality. This is the message Claudius gives Hamlet at their first meeting in the play:

> 'Tis sweet and commendable in your nature, Hamlet,
> To give these mourning duties to your father.
> But you must know your father lost a father,
> That father lost, lost his, and the survivor bound
> In filial obligation for some term
> To do obsequious sorrow. But to persever
> In obstinate condolement is a course
> Of impious stubbornness, . . .
>   Fie, 'tis a fault to heaven,
> A fault against the dead, a fault to nature
> To reason most absurd, whose common theme
> Is death of fathers. (1.2.87–94, 101–4)

The speech begins with patient understanding, but its commonsense message is insistently reiterated: there is nothing unnatural about death; the "common theme" of life is "death of fathers." Four months after his father's death, Hamlet is not yet in a position to accept death's place in the life cycle. His reactions – protracted mourning, morbid thoughts, inability to function or act decisively, anger at those such as his mother who have resumed normal life – are those of a person in the early stages of grief. His historical location in a world in which death is familiar (be it seventeenth-century England or twelfth-century Denmark) seems irrelevant: for him death is a shock.

He is not alone in his view that death is unnatural. Horatio describes Julius Caesar's death as accompanied by a plethora of unnatural phenomena: skeletons and ghosts "squeak and gibber in the Roman streets"; there are fiery stars, dews of blood, ominous activity in the sun, an eclipse

(1.1.114–20). The images cannot be attributed solely to assassination, for in act 5, a much calmer Hamlet uses Caesar as an example of the blunt reality in which all men, even kings and emperors, die: "Imperious Caesar, dead and turn'd to clay, / Might stop a hole to keep the wind away" (5.1.213–14). The two references to Caesar frame the play, with the second image of natural mortality providing a corrective to the first supernatural image.[1]

Acts 1 and 5 are further linked by images of death. An unnatural example of death – the intangible Ghost – is followed by a natural example – the material skull of Yorick (Maslen 1983: 10–12; Frye 1979; Garber 1981). Hamlet's agitated reaction to the first revenant contrasts with his acceptance of the second. Yorick's skull prompts meditations on the material (Hamlet questions the gravedigger about rates of decomposition, and comments on the skull's smell), but there is nothing hysterical or unhealthy about the conversation (Maslen 1983: 11). On the contrary: it concludes with Hamlet's blunt summary of man's journey to dust – "Alexander died, Alexander was buried, Alexander returneth to dust" (5.1.208–10). In the next scene, Hamlet assures Horatio that "death is certain" (as Justice Shallow puts it): "If it be now, 'tis not to come; if it be not to come, it will be now; if it be not now, yet it will come" (*Hamlet* 5.2.220–2). The tone throughout act 5 is that of a man who has come to accept death's place in the natural order.

The process of dealing with death is complicated by (and initially distorted by) memory. If *Hamlet* is a play about grief, it is also a play about memory, and the two are linked. The link is not as transhistorical as it seems. With its erasure of Catholic burial rites – of candles and wakes and ritual prayers and requiem masses – the Reformation swept away formal outlets for grief, leaving Protestants alone with their memories (Neill 1997: 244–6).

The play begins with memory in its strongest, and most disabling, form, an inability to forget: Hamlet sees his father in his mind's eye, contrasts his perfections with Claudius's vices, and dwells obsessively on his mother's remarriage. Bereavement and memory are obviously linked: "Heaven and earth, / Must I remember?" asks Hamlet in anguish (1.2.142–3). But memory, like mourning, is not a relentless reinforcer of absence, as

---

[1]   Horatio's description of the Roman portents appears in the Quarto text of 1604–5 but not in the Folio of 1623. The 1604–5 Quarto seems to be based on Shakespeare's manuscript, containing the play as he originally wrote it, the Folio on a version subsequently cut for performance.

Hamlet's rhetorical question here implies. Memory involves both absence and renewal, for it fills the void which it symbiotically creates. Thus, in the *Confessions* the fourth-century Bishop Augustine depicts his tears of bereavement as occupying the space of his friend: "Tears alone were sweet to me, for in my heart's desire they had taken the place of my dearest friend" (Augustine 1961: 76). In *King John* Constance expands Augustine's point. She defends her right to grieve, explaining the emotion's psychological function:

> Grief fills the room up of my absent child,
> Lies in his bed, walks up and down with me,
> Puts on his pretty looks, repeats his words,
> Remembers me of all his gracious parts,
> Stuffs out his vacant garments with his form;
> Then, have I reason to be fond of grief? (*KJ* 3.4.93–8)

Alexander Leggatt notes the same phenomenon in *Richard II*. When Leggatt observes that grief is "the only reality [Richard] has" (1988: 70), he means, *à l'*Augustine, that grief fills a void.

Grief is an emotion (or a myriad of emotions); mourning is an action. In *Titus Andronicus* Marcus views the static dumbshow of his bereaved family, "Even like a stony image, cold and numb," and tells Titus, "Now is a time to storm, why art thou still?" (3.1.258, 263). Mourning demands action, and in this it differs from grief; it is the *performance* of grief. Grief is internal – "I have that within which passes show, / These but the trappings and the suits of woe," declares Hamlet (1.2.85–6), distinguishing the costumed ritual of mourning from the internal grief it denotes. But if mourning is performative, Hamlet's grief cannot be expressed, for it is the performative which Hamlet mistrusts: inky cloaks, sighs, tears, dejected visage, "together with all forms, moods, shapes of grief, / ... / These ... are actions that a man might play" (1.2.82–4).

Shakespeare's plays are full of characters damaged by an inability to express grief (an inability caused externally by circumstance or internally by self). Actors are quick to pick up on this. Nicholas Woodeson points out that King John is given but one line to react to his mother's death. "My mother dead!" is John's only soliloquy (4.2.181) – three words. Any potential for expansion is prevented by the arrival of Hubert, and the angry tongue-lashing John gives him is clearly a displacement activity (Woodeson 1993: 91). David Troughton notes something similar in *Richard III*. "When speaking of his late father," Richard III becomes "comparatively lyrical" (Troughton 1998: 86). Troughton concludes that "Here is a man still mourning his father's death" (ibid.: 87). Richard's suppressed grief contrasts with the emotions of the three mothers in the play who exist primarily as mourners (Loraux 1998: 6; and see Brown 1998: 109 for a brilliant analysis of the different mourning modes of the three queens). Women in the histories can express what the men cannot. It is no coincidence then that in *Macbeth*, a tragedy which examines what it is to be a man, the bereaved Macduff, like the earlier Constance, defends his need to express grief: "I must also feel it as a man" (4.3.221). Malcolm encourages him: "Give sorrow words. The grief that does not speak / Whispers the o'er-fraught heart, and bids it break" (4.3.209–10).

Unlike Macduff, Hamlet cannot experience the cathartic performance of grief because he rejects mourning's theatrical aspect as insincere. The genuineness of the player's performance of Pyrrhus's grief in act 2 thus takes him by surprise. The actor's performance is no different from the mourner's performance; indeed, the tears, distraction, and broken voice of the mourner and the player are described *identically* (see 1.2.77–86 and 2.2.551–7). Hamlet thus encounters a dilemma. He is an actor who loves theater because it holds a mirror up to nature; he is a bereaved son who rejects the trappings of mourning as insincere. Yet the two are the same. Mourning is performance. And performance, as the entire Shakespeare canon reiterates, is an expression of nature, not a violation of it.

Hamlet begins to appreciate the symbiosis of mourning and theater in the Player's speech in act 2, but Denmark impedes his recovery because the rituals of mourning are truncated. The mourning period for Hamlet Senior is terminated by Gertrude's "o'er hasty marriage." Polonius has an "obscure funeral – / No trophy, sword, nor hatchment o'er his bones, / No noble rite nor formal ostentation" (4.5.214–16). Ophelia is denied full Christian burial. The play's children – Hamlet, Ophelia, and Laertes – wander through the play suffering a grief that is denied the ritual outlet of full mourning. This is a newly Protestant predicament. The characters are driven to find alternative forms of expression for their grief. For Hamlet and Laertes, revenge takes the place of mourning; for Ophelia, madness. Revenge and madness can both be performed when mourning cannot.

If mourning is maimed, so is its associated entity, theater: *The Mousetrap, or the Murder of Gonzago* is as truncated as the play's funeral rites. Drama, like grief, requires performance, for an interrupted play is as emotionally destabilizing as an incomplete mourning. The theatrical nature of the vocabulary in 5.2, as Hamlet and Horatio gaze at the court "*mutes* or *audience* to this act," leads to instructions for staging Hamlet's funeral: "let this same be presently *perform'd* / . . . Lest more mischance / On *plots* and errors happen. / . . . Bear Hamlet like a soldier . . . to the *stage*" (5.2.335, 393–4, 396). The first complete performance in the play is about to take place; mourning and theater finally coalesce.

Hamlet is a play about bereavement, about the interplay of death, memory, and performance. With this nexus in mind we might now return to the Ghost's plea for remembrance in act 1. "Remember me" are his last words before he returns to purgatory. But what does it mean to "remember me" in *Hamlet?*

Hamlet receives the instruction as a call to action, a not unreasonable interpretation given the Ghost's subsequent explicitness: "If thou didst ever thy dear father love – / . . . Revenge his foul and most unnatural murther" (1.5.23–5). However revenge leads ineluctably to inaction, because, as Harold Jenkins points out, if avenging one man means killing another, it is an action which a noble soul might naturally resist (Jenkins 1982: 144). Furthermore, the play's concentric circles of revenge (Hamlet's revenge action causes the murder of Polonius, thus inciting Laertes to avenge his father . . .) show that revenge achieves nothing: a second revenge action arises in response to the first (Frye 1986: 90).

"Remember me" might more usefully function as a verbal *memento mori*, a reminder to value the living and to seize the day, two actions which Claudius has already demonstrated so efficiently and which outrage Hamlet excessively. And here is the heart of Hamlet's problem, a problem typical of those in grief. Hamlet's outrage at the apparent fickleness of his mother, Claudius, and the Danish populace (who adored Hamlet Senior but now pay extravagant sums for portraits of Claudius) is a single outrage: it is outrage at those who have chosen the living over the dead, and the present over the past.

Denmark has decided that life must go on, but Hamlet is trapped in memory. His memory is the kind specific to the early stages of grief – idealization. He sees in his father Hyperion and casts Claudius as the satyr. This extreme bifurcation flies in the face of the evidence, for the Ghost refers to his "sins" and "imperfections" and, if we except his regicide, Claudius can, in production, seem every inch the statesman, as in Patrick Stewart's patient diplomat in the BBC film. Hamlet divides his world into good versus bad, genuine versus false, but the tension is actually dead versus alive. He believes that to cease mourning means to cease grieving, that to stop remembering means, in effect, to forget. (Branagh's film of *Hamlet* begins tellingly with workmen dismantling a statue of King Hamlet at the gates of Elsinore.) Hamlet's emotional journey, and the play's thematic journey, is how to negotiate these binaries of good/bad, genuine/false, dead/alive, how to control memory and how to cope with death.

Olivia makes the same journey in *Twelfth Night*, written at the same time as *Hamlet*. She begins with a grief even more socially disabling than Hamlet's: she has vowed to cloister herself for seven years, wear a veil, remain indoors, and cry daily, all "to season / A brother's dead love, which she would keep fresh / And lasting in her sad remembrance" (1.1.29–31). Olivia's excessive grief is quickly exposed by Feste:

> *Clown*:   Good madonna, why mourn'st thou?
> *Olivia*:   Good fool, for my brother's death.
> *Clown*:   I think his soul is in hell, madonna.
> *Olivia*:   I know his soul is in heaven, fool.
> *Clown*:   The more fool, Madonna, to mourn for your brother's soul, being
> in heaven. Take away the fool, gentlemen. (1.5.66–72)

It is one of the functions of Shakespearean fools to bring their masters/mistresses back to reality, or to attempt to do so. But there is no fool in *Hamlet*, or at least, no live fool. In a brilliant article Elizabeth Maslen reminds us of Yorick's occupation – court jester – and points out that, like the typical Shakespeare fool, Yorick offers "a balanced/balancing view, trying to restore the moral norm. In this play the function could only be served by a *dead* fool" (Maslen 1983: 12). After the encounter with Yorick in act 5, Hamlet's hysteria subsides and he talks acceptingly of death.

Shakespeare's father died in 1601; the death of fathers is prominent in Shakespeare's writing in 1600–1. As Ben Morgan observes,[2] in *Twelfth Night* the moment of recognition between Viola and Sebastian is anchored in the death of their father, for the death of Sebastian père verifies the twins' identity:

> *Viola*:   Sebastian was my father, . . .
> And died that day when Viola from her birth
> Had numb'red thirteen years.

---

[2]   I am indebted to Ben Morgan for an unpublished essay, and subsequent discussion, which prompted this section.

> *Sebastian:*   O, that record is lively in my soul!
> He finished indeed his mortal act
> That day that made my sister thirteen years. (5.1.232, 244–8)

Finding each other again, the twins in fact "find the body of their father, whose name, appearance and death they describe" (Morgan n.p.).

Much has been made of the tantalizing link between the death of Shakespeare's son, Hamnet, in 1596 and the writing of *Hamlet* in 1601. In exploring grief in *Hamlet* we should remember that Hamnet was not just a dead son but a dead twin. Twins in Shakespeare are associated with shipwreck, separation, bereavement (the Antipholi, the Dromios, Viola and Sebastian), and they provide a convenient dramatic shorthand for the psychological mechanisms of grief. In his essay on mourning and melancholia, Freud describes how, in extended grief, mourners cannot separate themselves from the lost object. They incorporate the lost person into their sense of self, embracing the dead object in an attempt to redeem the loss. Freud's classic explanation of grief may underlie the interpretation of W. W. Greg who viewed the Ghost in *Hamlet* as a figment of Hamlet's imagination. It may also have influenced the famous Royal Court production of *Hamlet* in 1969 in which the Ghost spoke from the prince's body. Reviewers made much of the fact that Nicol Williamson, who played Hamlet, had recently lost his father. As Ben Morgan points out, when Viola volunteers her own story of love and loss, she opens with a narrative about her father rather than about herself: "My father had a daughter lov'd a man" (2.4.107). Her identity has become inseparable from that of father and brother, both of whom merge in her speech: "Sebastian was my father, / Such a Sebastian was my brother too" (5.1.232–3).

John Caird notes that the scene in which Viola decides to dress as a eunuch shows her assimilating the news of Sebastian's death and deciding to dress as her brother. "There's something deep in the psychology of a twin, when the other twin dies, which would make her want to keep that twin alive by acting out his life as well as her own" (Caird in Billington 1990: 40). The psychology is not, as it happens, confined to twins although they provide a striking visual illustration of it. In Shakespeare grieving twins are mistaken for each other not because (or not just because) they are twins but because the mourners temporarily incorporate the lost one in themselves. "I am all the daughters of my father's house, / And all the brothers too," says Viola (2.4.120–1). When Sebastian is restored to Viola in act 5, his return marks the conclusion of her mourning (Morgan n.p.).

It also marks the conclusion of her cross-dressing: as John Caird observes, "The brother turns up, which means she doesn't have to be a boy any more" (Caird in Billington 1990: 40).

3   The Family

"the appalling dangers of family life" (Huxley 1969: 30)

Introduction

It might seem a bitter joke to include a section on the family in a chapter on suffering. But no one, least of all Shakespeare, ever pretended that family life was pain-free.

Sometimes the pain stems from loss or absence (see section 2, "Mourning"). Loss often has legal as well as emotional repercussions. In *Midsummer Night's Dream* the Indian boy becomes the center of a custody battle between Titania and Oberon (Dubrow 1999: 144–6). The death of Bertram's father in *All's Well that Ends Well* breaks up the family as the underage Bertram is sent to Paris to be a ward of court. In *Merchant of Venice* the death of Portia's father ties her to a marriage by lottery.

But matrimonial restrictions exist even without a parent's death. If Portia cannot marry without the approval of her dead father, Hermia cannot marry without the approval of her living father. (For good discussions of marriage negotiations see Cressy 1997: 233–376 and Cook 1991). Whether Hermia ever gains this approval is a moot point. Egeus is absent from the nuptial celebrations in the first Quarto text (1600), but is assigned all the speeches given to Philostrate, the court master of the revels, in the Folio text (1623). His Folio speech prefixes may indicate no more than that the actor who played Egeus doubled as Philostrate. Productions regularly qualify Hermia's nuptial happiness in act 5, like that of Jessica in *Merchant of Venice*, by stressing her awareness of the absent father.

Some family tensions seem to be timeless. Volumnia lives vicariously through her son's achievements in *Coriolanus*; Hal rebels against his father in *Henry IV*; Richard II is "the disappointing son of a brilliant father" (Leggatt 1988: 57). In *All's Well* people compare Bertram to his dead father and hope he has inherited his father's good qualities (Parker 1984: 101); these well-meaning statements inevitably irritate a young man trying to assert his independence, and their stochastic phrasing inadvertently tips optative compliment toward insulting skepticism.

Broken families often function metaphorically to indicate disruption in the state. The internecine feuds of the Wars of the Roses reach a despairing climax in two symbolic stage directions in *3 Henry VI*:

> . Enter a SON that hath kill'd his father, at one door, dragging in the dead body.
> Enter a FATHER that hath kill'd his son, at another door, bearing of his son.
> (2.5.54 SD, 78 SD)

The grief when the anonymous son and the anonymous father independently discover the identity of the corpses they bear is underlined by Henry VI's vicarious sorrow. The three characters, separate on stage and unknown to each other, are united in anaphoric lament:

> *Son*:   Was ever son so ru'd a father's death?
> *Father*:   Was ever father so bemoan'd his son?
> *King Henry*:   Was ever king so griev'd for subjects' woe? (2.5.109–11)

This accidental sundering of kinship replays tragically the comic scene in *1 Henry VI* when Joan La Pucelle repudiates her father (5.4). Joan's unnatural behavior indicates her villainy (contrast the sequence of three scenes where the Talbots, father and son, vie to demonstrate their loyalty to each other in *1 Henry VI* 4.5, 4.6, 4.7); but it also prefigures the way that war – and, later in the tetralogy, civil war – tears at the fabric of society.

Lack of maternal love is a problem for Richard of Gloucester in *Richard III*. He tells us that "love foreswore me in my mother's womb" (*3HVI* 3.2.153), a statement which provides a cue for actors and critics. David Troughton's Richard III evinced pain in the presence of his mother. His defensiveness in the face of continual rejection (his mother omits to bless him) inflected two-word utterances such as "my mother" with such compressed history that they guaranteed audience laughter (Troughton 1998: 91). Michael Neill explains, "Richard cannot know himself because he cannot love himself, and he cannot love himself because he has never been loved" (1988: 21). If one adds to Richard's vulnerability his recent bereavement (he is very much affected by the Duke of York's murder; Troughton 1998: 87), it is clear that he is unlikely to exit the moral maze in which he describes his confused self in *3 Henry VI*.

If maternal love creates problems in *Richard III*, paternal love precipitates tragedy in *King Lear*. The mother whose funeral has just taken place at the start of the source play, *King Leir* (1605), is conspicuously absent from Shakespeare's play. Mothers appear rarely in Shakespeare drama, probably in part because of casting requirements (the need for another boy actor). But the mother does not even get a mention in *King Lear* (contrast Jane Smiley's novel, *A Thousand Acres*, an updated version of *King Lear*, in which the daughters frequently discuss the mother and her death from breast cancer). The emphasis in *Lear* is firmly on the father–daughter relationship. This relationship merits closer inspection.

King Lear (1605–6)

King Lear is a play about love: love in human relationships and love in family dynamics. Famous families, rich families, royal families: none is exempt from family problems (as events in our own period illustrate only too well). *King Lear's* first scene introduces us to *two* dysfunctional families: those of King Lear and the Earl of Gloucester.

Edmund, the illegitimate son of the Earl of Gloucester, is making a rare public appearance (he has been abroad for nine years and will soon be sent away again). Gloucester, as we saw in section 1 of this chapter, introduces Edmund to a courtier with a salacious "nudge-nudge, wink-wink" attitude toward his son's illegitimate origin: "There was good sport at his making" (1.1.23). A slighting parental tone like this is perhaps enough to explain Edmund's creative malevolence in the play as he plots to disinherit his legitimate brother. However, Edmund's malignancy moves from the pragmatic (a desire to inherit land) to the vengeful: he silently acquiesces in the three plots to torture his father, to murder Lear, and to kill Lear's youngest daughter, Cordelia. While the plot for his brother's land may be an understandable, if immoral, consequence of illegitimate exclusion, the escalating violence is not. What are we to make of this?

In his dying moments Edmund cries out, "Yet Edmund was belov'd" (5.3.240), a reference to his love affairs with Goneril and Regan. In this sentence we hear not the macho boast of the Lothario but the desperate cry of the child seeking and needing love, seeking and needing proof that he is lovable. Romantic love compensates for his father's insouciance in 1.1.

This need of the child-adult Edmund is also the need of the child-adult Lear, and, in the play's opening scene, Lear takes steps to legislate love. He sets up a public love-test in which each of his three daughters has to compete with her siblings in declaring the greatest amount of love for her father. The winner will be awarded the largest third of Lear's kingdom as prize. The contest is a disaster from the start, for the simple and obvious reason that love is neither legislatable nor quantifiable. "There's beggary in the love that can be reckon'd," says Antony in *Antony and Cleopatra* (1.1.15). Lear's problem throughout the play is that he tries to reckon love. Goneril later offers hospitality to fifty of Lear's knights whereas Regan offers accommodation to only twenty-five. Lear therefore concludes that Goneril loves her father twice as much as does Regan. Cordelia, the youngest daughter, sees the problems in measuring love in this way and accordingly refuses to play the game. She has nothing to say as proof of her love, and is consequently disinherited by her father.

Cordelia's pointed refusal to cooperate is justifiable philosophically: love cannot be reduced to games or measurements or tests or proofs. But her behavior is not justifiable emotionally. If she were to think about the episode from her father's point of view, she would see that behind the love-test lies an old man's fear and vulnerability: a fear of being old and unloved. What the situation requires, then, is not a statement of truth but a gesture of reassurance. Technically Cordelia is correct when she offers the logical response that she can't love her father more than her future husband, but emotionally she misses the point completely. As a result, Lear, like Edmund, experiences a dark night of the soul and wanders through the play feeling betrayed and unloved.

The play seems pessimistic about humans' ability to give love. Goneril and Regan's attitude to their father is surely rooted in his attitude to them. Shakespeare does not offer any background, but father–daughter tensions were hinted at in the 1976 RSC production: Judi Dench's Regan had a stammer which only appeared in the presence of her father. In the final scene the only character who makes an effort to reconnect with society is the villain, Edmund, and although his effort is frustrated by timing, the intention is unmistakable: "Some good I mean to do, / Despite of mine own nature" (5.3.244–5). The line follows his reaction to the deaths of Goneril and Regan, the women who loved him. A villain attempts to do good because he has been given love.

If the family in *Lear* withholds love, so does Shakespeare by setting the play in pre-Christian Britain. There is no compensatory "love that passeth all understanding." Although critics determinedly detect Christian symbolism in Cordelia's "Father, / It is thy business that I go about" (4.4.23–4), and fasten on the image of the Pietà in the last scene, the oaths are consistently pagan: "By Apollo"; "by Jove." *Midsummer Night's Dream*, by contrast, gives us, in Bottom's parody of St. Paul, reassurance that humans exist in a world of love which will redeem their flaws (see chapter 2, "Love and Madness").

Although Lear is a flawed man, he is a father, and the father in Renaissance society commands respect. "To you your father should be as a god," Theseus tells Hermia in *Midsummer Night's Dream* (1.1.47). The language of *Lear* stresses nature and the unnatural; and nothing is more unnatural to Elizabethans and Jacobeans than the fracturing of family bonds. Gloucester lists the play's social disorders: "Love cools, friendship falls off, brothers divide: in cities, mutinies; in countries, discord; in palaces, treason; and the bond crack'd 'twixt son and father. This villain of mine comes under the prediction; there's son against father: the King falls from bias of nature; there's father against child" (1.2.106–12). When Lear contends with the elements, he acknowledges that he cannot accuse them of "unkindness" because "I never gave you kingdom, call'd you children" (3.2.16–17). "Unkind" is a strong word in the Renaissance: not a synonym for not-nice, it means unnatural, acting as if not kindred, not related by nature (Hamlet puns that his relation with his stepfather, Claudius, is "less than kind"; 1.2.65). The violent elements are natural because they are only behaving as elements should. When "the offices of nature, bond of childhood" are violated (2.4.178), however, the unnatural crime reflects disorder in the state.

Lynda Boose points out that disorder in the family does not simply reflect disorder in the state: it may cause it (Boose 1986: 60). She sets out to answer Lear's rhetorical question, "Is there any cause in nature that makes these hard hearts?" (3.6.77–8), concluding that state power and family power are similar: "the power to bestow or abate, enlarge or scant, whether measured by the size of a kingdom or the number of knights, represents, at its most important level, the power to confer or withhold love" (Boose 1986: 61). In what follows I am indebted to Boose's analysis.

The problems in *King Lear* begin when a daughter attempts to pass out of the family structure to establish herself independently. Marriage is, as we have seen, a moment of crisis in friendship, and it is no less fraught in father–daughter relationships. The Church of England marriage service is not just designed to join husband and wife but to separate father and daughter (Boose 1986: 64). Lear resists separation. He wants to give away his crown, yet remain king of his country; he wants to give away his daughter, yet remain king of her affections. Cordelia sees the contradiction: "Why have my sisters husbands, if they say / They love you all?" (1.1.99–100).

It matters little whether Cordelia speaks or stays silent, for both responses invalidate her future marriage. To declare love for Lear over a husband binds her exclusively to her father; when she remains silent, Lear withdraws her dowry, thus rendering her unmarriageable (Boose 1986: 65). Either way Lear gets what he wants. That France chooses to marry a dowerless bride is a happy accident of love. (The 1971 Russian film of *Lear* nicely indicated the genuineness of France's emotion by having him anxiously follow the father–daughter quarrel through a translator.) When France accepts the rejected Cordelia, he does so in language whose formality echoes the marriage service (Boose 1986: 66):

> Fairest Cordelia, that art most rich being poor,
> Most choice forsaken, and most lov'd despis'd,
> Thee and thy virtues here I seize upon,
> Be it lawful I take up what's cast away. (1.1.250–3)

France salvages the ritual which Lear unconsciously tries to prevent.

Boose notes the way in which the first scene's conversations about politics (the division of the kingdom) are twice interrupted by family issues: Edmund's bastardy, Cordelia's marriage. The father–sons plot mirrors the father–daughters plot as good children are rejected, and bad children inherit. But the bad children continue their malevolence irrationally, unnecessarily, indiscriminately, and inflict violence on the family – anyone's family. Acquisition does not bring them happiness, and so they seek to deprive: Lear loses his knights and his residences, Gloucester his house and his eyes. Regan is inexplicably involved in the plot against Edmund's father just as Edmund is involved in the plot to kill Lear. The motivation is not material greed (inheritance) but rage: "the insatiable rage of the neglected child vents itself indiscriminately against the world of the fathers" (Boose 1986: 61). The dynamic which Boose describes is one we have encountered already in Freud's analysis of Richard III – a dynamic of emotional ascesis and compensation in which a deprived child seeks reparation.

The "rage of the neglected child" accounts for *Lear*'s terrifying bleakness. That such destruction can be caused by a failure to express love is undeniably true (hence the terror). When Cordelia meets her estranged father in act 4, she asks for his blessing: "hold your hand in benediction o'er me" (4.7.57). Richard of Gloucester, whom love foreswore in the womb, desired the same from his mother. Cordelia's request, Boose writes (1986: 67), "summarizes the inchoate cries for love that emanate from every child and every parent in the play."

Macbeth (1606)

Macbeth is a play about duplication. The Thane of Cawdor is twice a traitor (the title belongs first to the character who assists Norway and then to the one who murders Duncan). Duncan visits the Macbeths "in double trust" (1.7.12). The witches traffic in double meanings. Lines are repeated and reasons multiplied (Braunmuller 1997: 26). But one entity in the play fails to duplicate or reproduce: the Macbeths themselves.[3]

The play is peopled with parents and children, both physically and metaphorically (Williams n.p.). Regicide is political patricide, and Lady Macbeth declares she could have murdered Duncan "had he not resembled / My father as he slept" (2.2.12–13). Banquo has a son, as does Siward; Duncan has two. Macduff has at least three children if we are to justify the adjective "all" which he uses five times and which clearly excludes his wife ("all my pretty chickens, and their dam"; 4.3.218). The witches' cauldron includes the finger of a dead baby. Part of the play's investigation of the "unnatural" is that parents – Siward, the Macduffs, the Macbeths – outlive their children, "if only by the few moments it takes to drag Lady Macduff offstage" (Williams n.p.).

However emotionally unnatural it is for parents to survive offspring, it was not unusual in the early modern period. Fifty percent of pregnancies ended in miscarriage (Cressy 1997: 47). Two seventeenth-century diaries, those of the clergymen Isaac Archer and Ralph Josselin, chronicle the physical and emotional perils of creating a family. After seventeen years of marriage, more than ten pregnancies, and several miscarriages, Anne and Isaac Archer had one surviving child. Several babies had died before they could be baptized (Cressy 1997: 29, 31). Jane Josselin had five miscarriages, fifteen pregnancies, ten live births, and an unknown number of subsequent infant deaths (Cressy 1997: 47). When Emilia announces the birth of the princess

---

[3] For extended discussions of childlessness see Braunmuller (1997: 15–23) and Rutter (1988: 53–72). I am indebted to Laurence Williams for an unpublished essay which prompted the discussion in this section.

Perdita in *Winter's Tale* she offers three pieces of information: the baby's sex, appearance, and chances of survival (2.2.24–6). In *Romeo and Juliet*, the Friar rhymes "womb" with its conceptual opposite "tomb" (2.3.9–10). In *Henry VIII*, Henry compares Katherine of Aragon's womb to a grave (2.4.187–92). Katherine had suffered five miscarriages and stillbirths; at the time of her divorce she was forty-three, with little chance of further pregnancy. At the start of the play the vengeful Surveyor, giving evidence against his master, the Duke of Buckingham, reports Buckingham's ambition for the crown "if the King / Should without issue die" (1.2.133–4). In the 1996 RSC production Henry sympathetically reached for Katherine's hand on this line, a shared moment of marital pain (Lapotaire 1998: 140).

Personal accounts of bereavement indicate deep parental grief. Robert Woodford experienced deep "affliction" when his week-old baby died. John Evelyn recorded his "great grief and affliction" when children and grandchildren died. Henry Newcome experienced "pain and grief" at his son's death. Edmund Verney's "heart" was "incurably pierced with grief" at the loss of his child (Cressy 1997: 394). Religion offered some consolation, as when Ben Jonson reassures himself that his six-month-old daughter, Mary, is with Mary the Queen of Heaven. Gender considerations also mitigated pain. Isaac Archer notes that "the loss is the less because 'twas a girl, though we could have wished the life of it" (Cressy 1997: 33). Gender may explain the philosophical grief of Ben Jonson's poem on the death of his daughter in comparison to the anguish expressed on the death of his son, although the difference in ages (the six-month-old Mary versus the seven-year-old Benjamin) may also be relevant.

Shakespeare's only son, Hamnet, died in 1596, aged eleven. In the early modern period, as Katherine Duncan-Jones points out, bereaved parents often determinedly created another heir. This did not happen in Shakespeare's case, and it seems never to have been an option: Duncan-Jones suggests that conjugal relations between the Shakespeares had long since ceased (2001: 91). In *Macbeth* reproduction is still viewed as a possibility: "bring forth men-children only," Macbeth commands and compliments his wife (1.7.72). But the Macbeths have neither he-children nor she-children. This lack is at the center of their tragedy.

Children are politically important. They link the personal and the national, the biological and the dynastic. In *Winter's Tale* Mamillius is important as a prince rather than as a child. As soon as his legitimacy is challenged he loses dynastic significance, and thus promptly dies (Elisabeth Glover, personal communication). Banquo is "lesser than Macbeth, and greater" because he shall "get kings," though he himself be none (1.3.65, 67). *Macbeth* was written as a compliment to James VI and I who not only owed his position as King of England to Elizabeth I's childlessness but traced his ancestry to Banquo. As Laurence Williams points out, the man who can reproduce (Banquo, James) triumphs over the monarch who cannot (Macbeth, Elizabeth).

Having children is a way of creating the future in the instant. Duncan nominates his biological son as his political heir (an important gesture because not an inevitable succession in a system of thanist election). He economically fuses the political and the biological (Braunmuller 1997: 1) in a way that gubernatorial metaphors – father of the state, head of the country – have long done. Malcolm is son and successor, the present and the future. In *Macbeth* procreation (and procreative failure) are important, for given *Macbeth*'s stress on manipulating time, it is clear that biology is an alternative to murder: reproduction legally, socially and responsibly manipulates the future in a way that regicide cannot.

But the center of *Macbeth* is not just lack of children but loss of children. "I have given suck, and know / How tender 'tis to love the babe that milks me" says Lady Macbeth (1.7.54–5). Historically Lady Macbeth had a son by her first husband. Shakespeare omits this detail and Jacobean audiences are unlikely to supply it, given that arcane details of Scottish history would not be at their fingertips. In the play, we are entitled to assume that the Macbeths had a child who has died (this is the assumption behind the 1986 RSC production, below). Whichever narrative we prefer, the facts are: the Macbeths are a childless couple; at least one of them has experienced parenthood.

Macduff assumes that Macbeth's tyranny and his childlessness are related. " 'He has no children' means 'Only because he is himself childless could he murder my children.' " The explanation is Freud's, from his 1915 essay "Some Character Types Met With in Psycho-Analytic Work" (Freud 1953–74: 329). Harold Bloom expresses more clearly the causal relationship which Freud hints at: "unable to beget children, Macbeth slaughters them" (Bloom 1999: 529).

It is not physical inability but emotional compensation which motivates Macbeth. Freud discusses "The Exceptions": people who commit moral wrong because they feel the world has been unjust to them. Their desire for reparation overrides morality: "I have a right to be an exception. I may do wrong myself, since wrong has been done to me" (Freud 1953–74: 322). By this line of thinking, Macbeth's child slaughter has an emotional rather than (or as well as) a political motivation: "if I can't have children, no one else shall."

In Holinshed it is ten years before Macbeth targets Banquo's or Macduff's children. There is no urgency. To prevent the witches' prophesy to Banquo coming true Macbeth must dispose of Fleance some time, any time. In Shakespeare Macbeth immediately and pointlessly attacks children (just as in *King Lear* Edmund's motivated violence against his own father develops senselessly into violence against another father, Lear). Grief becomes indiscriminate rage. Productions of *Macbeth* frequently highlight the issues of childlessness and child abuse. The 1986 RSC production was populated by children with whom Macbeth, père manqué, played lovingly. Sinead Cusack had just given birth to her second son when she played Lady Macbeth, and she approached the part from two linked perspectives: "the death of a child is the ultimate grief; the abuse of a child is the ultimate taboo" (Rutter 1988: 56).

The Macbeths employ each of these points against each other. For Cusack's Lady Macbeth, "I have given suck" was her "secret weapon" (Rutter 1988: 64), a point Derek Jacobi, who played Macbeth at the RSC in 1993, acknowledges from the husband's point of view: the line was a "vulnerable point" for his Macbeth, triggering his emotional defenses (Jacobi 1998: 201). Lady Macbeth uses it as emotional leverage: despite her "tender love" of her nursing infant she would rather commit infanticide than renege on her word. (Lady Macbeth's commitment to motherhood is indicated by the unexpectedness of her having "given suck": aristocratic women, as Braunmuller reminds us [1997: 38], employ wet nurses, although Shakespeare's Queen Hermione in *Winter's Tale* objects to having her newborn infant plucked from her nursing breast [3.2.98–101].) When Macbeth grows apart from his wife, his emotional distance is signaled by irremediable child abuse: murder. Cusack records her character's horror when she first realized the threat to Fleance: "oh my god, he's going *to kill the child*" (Rutter 1988: 67).

The only way Macbeth can defeat the witches' prophesy is by having children. Although the play presents him verbally as full of sexual energy, the energy is misdirected. Macbeth is bridegroom to Bellona, the goddess of war (1.2.54) and the minion of Valour (1.2.19). His regicide is figured as rape (he approaches Duncan with "Tarquin's ravishing strides"; 2.1.55). After the physical climax of murder Macbeth is presented as detumescent: Bloom glosses the line "Your constancy / Hath left you unattended" (2.2.65–6) as "your firmness has deserted you" (Bloom 1999:

530–1). Murder becomes Macbeth's "mode of sexual expression" (Bloom 1999: 529).

Tragedy, like drama generally, is about fertility and regeneration (see chapter 1). But any feeling of growth and regeneration is conspicuously absent from *Macbeth*. The incomplete catharsis which Turner notes (Holderness, Potter, and Turner 1988: 147) is linked to the incomplete family.

Nigel Rees's published collection of graffiti contains the following statement observed in a men's urinal in St. Andrews University: "the future of Scotland is in your hands" (1979: 43). Given the noticeable lack of children at the end of *Macbeth*, it is not clear where the future of Scotland lies.

4   Anger and Revenge

"Yond man is very angry. Go,
Let him have a table by himself,
For he does neither affect company,
Nor is he fit for't" (*Timon* 1.2 29–32)

Introduction

The Elizabethan poet, courtier, and critic Sir Philip Sidney found drama helpful in understanding anger. Describing Ajax's mad rage in Sophocles, he challenged, "tell me if you have not a more familiar insight into anger than finding in the schoolmen his genius and difference" (1965: 108). The Stoic philosophers viewed anger as a temporary madness and it is the anger/insanity nexus that Sidney describes. But his point about drama's usefulness in understanding this complex emotion applies well to the varieties of anger in Shakespeare's plays.

Since anger expresses passion, it creates excitement and drama; consequently, fiery temperaments can be attractive. In *Twelfth Night* Olivia sighs, "O, what a deal of scorn looks beautiful / In the contempt and anger of his lip!" (3.1.145–6). In *As You Like It* the cross-dressed Rosalind realizes that Phoebe will "fall in love with my anger" (3.5.67). In both examples the anger is superficial, very different in cause and effect from the threatening ire enacted by Diomedes in *Troilus and Cressida* (see chapter 2, "Love and Abuse").

When anger becomes a permanent characteristic it becomes self-destructive, as when Coriolanus's emotion overrides both diplomacy and self-preservation: "His heart's his mouth; / What his breast forges, that his tongue must vent, / And, being angry, does forget that ever / He heard the name of death" (3.1.256–9). In the same play Volumnia's anger is characterized in a dangerous oral image: "Anger's my meat; I sup upon myself, / And so shall starve with feeding" (4.2.50–1). The combination of cannibalism and inanition illustrates anger's circularity: it is its own, non-nutritive end. But it needn't be. The digestive metaphor appears in a healthier form in *1 Henry VI* when the king instructs his factious nobles: "digest / Your angry choler on your enemies" (4.1.167–8). By directing their anger outwards, the nobles avoid self-consumption. Alcibiades's professional anger as a military captain is similarly directed against the enemy in *Timon of Athens*: "So they were bleeding new, my lord, there's no meat like 'em" (*Timon* 1.2.78–9).

Anger is constructive when it challenges injustice. In *King Lear* Cornwall chastises the servant Kent/Caius for his vituperation: "Peace, sirrah! / You beastly knave, know you no reverence?" Kent justifies his behavior: "anger hath a privilege," i.e., anger has the right to protest, even when such speech seems indecorous (2.2.68–70). Kent then inveighs against Oswald's hypocrisy.[4] In *Taming of the Shrew* Katherine's angry speech (her alleged shrewishness) is a mechanism for social protest: "My tongue will tell the anger of my heart, / Or else my heart concealing it will break" (4.3.77–8). Her reference to heartbreak reminds us of the serious emotional consequences of repressed anger.

Because of the surge of adrenalin that facilitates all animals' "fight or flight" reactions, human beings gain physical strength when they are angry. "O, I could hew up rocks and fight with flint, / I am so angry," fulminates the Duke of York in *2 Henry VI* (5.1.24–5). "To be furious / Is to be frighted out of fear, and in that mood / The dove will peck the estridge [goshawk]," observes Enobarbus (*A&C* 3.13.194–5). The most extraordinary Shakespearean example of anger-induced power comes at the end of *King Lear*. Cordelia has just been hanged by a servant acting under Cornwall's orders. Lear – frail, old, and half-crazed with a combination of the play's injustices and localized grief – enters with the dead Cordelia in his arms. In a line that is easily neglected, he says, "I kill'd the slave that was a-hanging thee." An anonymous Gentleman offers confirmation: " 'Tis true, my lords,

---

[4]   Cf. Pembroke's "Impatience hath his privilege" in *King John* 4.3.32; impatience and anger are closely related.

he did" (5.3.275–6). The Gentleman has no other line in the scene; his is one of the smallest speaking roles (a half-line!) in Shakespeare. But the director Harley Granville-Barker told his actors that this was one of the most important utterances in the play: the Gentleman has to convince the audience that a sick octogenarian was indeed capable of killing a young hitman. Anger gives Lear this strength. Every part of him protests against the injustice of Cordelia's murder by killing her assailant.

Anger is often the partner to grief. It can be an early stage of bereavement, an expression of, or displacement of, sorrow, as we saw in *King John* where John's tirade at Hubert substitutes for the grief at his mother's death which circumstances prevent him from expressing. In *Julius Caesar* Brutus's anger at Cassius follows the news of Portia's death; anger provides an alternative outburst to Brutus's unexpressed (because interrupted) grief.

The progress from grief to anger becomes dangerous, however, when anger leads to revenge. "Here is a mourning Rome, a dangerous Rome," observes Mark Antony after Caesar's assassination (*JC* 3.1.288); revenge is the unspoken middle term. Queen Margaret self-consciously redirects her grief over Suffolk's death in *2 Henry VI* to revenge:

> Oft have I heard that grief softens the mind,
> And makes it fearful and degenerate;
> Think therefore on revenge and cease to weep. (*2HVI* 4.4.1–3)

Malcolm offers Macduff the same advice in *Macbeth*: "Let's make us med'cines of our great revenge / To cure this deadly grief" (4.3.214–15). The Wars of the Roses in the *Henry VI* plays form a cycle of death–grief–revenge, expressed most hopelessly in the first act of *3 Henry VI*, where Clifford's insistent refrain "thy father slew my father" and its variants (1.3.5, 21–2, 39, 47) indicates the circularity of revenge.

Revenge tragedy was one of the dominant genres in the theaters of the 1580s and 1590s. Shakespeare's earliest excursions into tragedy – the *Henry VI* plays (the original title of *3 Henry VI* was *The True Tragedy of Richard Duke of York*) and *Titus Andronicus* – chronicle the repetitive, and hence self-defeating, anger of revenge.

Titus Andronicus (1592)

The traveling players in Stoppard's *Rosencrantz and Guildenstern are Dead* have a revenge tragedy in their repertory. The Head Player's artistic summary outlines the genre's essential ingredients:

> We're ... of the blood, love and rhetoric school. ... I can do you blood and love without the rhetoric, and I can do you blood and rhetoric without the love, and I can do you all three concurrent or consecutive, but I can't do you love and rhetoric without the blood. Blood is compulsory. (Stoppard 1998: 1087)

The blood used on the Elizabethan stage was real. The Rose Theatre on the South Bank, where *Titus Andronicus* was first performed, was close to a slaughterhouse where Philip Henslowe, the theater manager, bought pigs' livers, sheep's bladders, animal tongues, etc. The Elizabethan stage cannot have been the most hygienic place: the rushes were changed (or supplemented) regularly, but the costumes could hardly be drycleaned. Kyd's *The Spanish Tragedy* concludes with Hieronimo biting out his tongue; Gloucester's eyes are gouged out in *King Lear*; in the anonymous *Selimus* a character suffers blinding, has his hands amputated and his chest cut open to function as a pouch for his disembodied hands; in Middleton's *Revenger's Tragedy* the Duke's tongue is nailed to the floor; *Titus Andronicus* has six dismembered body parts (one tongue, two heads, three hands); and the body count is high at the end of all revenge tragedies. Clearly, a high tolerance of blood is an essential critical requirement.

The rhetoric which Stoppard's Head Player advertises is Senecan in origin. Senecan tragedy was essentially declamatory (this partly explains Marcus's reaction to Lavinia's mutilation in *Titus Andronicus*: he delivers a forty-seven-line speech rather than first aid). The Head Player's "love" is not a dominant feature of revenge tragedy, but it is relevant to *Titus Andronicus* where Titus, like Lear, does not learn what love is until he has suffered. Revenge, which the player omits from his list, is too obvious to require mention.

Revenge was an ambivalent moral area for the Elizabethans. On the one hand, "vengeance is mine, I will repay, saith the Lord" (Romans 12:19); on the other hand, the Lord works through human agents. On the first hand again, Mosaic law sanctioned *lex talionis*, the principle of compensation: "an eye for an eye, tooth for a tooth" (see Exodus 21:12–35); on the other hand, Elizabethan authors stressed the social dangers when citizens took law into their own hands. Bacon's essay "On Revenge" complicates the ethical dilemma further by dividing revenge into public and private actions. Public revenge is enacted by the legal system, private revenge by "vindictive persons."

In *Titus Andronicus*, as in the later *Hamlet*, Shakespeare gives us both private and public revenge. Hamlet's father has been murdered, prompting Hamlet to take private revenge; but because his father was the King of Denmark, and the murderer "now wears his crown" (1.5.40), Hamlet's revenge concerns the public good. In *Hamlet*, as in *Titus Andronicus*, revenge is both a triumph and self-defeating futility. Hamlet avenges the murder of his father, but in the course of his action, kills another man's father. A second revenge action therefore arises in response to the first for Laertes now has to avenge the death of *his* father. The accidental killing of Polonius which links the plots (and which makes Hamlet the revenger in one plot and the victim of revenge in another) is Shakespeare's way of showing revenge's tendency toward self-perpetuation. The effect is to "neutralize the sense of the restoring of moral balance that a revenge is supposed to give us … Revenge does not complete anything; it merely counters something" (Frye 1986: 90).

Kyd, at the end of *The Spanish Tragedy*, refers to "*endless* tragedy" (4.5.48). The endlessness of revenge is illustrated in *Titus* whose plot, as Ronald Broude demonstrates, is structured round four causally related but ethically discrete revenge codes. A revenge which is appropriate in one context (religious, social) has tragic repercussions in another (civil relations, international diplomacy). It therefore achieves nothing.

The play begins with Rome victorious in the recent war against the Goths. Rome's military hero, Titus, prepares to sacrifice Alarbus, a Gothic prisoner. The vengeance is traditional, sanctioned by state religion: the Greco-Roman world believed that the shades of those killed violently were unable to rest in peace unless propitiated by the retaliatory sacrifice of their killers (Broude 1979: 496). The vengeance is therefore desirable on religious grounds. But it is disastrous on political grounds, as the reaction of Tamora, Queen of the Goths and mother of Alarbus, makes clear – she immediately plans a counter-revenge.

Tamora's action is a different kind of revenge: blood revenge, what Bacon calls "private revenge," what our century knows as a "vendetta" (Broude 1979: 497). As Broude points out (ibid.: 498), blood revenge operates to protect the family, the clan, the social group, and usually takes place in situations when no state protection is available. The Gothic Tamora is outside Rome's legal system so she takes the law into her own hands. Elizabethan society acknowledged that kinship hath a privilege (next-of-kin were treated leniently by the prosecution in murder trials), but it was nonetheless concerned that private revenge might interfere with the good of the commonwealth (Broude 1979: 498–9). This is exactly what happens with the rape and dismemberment of Titus's daughter, Lavinia, and the murder of her husband, Bassianus – acts of violent revenge perpetrated by Alarbus's brothers, Chiron and Demetrius, and supported by Tamora and her lover Aaron. The violence is both physical and symbolic: Tamora's revenge affects not just the human body but the body politic.

The Goths' crimes – rape and murder – prompt a third type of revenge: civic justice. Titus seeks justice for the crimes perpetrated by the Gothic brothers. The legal system operates effectively in a healthy body politic, but in Rome's partial regime (the emperor, Saturninus, assumes the Andronici's guilt) justice has fled. Many revenge tragedies are actually tragedies of failed justice. Kyd's Hieronimo turns to revenge only because his attempts to obtain justice are frustrated: the Machiavel Lorenzo repeatedly blocks his access to the King. Similarly, when the state fails to dispense the civic justice Titus requests in act 3, he seeks revenge.

This revenge is of a fourth type: divine Providence with Titus as human agent. Broude shows how the vocabulary in act 4 stresses divine intervention. Titus's brother, Marcus, invokes "Apollo, Pallas, Jove, or Mercury" to "inspire" him to find Lavinia's violators (4.1.66–7); immediately he forms the idea of writing in the sand, whereupon "God" and "Heaven" guide Lavinia's staff (4.1.74–5). Titus's revenge action, like those of Hieronimo and Hamlet, is ethically more palatable to the Elizabethans because of the characters' civic authority: Hieronimo is knight marshal of Spain (the Spanish equivalent of lord chief justice), Hamlet a prince, Titus a statesman. These are not cavalier citizens willfully taking the law into their own hands.

It could be argued that Titus's revenge action differs little from that of Tamora, since both characters take steps to avenge wrongs done to their family. Broude (1979: 503) points out the crucial differences between Titus's actions and those of Tamora and her family. Titus responds only to wrongs, whereas Tamora's sons operate from mixed motives: lust and revenge. Titus targets only the guilty – Tamora and her sons – whereas Tamora targets the innocent Lavinia and Bassianus. Titus publicizes his action as soon as he has achieved his goal rather than concealing it, as does Tamora. And his revenge feeds justice not itself.

Revenge, nonetheless, is presented dually in *Titus Andronicus*. Broude (1979: 505) concludes that revenge, like anger, has the "potential both for good and for ill."

Titus Andronicus, like revenge tragedy in general, was popular in the late sixteenth century. Since then it has had a bad press. Dr. Johnson objected to the play's "barbarity," and T. S. Eliot called it "one of the stupidest and most uninspired plays ever written" (1932: 82). However, it has been successfully performed in Europe since the 1950s: one thinks of Peter Brook's stylized RSC production in 1955 (Vivien Leigh's Lavinia trailed red ribbons for blood), Deborah Warner's realistic version for the RSC in 1985 (as Marcus approached his mutilated niece, he spent forty-seven lines ripping his garments and bandaging Lavinia), and Julie Taymor's Hollywood film (2000), a nightmarish world in which children's play violence becomes adult reality. The development of a twentieth-century dramatic genre which parallels Elizabethan revenge tragedy may account for *Titus*'s popularity in the twentieth century: Theater of Cruelty.

Theater of Cruelty seeks to shock, to expose the barbaric core of human behavior. From Artaud, through Camus and Genet to Edward Bond, Theater of Cruelty highlights rhythm, movement, gesture, humankind without the veneers of civilizing behavior, symbolism rather than language. The mute Lavinia is clearly a very important character in this respect (when language is removed, her body becomes a symbolic alphabet), but the larger stage emblems are also significant. In this early play Shakespeare is already very conscious of visual theater (note the number of occasions on which characters kneel and plead). Thus, the twentieth century discovered a theatrical genre that reaffines us with the Elizabethan atmosphere of *Titus*. And after Theater of Cruelty? We live in a world with snuff movies, video nasties, slasher films, Quentin Tarantino. Anger and violence, the respective cause and effect of revenge tragedy, are still very much to the fore.

There is only one antidote to revenge – forgiveness. That is the subject of the next section.

5   Forgiveness

"*For children are innocent and love justice; while most of us are wicked and naturally prefer mercy*" (Chesterton 1938: 195)

Pericles (1607); *Winter's Tale* (1609); *Cymbeline* (1610);
Tempest (1611); *Henry VIII* (1611); *Two Noble
Kinsmen* (1613–14)

Although the *Riverside Shakespeare*, in common with most *Collected Works*, groups all of the above plays, except *Henry VIII*, in a generically separate section called "Romances," the first collected works of Shakespeare, the Folio of 1623, distributes them differently or ignores them altogether. *Cymbeline* is included in the Tragedies (perhaps because, like Lear, the eponymous hero is a suffering king of ancient Britain), *Winter's Tale* and *Tempest* are in the Comedies, *Henry VIII* in the Histories, and *Pericles* and *Two Noble Kinsmen* are excluded from the volume entirely (for reasons not clearly discernible).[5] *Henry VIII*, despite its title, is not a history play in the way the other *Henry* or *Richard* plays are – England is not "at war or under threat of war" (Schoenbaum 1967: xxxvi) – nor is Henry its principal character, a fact reflected in the title under which the play was first performed, *All is True*. Heminge and Condell titled the play *Henry VIII* when they included it in the Histories in the First Folio. Nonetheless, it is closer in theme and structure to the romances Shakespeare was writing at the same time; I therefore include it in this section on "Forgiveness."

Although these six plays have something in common with tragedy (their suffering is real and irreversible) and with comedy (celebratory, often nuptial, endings), their specific indebtedness to romance makes separate generic categorization advisable. To the Renaissance, romance meant Greek narrative romance. The genre had expected conventions, seen in works as chronologically separate as the anonymous *The Adventures of Apollonius of Tyre* (second century CE) and Robert Greene's *Pandosto; or the Triumph of Time* (1588), the sources of *Pericles* and *Winter's Tale* respectively. Romance stories are elaborate, exciting, episodic; plot matters more than characterization; perilous journeys and quests abound; good and evil are stereotypically demarcated; improbable and miraculous events occur; lengthy time schemes enable events to complicate and resolve; and a narrator is prominent.

Clearly, transferring these prose traditions to drama is difficult, and Shakespeare's romances run ostentatiously counter to the classical dramaturgy of Ben Jonson, who criticized *Pericles* as a "mouldy old tale," and the Augustan tastes of Dr. Johnson, who dismissed *Cymbeline* as "unresisting imbecility" (Wimsatt 1960: 136). They also appear to run counter to the central claim of this book: that Shakespearean drama is centered on

---

[5]   John Fletcher, who was to succeed Shakespeare as the King's Men's principal dramatist, coauthored *Henry VIII* and *Two Noble Kinsmen*. Shakespeare's previous known collaborations include *2* and *3 Henry VI*, written with someone variously and tentatively identified as George Peele, Christopher Marlowe, or Robert Greene; *Macbeth*, written with Thomas Middleton; and the lost *Cardenio* (1612–13), the manuscript of which survived till at least 1770 (Wells and Taylor 1987: 133), written with Fletcher.

character and psychology. Theater practitioners note the shallowness of characterization in the romances. Elijah Moshinsky viewed the dramatis personae in *Cymbeline* as functions rather than as rounded characters (Alexander 1983: 23). Henry Fenwick noted the "heavy demands [in *Pericles*] on actors more used to psychological subtlety" (Alexander 1984: 24). Critics comment on Prospero's opacity in *Tempest*. Paul Jesson, who played Henry VIII at Stratford in 1996, observes Henry's lack of "psychological depth" (Jesson 1998: 116), and John Wilders summarizes the critical view of Henry as "an indistinct, tentatively sketched character" (Alexander 1979b: 16). Clifford Leech felt that readers and directors were "put off" the romances by their less complex characterization (1977: xxxvii).

However, the characters' emotions and reactions are highly realistic. Leontes's hasty suspicion of his wife's fidelity is linked to Hermione's advanced state of pregnancy. It is not unusual for men to entertain unfounded sexual suspicions during their partner's pregnancy (a phenomenon sometimes referred to by psychologists as the Leontes syndrome): women, obviously, know the identity of their child's mother, but fathers cannot experience the same certainty. Similar vulnerability underlies Posthumus's rapid acceptance of Imogen's alleged infidelity. All relationships entail the prospect of loss; jealousy and suspicion are simply the constant anticipation of loss. When Posthumus believes his worst fears, he is thus relieved of the strain of constantly fearing the worst (Walter 1993: 208). Pericles may be characterized simply and superficially as the man who gets a raw deal from Fortune, but his anguish and incomprehension in the face of repeated suffering is Lear-like: "O you gods! / Why do you make us love your goodly gifts / And snatch them straight away?" (3.1.22–4). Prospero may be a magician but this does not prevent him experiencing recognizably human – and flawed – emotions such as a desire to avenge himself on his usurping brother, Antonio. In *Two Noble Kinsmen* the Jailer's Daughter moves from romantic comedy to love melancholy to hunger, isolation, exhaustion, and madness (Leech 1977: xxxii). One is uncertain whether her acceptance of the local wooer-as-Palamon (the Athenian prince with whom she is in love) is the result of her madness or clear-sighted resignation which chooses to turn a blind eye. (The RSC production of 1986 emphasized the way in which the play's marriages are noncelebratory short straws for both Emilia and the Jailer's Daughter: the production ended with the two women, dressed bridally, facing each other alone on stage.) Thus the emotions and reactions in the romances are realistic; the events are not. However, it is an odd fact of literature that one improbable event compromises credibility, whereas several improbable events simply create a world where improbable events happen.

These six plays are in many respects very different. *Cymbeline* explores national identity as Britain rebels against the yoke of Rome; the play is set in the first century CE, with Britain still paying – or refusing to pay – tribute money to Augustus Caesar for Julius Caesar's conquest. Imogen's willingness to explore her identity beyond the shores of her native land – "Hath Britain all the sun that shines?" (3.4.136) – contrasts with Cloten's personal and geographic insularity: "Britain's a world / By itself" (3.1.12–13). *The Tempest* investigates colonialism, the politics and ethics of assuming ownership of a land that is already inhabited. Prospero rules (occupies) an island previously inhabited by Caliban and claimed by him through hereditary right: "This island's mine by Sycorax my mother" (1.2.331). The issue was topical in 1610 when *Tempest* was written: England had established the colony of Virginia in 1609, with an expedition whose flagship was lost for almost a year, having run aground on Bermuda. *Pericles* analyzes good government and good fatherhood (the two are linked), with disparate geographical examples of good and bad rulers and parents. *Winter's Tale* debates art, nature, and deception, from the dialogue in Bohemia about improving nature through artifice – grafting flowers – to the "trumpery" (from the French *tromper*, to deceive) of the rogue-pedlar Autolycus's *bric-à-brac* and the *trompe-l'oeil* (also from the French *tromper*) "statue" of Hermione which Paulina brings to life. The debate is continued in *Tempest* where Prospero distracts the drunken clowns Stephano and Trinculo with fine clothing – "trumpery."

Henry VIII depicts the transience of earthly glory as Buckingham, then Katherine, then Wolsey fall from ascendance. The prologue explains: "Think you see them great. / ... Then, in a moment, see / How soon this mightiness meets misery" (27, 29–30). *Two Noble Kinsmen* is Shakespeare's harshest exposé of the inadequacies of marriage as an emotional resolution or comedic solution. As in *Measure for Measure*, marriage is imposed not chosen. Having declared she will never love men, Emilia is mandated to marry Palamon; the Wooer is presented to the Jailer's Daughter as a corrective to madness. The plot concludes bathetically – Palamon is the loser who "wins" the competition for Emilia only because his successful rival, Arcite, dies, the Wooer is not the Jailer's Daughter's first choice – and the tone is funereal: the play ends, as it began, with a combination of funeral and marriage. But despite their disparate political and aesthetic concerns, the romances are linked in ways that bring us back to the first chapters of this book.

The plays are stories, and they are about stories. In *Pericles* the twelfth-century poet Gower is resurrected as a narrator "to sing a song that old was sung" (1.Chorus.1). *Two Noble Kinsmen* turns to Gower's contemporary, Chaucer, to retell a story familiar to audiences from *The Knight's Tale*. The title of *Winter's Tale* stresses its fabular nature, and frequent references in the play underline it: sad tales, ballads, old tales. *Tempest* begins with Prospero relating a strange and soporific tale to Miranda. The plays present lengthy and complicated stories, and the appearance of Time as Chorus in *Winter's Tale* and Gower as narrator in *Pericles* serves the function of today's program notes.

In *Pericles*, however, Gower is not the only character to narrate: all the characters tell a story at some stage. The governor of famine-struck Tharsus invites his wife to join him in relating others' suffering as a means to assuage their own (1.4.1–3). In act 5 Pericles invites Marina to tell her story, to put his sufferings in perspective (5.1.134–7). The goddess Diana commands Pericles to go to her temple at Ephesus and reveal his story (5.1.240–9). As in *Titus Andronicus* narrative is presented as revelatory and cathartic.

The romances also present the search for identity which has preoccupied all the plays in this book. We see this most obviously in *Pericles* where the geographical variety enables – as does the voyage in all quest literature or today's gap-year and junior-year abroad – the search for identity. *Pericles* is the only Shakespeare play for which editors provide a map of the Mediterranean. Throughout the Mediterranean Pericles learns about life and self. In Antioch he discovers the serpent in Eden, as he uncovers the incest of Antiochus and his daughter. In Pentapolis he experiences good rulership (he questions the fishermen's description of their king as "good Simonides"; 2.1.99), finds his identity as a son (he wears his father's armor), and receives a new identity as a husband. In act 3 he receives a new identity by becoming a father; and so on. The episodic structure of *Henry VIII*, with its three emotional foci – Buckingham, Katherine, and Wolsey – shows characters acquiring self-knowledge through tragedy. The three situations are different – Katherine is innocent, Wolsey guilty, Buckingham's "guilt or innocence … uncertain" (Wilders in Alexander 1979b: 14) – but the dramatic and emotional pattern is invariable: demotion and death or divorce are prefaced by self-awareness. The point is insistently underlined. "I know myself now," says Wolsey (3.2.378); later, Katherine's gentlemen usher tells her that Wolsey's "overthrow heap'd happiness upon him, / For then, and not till then, he felt [knew] himself" (4.2.64–5). The eponymous king, who oversees (and partly causes) the characters' descent from power, grows in the play from ignorance of subjects and self to political awareness and self-awareness. His political and personal growths are symbiotic. Norfolk, aware of Wolsey's machinations, hopes that "the King will know him one day," to which Suffolk replies, "Pray God he do, he'll never know himself else" (2.2.21–2). Thus Pericles is a peripatetic monarch, Henry a static, but the effect is the same: exploration of identity.

In *Cymbeline* identity is explored through assuming another. Imogen ceases to be a princess, becomes a franklin's housewife for her journey to Wales, learning how to change "command into obedience" (3.4.154–5); she becomes a man, sleeping rough and living in a cave; she becomes a page, Fidele. Her estranged husband, Posthumus, enters Britain in "Italian weeds" (5.1.23), seeks suicide as a British peasant, then as a Roman. The characters are constantly aware of the way in which the world looks different from their new vantage point. "I see a man's life is a tedious one," laments Imogen (3.6.1), a negativity which runs counter to the experience of all other cross-dressed Shakespeare heroines; her experience of hospitality in the Welsh caves, however, is positive, enabling her to reject courtiers' reports that "all's savage but at court" (4.2.33). The play's many speeches about visual and spatial perspective are relevant to the theme of identity: as the rustics/princes ascend the hill, Belarius reminds them that things look different from above (3.3.11–17).

The romances embody most overtly the tripartite pattern of comedy described in chapter 1. Although the theology of the plays is mixed (*Winter's Tale* refers to Apollo, Dis, Phoebus, Judas Iscariot, and Whitsun), the tripartite structure is heavily Christian: loss–suffering–resurrection describes the plots; sin–penance–forgiveness describes the emotional journeys. Throughout the plays, characters suffer, whether because of their errors or because of life's whimsical capacity to inflict suffering. David Jones, who directed the BBC *Pericles*, summarizes Pericles's story: "This is a guy who gets hit over the head and he gets up and says that's fine with him and he gets hit over the head again and he gets up and says don't worry, I don't hold it against you and he gets hit over the head again. He's a man to whom a long list of awful things happens" (Alexander 1984: 26). If Pericles is a passive recipient of misfortune, others' sufferings are caused by errors of colossal proportions. Leontes suspects, imprisons, and arraigns his innocent wife. She is lost to him (concealed by her waiting-woman but reported dead) for sixteen years, during which time Leontes performs a "saint-like sorrow." Sometimes the errors are smaller in scale. Prospero may be a good magus but he was a bad ruler, preferring his books to government; Cymbeline is misled by his second wife who has her son's interests at heart rather than those of her stepdaughter, her husband, or the British crown. Even the good characters are imperfect. The wronged courtier, Belarius, kidnaps Cymbeline's two baby sons in a quid pro quo revenge, "thinking to bar thee [Cymbeline] of succession, as / Thou refts me of my lands" (3.3.102–3). The princes' innate nobility later shines through their rustic upbringing, but Prince Guiderius displays a far from noble attitude to law and justice: "The law / Protects not us; then why should we be tender / To let an arrogant piece of flesh threat us, . . . / For we do fear the law" (4.2.125–9). Most of the characters in the romances err and misjudge. Their capacity to mistake is seen most alarmingly in *Cymbeline* where the Roman soothsayer misinterprets his dream vision, erroneously predicting success to the Romans (4.2.352). If a *professional* interpreter misinterprets life, how can humans expect to judge events and people correctly?

We can't. To err is human, as Alexander Pope bluntly puts it. But he offers a consolatory extension: "to forgive, divine." In the romances some benevolent force gives flawed humans a second chance. Lost children are found (Marina in *Pericles*, Perdita in *Winter's Tale*, Guiderius and Arviragus in *Cymbeline*) and new ones born (Princess Elizabeth in *Henry VIII*); dead wives are restored (Thaisa in *Pericles*, Hermione in *Winter's Tale*, Imogen in *Cymbeline*); a dukedom reclaimed and insular exile ended (*Tempest*). Damage cannot be undone – Mamillius and Arcite remain dead, Katherine divorced, years of marital and parental separation unrestored or reversed – but forgiveness and reconciliation dominate the dénouements, redeeming earlier sins. As Ferdinand says, "Though the seas threaten, they are merciful" (*Tempest* 5.1.178).

We may see in this structure a specifically Christian ambience. The word "peace" is repeated five times in the last two speeches in *Cymbeline*, and, given the play's historical location (a few years before the birth of Christ), the countdown to Christian peace is inescapable. The stress on spiritual renewal through physical resurrection (Thaisa, Perdita, Hermione) and birth (Elizabeth) is further underlined by the practicalities of casting in *Winter's Tale* where the boy actor who played the dead Mamillius most logically doubled the role of his dead and restored sister, Perdita. Sometimes in contemporary productions renewal is signified through set design. The Sicilian first half of *Winter's Tale* is usually wintery, frosty, with characters draped in furs; the pastoral second half can be floral, rural, and agricultural (a colleague characterized one production we attended as "Romanovs meet *Oklahoma!*"). In Adrian Noble's RSC production in 1992–3, the transition "from darkness into light" was fantastical rather than realistic. Autolycus descended "on a sort of tree whose multi-coloured branches sprouted balloons" (McCabe 1998: 63).

As this production showed, the vision of light and renewal need not be specifically Christian. The plays' optimism might be rooted in politics. The discovery of the New World must have seemed to Europeans like a new beginning, a second chance to build society (Gonzalo offers his vision of the ideal Commonwealth in act 2 of *Tempest*). Or the plays' optimism may be related to biography. Shakespeare's daughters were of marriageable age – Judith was twenty-five in 1610, Susanna twenty-seven (although Shakespeare heroines marry in their teens, ordinary women did not). In the romances the younger generation is seen as miraculously able to regenerate the older: "thou that beget'st him that did thee beget" is how Pericles addresses his daughter, Marina (5.1.195) as he receives new life from her mature existence and marriageable future, and Cranmer prophesies happiness to England from the infant Elizabeth (*HVIII* 5.5.14–54). Or, the plays' optimism may be linked to Shakespeare's professional state: a man on the verge of retirement, looking back on life, reflecting mellowly on a world in which humans suffer and survive to begin again.

The realism of the romances is seen in the ways in which characters dispense forgiveness against their instincts, against their intentions, or against our expectations. Henry VIII rescues Cranmer from humiliation in act 5, thus frustrating the play's pattern of downfall. Pardon replaces revenge in *Tempest* but the quality of Prospero's mercy seems strained (even as he pardons Antonio he reminds him of his sins), and given Antonio's (sullen?) silence one feels that Prospero may be premature in breaking his staff and abjuring magic. "I would we were of one mind and one mind good," says the Jailer in *Cymbeline*, articulating a vision of universal peace. That vision is closest to realization in *Cymbeline* where forgiveness and generosity prove infectious. Posthumus forgives the villain, Iachimo, who had misled him about his wife's loyalty: "The pow'r that I have on you is to spare you; / The malice towards you, to forgive you. Live, / And deal with others better" (*Cymbeline* 5.5.418–20). Cymbeline follows suit: "We'll learn our freeness of a son-in-law: / Pardon's the word to all" (5.5.421–2). The "freeness" becomes political as well as personal: although the victor in battle, Cymbeline agrees to submit to Caesar (5.5.460). *Cymbeline* suggests that you can never have too much generosity, too much freeness, too much forgiveness.

Although such eirenic views of the romances were popular in the criticism of the 1950s onward, they have been marginalized in recent years by new historicism which stresses the romances' political aspects and historical locations. Attractive and convincing though such readings are, in performance the spiritual aspects dominate. The theme of forgiveness seems an appropriate topic with which to end a book that has focused on human lives, private and public. In the epigraph which prefaces this chapter, Chesterton reminds us that children love justice because they have not lived long enough to need mercy. By the time of the romances Shakespeare was old enough to prefer mercy.

Works Cited

Adams, Howard C. 1991: "What Cressid Is." In *Sexuality and Politics in Renaissance Drama*. Ed. Carole Levin and Karen Robertson. New York: Mellen Press, pp. 75–93.

Adamson, Jane 1987: *Troilus and Cressida*. Boston: Twayne.

Alexander, Peter 1978: See Shakespeare, *Richard II*.

—— 1979a: See Shakespeare, *Twelfth Night*.

—— 1979b: See Shakespeare, *Henry VIII*.

—— 1981: See Shakespeare, *Antony and Cleopatra*.

—— 1983: See Shakespeare, *Cymbeline*.

—— 1984: See Shakespeare, *Pericles*.

—— 1986: See Shakespeare, *King John*.

Anon ca. 1550: *A Merry Jest of a Shrewd and Curst Wife Wrapped in Morel's Skin for her Good Behaviour*. London.

Anon 2000: "Passnotes: Lady Macbeth." *Guardian*, August 9.

Atkinson, Max 1984: *Our Masters' Voices: The Language and Body Language of Politics*. London: Routledge.

Auden, W. H. 1966: *Collected Shorter Poems 1927–57*. London: Faber and Faber.

Augustine, Bishop 1961: *Confessions*. Ed. R. S. Pine-Coffin. Harmondsworth: Penguin.

Augustine, Norman and Adelman, Kenneth 1999: *Shakespeare in Charge: The Bard's Guide to Leading and Succeeding on the Business Stage*. New York: Hyperion.

Austin, J. L. 1962: *How To Do Things with Words*. Cambridge, MA: Harvard University Press.

Bacon, Francis 1966: *The Advancement of Learning and New Atlantis*. London: Oxford University Press.

Bamber, Linda 1982: *Comic Women, Tragic Men*. Stanford, CA: Stanford University Press.

Barber, C. L. and Wheeler, Richard 1988: "Savage Play in *Richard III*." In *William Shakespeare's "Richard III*." Ed. Harold Bloom. New York: Chelsea House, pp. 101–16.

Barkan, Leonard 1978: "The Theatrical Consistency of *Richard II.*" *Shakespeare Quarterly* 29, 5–19.

Barton, John 1984: *Playing Shakespeare.* London: Methuen and Channel 4.

Bassnett, Susan 1988: *Elizabeth I: A Feminist Perspective.* Oxford: Berg.

Bate, Jonathan 1992: *The Romantics on Shakespeare.* Harmondsworth: Penguin.

Belsey, Catherine 1993: "The Name of the Rose." *Yearbook of English Studies* 23, 126–42.

Bennett, Alan 1992: *The Madness of George III.* London: Faber and Faber.

—— 1995: *The Madness of King George.* London: Faber and Faber.

Berry, Ralph 1972: *Shakespeare's Comedies.* Princeton, NJ: Princeton University Press.

—— 1981: "*Julius Caesar:* A Roman Tragedy." *Dalhousie Review* 61, 325–33.

—— 1988: *Shakespeare and Social Class.* Atlantic Highlands, NJ: Humanities Press International.

Bevington, David 1998: See Shakespeare, *Troilus and Cressida.*

Billington, Michael (Ed.) 1990: *Directors' Shakespeare: Approaches to "Twelfth Night."* London: Nick Hern Books.

Bishop, Elizabeth 1991: *Complete Poems.* London: Chatto and Windus.

Blakemore, Colin and Jennett, Sheila (Eds.) 2001: *The Oxford Companion to the Body.* Oxford: Oxford University Press.

Blanpied, John W. 1988: "The Dead-End Comedy of *Richard III.*" In *William Shakespeare's "Richard III."* Ed. Harold Bloom. New York: Chelsea House, pp. 61–72.

Bloom, Harold (Ed.) 1988: *William Shakespeare's "Richard III."* New York: Chelsea House.

—— 1999: *Shakespeare: The Invention of the Human.* London: Fourth Estate.

Boose, Lynda E. 1982: "The Father and the Bride in Shakespeare." *PMLA* 97, 325–47.

—— 1986: "An Approach through Theme: Marriage and the Family." In *Approaches to Teaching Shakespeare's King Lear.* Ed. Robert H. Ray. New York: MLA, pp. 59–68.

Bowker, John 1998: *The Complete Bible Handbook.* London: Dorling Kindersley.

Bradley, A. C. 1904: *Shakespearian Tragedy.* London: Macmillan.

Bradshaw, Graham 1987: *Shakespeare's Scepticism.* Ithaca, NY: Cornell University Press.

Braunmuller, A. R. 1988: "*King John* and Historiography." *English Literary History* 55, 309–32.

—— 1989: See Shakespeare, *King John.*

—— 1997: See Shakespeare, *Macbeth.*

Brockbank, Philip 1989a: *J. P. Brockbank on Shakespeare.* Oxford: Blackwell.

—— (Ed.) 1989b: *Players of Shakespeare 1.* Cambridge: Cambridge University Press.

Broude, Ronald 1979: "Four Forms of Vengeance in *Titus Andronicus.*" *Journal of English and Germanic Philology* 78, 494–507.

Brown, Susan 1998: "Queen Elizabeth in *Richard III.*" In *Players of Shakespeare 4*. Ed. Robert Smallwood. Cambridge: Cambridge University Press, pp. 101–13.

Bullough, Geoffrey 1962: *Narrative and Dramatic Sources of Shakespeare*. Vol. 4. London: Routledge and Kegan Paul.

Burnett, Mark Thornton 1993: "Giving and Receiving: *Love's Labour's Lost* and the Politics of Exchange." *English Literary Renaissance* 23, 287–313.

Burns, Edward 1990: *Character: Acting and Being on the Pre-Modern Stage*. London: Macmillan.

Butler, Judith 1997: *Excitable Speech*. London: Routledge.

Carroll, Clare 1996: "Humanism and English Literature in the Fifteenth and Sixteenth Centuries." In *The Cambridge Companion to Renaissance Humanism*. Ed. Jill Kraye. Cambridge: Cambridge University Press, pp. 246–68.

Cerasano, S. P. 1992: "Half a Dozen Dangerous Words." In *Gloriana's Face: Women, Public and Private, in the English Renaissance*. Ed. S. P. Cerasano and Marion Wynne-Davies. Brighton: Harvester Press, pp. 167–83.

Charnes, Linda 1989: "'So Unsecret to Ourselves': Notorious Identity and the Material Subject in Shakespeare's *Troilus and Cressida.*" *Shakespeare Quarterly* 40, 413–40.

Chesterton, G. K. 1938: "On Household Gods and Goblins." In *The Coloured Lands*. London: Sheed and Ward, pp. 195–200.

Cook, Ann Jennalie 1991: *Making a Match*. Princeton, NJ: Princeton University Press.

Cornford, Francis M. 1934: *The Origins of Attic Comedy*. Cambridge: Cambridge University Press.

Cressy, David 1997: *Birth, Marriage and Death*. Oxford: Oxford University Press.

Daniell, David 1998: See Shakespeare, *Julius Caesar*.

Davis, Kenneth C. 1998: *Don't Know Much About the Bible*. New York: Eagle Brook.

Dawson, Anthony B. 1978: *Indirections: Shakespeare and the Art of Illusion*. Toronto: University of Toronto Press.

Dent, R. W. 1983: "Imagination in *A Midsummer Night's Dream.*" In *A Midsummer Night's Dream: A Casebook*. Ed. Antony W. Price. London: Macmillan, pp. 124–42.

Derrida, Jacques 1992: "L'aphorisme à contretemps," translated as "Aphorism Countertime." In *Acts of Literature*. Ed. Derek Attridge. London: Routledge, pp. 414–33.

Dixon, Peter 1971: *Rhetoric*. London: Methuen.

Dolan, Frances E. 1996: See Shakespeare, *The Taming of the Shrew*.

Dubrow, Heather 1987: *Captive Victors: Shakespeare's Narrative Poems and the Sonnets*. Ithaca, NY: Cornell University Press.

—— 1999: *Shakespeare and Domestic Loss: Forms of Deprivation, Mourning and Recuperation*. Cambridge: Cambridge University Press.

Duncan-Jones, Katherine 2001: *Ungentle Shakespeare: Scenes from his Life*. London: Thomson Learning.

Dusinberre, Juliet 1975: *Shakespeare and the Nature of Women*. London: Macmillan. Rpt. 1996.

Eagleton, Terry 1983: *Literary Theory: An Introduction*. Oxford: Blackwell.

Eliot, T. S. 1932: "Seneca in Elizabethan Translation." In *Selected Essays 1917–1932*. London: Faber and Faber, pp. 65–105.

—— 1954: *Selected Poems*. London: Faber and Faber.

Erne, Lukas 2003: *Shakespeare as Literary Dramatist*. Cambridge: Cambridge University Press.

Evans, G. B. (Gen. Ed.) 1974: *The Riverside Shakespeare*. Boston, MA: Houghton Mifflin.

Evans, Maurice (Ed.) 1977: *Elizabethan Sonnets*. London: J. M. Dent.

Evans, Patricia 1992: *The Verbally Abusive Relationship*. Holbrook, MA: Adams Media Corporation. Rpt. 1996.

—— 1993: *Verbal Abuse Survivors Speak Out*. Holbrook, MA: Bob Adams Publishers.

Fawcett, Mary Laughlin 1983: "Arms/Words/Tears: Language and the Body in *Titus Andronicus*." *English Literary History* 50, 261–77.

Fischer, Sandra K. 1989: "'He Means to Pay': Value and Metaphor in the Lancastrian Tetralogy." *Shakespeare Quarterly* 40, 149–64.

Flahiff, Fred 1986: "Lear's Map." *Cahiers Elisabéthains* 30, 17–33.

Foakes, R. A. and Rickert, R. T. (Eds.) 1991: *Henslowe's Diary*. Cambridge: Cambridge University Press.

Forward, Susan 1986: *Men Who Hate Women and the Women Who Love Them*. London: Bantam.

Freud, Sigmund 1953–74: "Some Character Types Met With in Psycho-Analytic Work" (1915). In *The Complete Psychological Works of Sigmund Freud*. Gen. Ed. James Strachey. London: Hogarth Press.

Frye, Northrop 1986: *Northrop Frye on Shakespeare*. Ed. Robert Sandler. New Haven, CT: Yale University Press.

Frye, Roland Mushat 1979: "Ladies, Gentlemen, and Skulls: Hamlet and the Iconographic Traditions." *Shakespeare Quarterly* 30, 15–28.

Garber, Marjorie 1981: "'Remember Me': Memento Mori Figures in Shakespeare's Plays." *Renaissance Drama* 12, 3–25.

Garner, Shirley Nelson 1998: "*The Taming of the Shrew*: Inside or Outside of the Joke?" In *"Bad" Shakespeare: Revaluations of the Shakespeare Canon*. Ed. Maurice Charney. Toronto: Associated University Presses, pp. 105–19.

Gibbens, Nicholas 1601: *Questions and Disputations Concerning the Holy Scripture*. London.

Gillies, John 1994: *Shakespeare and the Geography of Difference.* Cambridge: Cambridge University Press.

Goddard, Harold C. 1951: *The Meaning of Shakespeare.* 2 vols. Chicago: University of Chicago Press.

Grant, Hugh 2001: Interview. *Elle* magazine (April), pp. 136–40.

Granville-Barker, Harley 1930: *Prefaces to Shakespeare.* Vol. 4. London: Bathurst.

Greenblatt, Stephen 2001: *Hamlet in Purgatory.* Princeton, NJ: Princeton University Press.

Greg, W. W. 1917: "Hamlet's Hallucination." *Modern Language Review* 12, 393–421.

Hammond, Antony 1987: "Prologue and Plural Text in *Henry V.*" In *Fanned and Winnowed Opinions: Shakespearean Essays Presented to Harold Jenkins.* Ed. John W. Mahon and Thomas A. Pendleton. London: Methuen, pp. 133–50.

Hartley, L. P. 1972: *The Go-Between.* London: Hamish Hamilton.

Hartwig, Joan 1982: "Horses and Women in *The Taming of the Shrew.*" *Huntington Library Quarterly* 44, 285–94.

Healy, Thomas 1994: *Christopher Marlowe.* Plymouth, UK: Northcote House and the British Council.

Heilman, Robert B. 1963: See Shakespeare, *The Taming of the Shrew.*

Hirsch, James E. 1986: "An Approach through Dramatic Structure." In *Approaches to Teaching Shakespeare's "King Lear."* Ed. Robert H. Ray. New York: MLA, pp. 86–90.

Hoban, Russell 1975: *Turtle Diary.* London: Jonathan Cape.

Hodgdon, Barbara 1997: "Race-ing *Othello,* Re-engendering White-out." In *Shakespeare, The Movie.* Ed. Lynda E. Boose and Richard Burt. London and New York: Routledge, pp. 23–44.

Hodson, Beverley 2001: "Don't Just Keep the Books – Read Some." *Guardian,* March 17. Available online at www.guardian.co.uk.

Holderness, Graham, Potter, Nick, and Turner, John 1988: *Shakespeare: The Play of History.* Iowa City: University of Iowa Press.

Holme, J. W. 1914: See Shakespeare, *As You Like It.*

Hopper, Zoë n.p.: "The Fashioning of Identity as a Manipulable Process." Unpublished paper.

Howard, Jean E. and Rackin, Phyllis 1997: *Engendering a Nation: A Feminist Account of Shakespeare's English Histories.* London: Routledge.

Humphreys, A. R. 1984: See Shakespeare, *Julius Caesar.*

Hunter, G. K. 1975: See Shakespeare, *Macbeth.*

—— 1983: "Contrast Rather than Interaction." In *A Midsummer Night's Dream: A Casebook.* Ed. Antony W. Price. London: Macmillan, pp. 120–3.

Huxley, Aldous 1969: *Brave New World.* London: Chatto and Windus.

Jackson, Russell and Smallwood, Robert (Eds.) 1993: *Players of Shakespeare 3.* Cambridge: Cambridge University Press.

Jacobi, Derek 1998: "Macbeth." In *Players of Shakespeare 4*. Ed. Robert Smallwood. Cambridge: Cambridge University Press, pp. 193–210.

James VI, King 1944: *The Basilikon Doron of King James VI*. Ed. James Craigie. Edinburgh: William Blackwood and Sons.

Jenkins, Harold 1982: See Shakespeare, *Hamlet*.

Jesson, Paul 1998: "Henry VIII." In *Players of Shakespeare 4*. Ed. Robert Smallwood. Cambridge: Cambridge University Press, pp. 114–31.

Johnson, Samuel. See Wimsatt 1960.

Jones, Ann Rosalind and Stallybrass, Peter 2000: *Renaissance Clothing and the Materials of Memory*. Cambridge: Cambridge University Press.

Jones, Robert C. 1985: "Truth in *King John*." *Studies in English Literature* 25, 397–417.

Jonson, Ben 1947: *Timber: or, Discoveries*. In *Ben Jonson*. Ed. C. H. Herford and Percy and Evelyn Simpson. Vol. 7. Oxford: Clarendon Press.

—— 1975: *Poems*. Ed. Ian Donaldson. London: Oxford University Press.

—— 1987: *The Alchemist*. Ed. Peter Bement. London: Routledge.

—— 2000: *The Devil is an Ass and Other Plays*. Ed. M. J. Kidnie. World's Classics. Oxford: Oxford University Press.

Kahn, Coppélia 1981: *Man's Estate: Masculine Identity in Shakespeare*. Berkeley, Los Angeles, and London: University of California Press.

—— 1997: *Roman Shakespeare: Warriors, Wounds, and Women*. London: Routledge.

Kant, Immanuel 1964: *Critique of Judgment*. In *Philosophies of Art and Beauty*. Ed. Albert Hofstadter and Richard Kuhns. New York: Random House.

Kastan, David S. 1983: "'To Set a Form Upon that Indigest': Shakespeare's Fictions of History." *Comparative Drama* 17, 1–15.

—— 1985: "*All's Well that Ends Well* and the Limits of Comedy." *English Literary History* 52, 575–89.

Kermode, Frank 2000: *Shakespeare's Language*. London: Penguin.

Knox, John 1558: *The First Blast of the Trumpet against the Monstrous Regiment of Women*. London.

Kuhn, Maura Slattery 1977: "Much Virtue in 'If.'" *Shakespeare Quarterly* 28, 40–50.

Kyd, Thomas 1970: *The Spanish Tragedy*. Ed. J. R. Mulryne. New Mermaids. London: Ernest Benn.

Lacan, Jacques 1977: *Écrits: A Selection*. Trans. Alan Sheridan. New York: W. W. Norton.

Lanier, Douglas 1993: "'Stigmatical in Making': The Material Character of *The Comedy of Errors*." *English Literary Renaissance* 23, 81–112.

Lapotaire, Jane 1998: "Queen Katherine in *Henry VIII*." In *Players of Shakespeare 4*. Ed. Robert Smallwood. Cambridge: Cambridge University Press, pp. 132–51.

Laroque, François 1991: *Shakespeare's Festive World: Elizabethan Seasonal Entertainment and the Professional Stage*. Trans. Janet Lloyd. Cambridge: Cambridge University Press.

Leech, Clifford 1977: See Shakespeare, *The Two Noble Kinsmen.*

Leggatt, Alexander 1971: *"All's Well that Ends Well:* The Testing of Romance." *Modern Language Quarterly* 32, 21–41.

—— 1974: *Shakespeare's Comedy of Love.* London: Methuen.

—— 1988: *Shakespeare's Political Drama.* London and New York: Routledge.

—— 1998: "Dramatic Perspective in *King John." Shakespeare Criticism* 41, 205–14. First published in *English Studies in Canada* 3 (1977), 1–17.

Lerner, Gerda 1986: *The Creation of Patriarchy.* New York: Oxford University Press.

Lewis, Cynthia 1992: "Teaching 'A Thing Perplex'd': Drawing Unity from the Confusion of *Cymbeline."* In *Approaches to Teaching Shakespeare's "The Tempest" and Other Late Romances.* Ed. Maurice Hunt. New York: MLA, pp. 72–9.

Loraux, Nicole 1998: *Mothers in Mourning.* Trans. Corinne Pache. Ithaca, NY: Cornell University Press.

Lower, Charles B. 1998: "Character Identification in Two Folio Plays, *Coriolanus* and *All's Well:* A Theater Perspective." In *Textual Formations and Reformations.* Ed. Laurie E. Maguire and Thomas L. Berger. Newark, DE: University of Delaware Press, pp. 231–50.

Lucking, David 1985: "'That Which We Call a Name': The Balcony Scene in *Romeo and Juliet." English* 44, 1–16.

Luscombe, Christopher 1998: "Launcelot Gobbo in *The Merchant of Venice."* In *Players of Shakespeare 4.* Ed. Robert Smallwood. Cambridge: Cambridge University Press, pp. 18–29.

Lyons, Clifford P. 1964: "The Trysting Scenes in *Troilus and Cressida."* In *Shakespearean Studies.* Ed. Alwin Thaler and Norman Sanders. Knoxville: University of Tennessee Press, pp. 105–20.

Lynch, Stephen J. 1984: "Shakespeare's Cressida." *Philological Quarterly* 63, 357–68.

McCabe, Richard 1998: "Autolycus in *The Winter's Tale."* In *Players of Shakespeare 4.* Ed. Robert Smallwood. Cambridge: Cambridge University Press, pp. 60–70.

MacCallum, M. W. 1967: *Shakespeare's Roman Plays and their Background.* New York: Russell and Russell.

McDiarmid, Ian 1988: "Shylock in *The Merchant of Venice."* In *Players of Shakespeare 2.* Ed. Russell Jackson and Robert Smallwood. Cambridge: Cambridge University Press, pp. 45–54.

Machiavelli, Niccolò 1977: *The Prince.* Trans. George Bull. Harmondsworth: Penguin.

Maguire, Laurie E. and Berger, Thomas L. (Eds.) 1998: *Textual Formations and Reformations.* Newark, DE: University of Delaware Press.

Makaryk, Irena R. 1996: "'Dwindling into a Wife?': Cleopatra and the Desires of the (Other) Woman." *The Elizabethan Theatre* 14, 109–25.

Mallette, Richard 1995: "Same-Sex Erotic Friendship in *The Two Noble Kinsmen." Renaissance Drama* 26, 29–52.

Mangan, Michael 1996: *A Preface to Shakespeare's Comedies.* London: Longman.

Maslen, Elizabeth 1983: "Yorick's Place in *Hamlet*." *Essays and Studies* 36, 1–13.

Maveety, Stanley 1973: "'A Second Fall of Cursed Man': The Bold Metaphor in *Richard II*." *Journal of English and Germanic Philology* 72, 175–93.

Mikalachki, Jodi n.p. "Lear and the Land's History." Unpublished paper.

—— 1998: *The Legacy of Boadicea: Gender and Nation in Early Modern England*. London and New York: Routledge.

Miller, Stephen B. 1998: "*The Taming of a Shrew* and the Theories; or, 'Though this be badness, yet there is method in't.'" In *Textual Formations and Reformations*. Ed. Laurie E. Maguire and Thomas L. Berger. Newark, DE: University of Delaware Press, pp. 251–63.

Miola, Robert S. 1983: *Shakespeare's Rome*. Cambridge: Cambridge University Press.

More, Sir Thomas 1978: *Utopia*. Harmondsworth: Penguin.

Morgan, Ben n.p. "Shakespeare and the Mirror of Art in the Comedies." Unpublished paper.

Morgan, Stephen M. 1982: *Conjugal Terrorism*. Palo Alto, CA: R and E Research Associates.

Morgan, Victor 1979: "The Cartographic Image of 'The Country' in Early Modern England." *Transactions of the Royal Historical Society* 29, 129–54.

Muir, Kenneth 1977: "*Timon of Athens* and the Cash-Nexus." In Muir, *The Singularity of Shakespeare*. Liverpool: Liverpool University Press, pp. 56–75. First published in *Modern Language Miscellany* 1 (1947).

Neill, Michael 1988: "Shakespeare's Halle of Mirrors: Play, Politics, and Psychology in *Richard III*." In *William Shakespeare's "Richard III."* Ed. Harold Bloom. New York: Chelsea House, pp. 15–43. First published in *Shakespeare Studies* 8 (1975).

—— 1994: See Shakespeare, *Antony and Cleopatra*.

—— 1997: *Issues of Death: Mortality and Identity in English Renaissance Tragedy*. Oxford: Oxford University Press.

Nettles, John 1998: "Brutus in *Julius Caesar*." In *Players of Shakespeare 4*. Ed. Robert Smallwood. Cambridge: Cambridge University Press, pp. 177–92.

Niccholes, Alexander 1615: *A Discourse of Marriage and Wiving*. London.

Okerlund, Arlene N. 1980: "In Defense of Cressida: Character as Metaphor." *Women's Studies* 7, 1–17.

Overbury, Sir Thomas 1890: *Miscellaneous Works in Prose and Verse*. Ed. Edward F. Rimbault. London: Reeves and Turner.

Parker, Kenneth 2000: *Antony and Cleopatra*. Tavistock, Devon: Northcote House and the British Council.

Parker, R. B. 1984: "War and Sex in *All's Well that Ends Well*." *Shakespeare Survey* 37, 99–113.

Pearlman, E. 1972: "Shakespeare, Freud, and the Two Usuries, or, Money's a Meddler." *English Literary Renaissance* 2, 217–36.

Phillips, Edward 1658: *New World of English Words, or A General Dictionary.* London.

Plutarch 1957–72: *Moralia.* 15 vols. London: Heinemann; Cambridge, MA: Harvard University Press.

Price, Antony W. (Ed.) 1983: *A Midsummer Night's Dream: A Casebook.* London: Macmillan.

Rabkin, Norman 1977: "Rabbits, Ducks and Henry V." *Shakespeare Quarterly* 28, 279–96.

Rackin, Phyllis 1989: "Patriarchal History and Female Subversion." In *King John: New Perspectives.* Ed. Deborah T. Curren-Aquino. Newark, DE: University of Delaware Press, pp. 76–90.

Ranald, Margaret Loftus 1974: "The Manning of the Haggard; or, *The Taming of The Shrew.*" *Essays in Literature* 1, 149–65. Reprinted as chapter 4 of *Shakespeare and his Social Context.*

—— 1987: *Shakespeare and his Social Context.* New York: AMS Press.

Ray, Robert H. (Ed.) 1986: *Approaches to Teaching Shakespeare's "King Lear."* New York: MLA.

Rees, Nigel 1979: *Graffiti Lives OK.* London: Unwin.

Rich, Barnaby 1578: *Alarm to England.* London.

Riefer, Marcia 1984: "'Instruments of Some More Mightier Member': The Constriction of Female Power in *Measure for Measure.*" *Shakespeare Quarterly* 35, 157–69.

Roberts, Jeanne Addison 1983: "Horses and Hermaphrodites: Metamorphoses in *The Taming of the Shrew.*" *Shakespeare Quarterly* 34, 159–71.

Rutter, Carol 1988: *Clamorous Voices.* London: Women's Press.

Ryan, Kiernan 1988: "*Romeo and Juliet*: The Language of Tragedy." In *The Taming of the Text.* Ed. Willie van Peer. London: Routledge, pp. 106–21.

Schoenbaum, Samuel 1967: See Shakespeare, *Henry VIII.*

Seward, Desmond 1987: *Henry V as Warlord.* London: Sidgwick and Jackson.

Shakespeare, William 1981: *Antony and Cleopatra.* Ed. Peter Alexander. BBC Shakespeare. London: BBC.

—— 1994: *Antony and Cleopatra.* Ed. Michael Neill. Oxford: Oxford University Press.

—— 1914: *As You Like It.* Ed. J. W. Holme. Arden edition. London: Methuen.

—— 1983: *Cymbeline.* Ed. Peter Alexander. BBC Shakespeare. London: BBC.

—— 1982: *Hamlet.* Ed. Harold Jenkins. Arden 2. London: Methuen.

—— 1967: *Henry VIII.* Ed. Samuel Schoenbaum. New York: New American Library.

—— 1979: *Henry VIII.* Ed. Peter Alexander. BBC Shakespeare. London: BBC.

—— 1984: *Julius Caesar.* Ed. A. R. Humphreys. Oxford: Oxford University Press.

—— 1998: *Julius Caesar.* Ed. David Daniell. Arden 3. London: Thomas Nelson.

—— 1986: *King John.* Ed. Peter Alexander. BBC Shakespeare. London: BBC.

—— 1989: *King John.* Ed. A. R. Braunmuller. Oxford: Oxford University Press.

—— 1975: *Macbeth*. Ed. G. K. Hunter. Harmondsworth: Penguin.

—— 1997: *Macbeth*. Ed. A. R. Braunmuller. Cambridge: Cambridge University Press.

—— 1984: *Pericles*. Ed. Peter Alexander. BBC Shakespeare. London: BBC.

—— 1961: *Richard II*. Ed. Peter Ure. Arden 2. London: Methuen.

—— 1978: *Richard II*. Ed. Peter Alexander. BBC Shakespeare. London: BBC.

—— 1963: *The Taming of the Shrew*. Ed. Robert B. Heilman. New York: New American Library.

—— 1996: *The Taming of the Shrew*. Ed. Frances E. Dolan. Boston: Bedford Books of St. Martin's Press.

—— 1998: *Troilus and Cressida*. Ed. David Bevington. Arden 3. London: Thomas Nelson.

—— 1979: *Twelfth Night*. Ed. Peter Alexander. BBC Shakespeare. London: BBC.

—— 1977: *The Two Noble Kinsmen*. Ed. Clifford Leech. In *The Two Noble Kinsmen, Titus Andronicus and Pericles*. New York: New American Library.

Shapiro, James 1996: *Shakespeare and the Jews*. New York: Columbia University Press.

Shaw, Bernard 1967: *Three Plays for Puritans*. Harmondsworth: Penguin.

Shewring, Margaret 1996: *Richard II*. Manchester: Manchester University Press.

Siberry, Michael 1998: "Petruccio in *The Taming of the Shrew*." In *Players of Shakespeare 4*. Ed. Robert Smallwood. Cambridge: Cambridge University Press, pp. 45–59.

Sidney, Sir Philip 1965: *An Apology for Poetry*. Ed. Geoffrey Shepherd. London: Thomas Nelson.

Simkin, Stevie 2001: *Marlowe: The Plays*. Basingstoke: Palgrave.

Sinden, Donald 1989: "Malvolio in *Twelfth Night*." In *Players of Shakespeare 1*. Ed. Philip Brockbank. Cambridge: Cambridge University Press, pp. 41–66.

Sinfield, Alan 1992: *Faultlines: Cultural Materialism and the Politics of Dissident Reading*. Berkeley and Los Angeles: University of California Press.

Slater, Ann Pasternak 1982: *Shakespeare the Director*. Brighton: Harvester Press.

Smallwood, Robert (Ed.) 1998: *Players of Shakespeare 4*. Cambridge: Cambridge University Press.

Smiley, Jane 1992: *A Thousand Acres*. London: Flamingo.

Smith, Alex Duval 1999: "Return of the Rebels." *Independent*, August 5, *Review*, p. 1.

Smith, Henry 1591: *The Examination of Usury*. London.

Snyder, Susan 1992: "'The King's Not Here': Displacement and Deferral in *All's Well that Ends Well*." *Shakespeare Quarterly* 43, 20–32.

Stanislavski, Constantin 1936: *An Actor Prepares*. Trans. Elizabeth R. Hapgood. New York: Theatre Arts Inc.

Stanton, Kay 1992: "*All's Well* in Love and War." In *Ideological Approaches to Shakespeare: The Practice of Theory*. Ed. Robert P. Merrix and Nicholas Ranson. Lewiston, NY: Edwin Mellen Press, pp. 155–63.

Steed, Maggie 1993: "Beatrice in *Much Ado about Nothing*." In *Players of Shakespeare 3*. Ed. Russell Jackson and Robert Smallwood. Cambridge: Cambridge University Press, pp. 42–51.

Stewart, Patrick 1989: "Shylock in *The Merchant of Venice*." In *Players of Shakespeare 1*. Ed. Philip Brockbank. Cambridge: Cambridge University Press, pp. 11–28.

Stoppard, Tom 1998: *Rosencrantz and Guildenstern are Dead*. In *Drama, Classical to Contemporary*. Ed. John C. Coldewey and W. R. Streitberger. Upper Saddle River, NJ: Prentice Hall, pp. 1077–1115.

Styan, J. L. 1984: *All's Well that Ends Well*. Manchester: Manchester University Press.

Taylor, Gary 1996: *Cultural Selection*. New York: Harper Collins.

Tennant, David 1998: "Touchstone in *As You Like It*." In *Players of Shakespeare 4*. Ed. Robert Smallwood. Cambridge: Cambridge University Press, pp. 30–44.

Tilley, Morris Palmer 1950: *A Dictionary of the Proverbs in England in the Sixteenth and Seventeenth Centuries*. Ann Arbor, MI: University of Michigan Press.

Troughton, David 1998: "Richard III." In *Players of Shakespeare 4*. Ed. Robert Smallwood. Cambridge: Cambridge University Press, pp. 71–100.

Ure, Peter 1961: See Shakespeare, *Richard II*.

Van de Water, Julia C. 1960: "The Bastard in *King John*." *Shakespeare Quarterly* 11, 137–46.

Varholy, Cristine n.p. "On Their Backs: Clothing and the Early Modern Sex Trade." Unpublished paper.

Vaughan, Virginia M. 1984: "Between Tetralogies: *King John* as Transition." *Shakespeare Quarterly* 35, 407–20.

Velz, John W. 1968: "'If I Were Brutus Now . . .': Role-Playing in *Julius Caesar*". *Shakespeare Studies* 4, 149–59.

Vickers, Brian 1968: *The Artistry of Shakespeare's Prose*. London: Methuen.

—— 1976: *Coriolanus: Studies in English Literature*. London: Edward Arnold.

—— 1977: "Teaching *Coriolanus*: The Importance of Perspective." In *Teaching Shakespeare*. Ed. Walter Edens, Christopher Durer, Duncan Harris, Keith Hull, and Walter Eggers. Princeton, NJ: Princeton University Press, pp. 228–70.

Voss, Philip 1998: "Menenius in *Coriolanus*." In *Players of Shakespeare 4*. Ed. Robert Smallwood. Cambridge: Cambridge University Press, pp. 152–64.

Walker, Alice 1953: *Textual Problems of the First Folio*. Cambridge: Cambridge University Press.

Walter, Harriet 1993: "Imogen in *Cymbeline*." In *Players of Shakespeare 3*. Ed. Russell Jackson and Robert Smallwood. Cambridge: Cambridge University Press, pp. 201–19.

Watson, Robert N. 1990: "Tragedy." In *The Cambridge Companion to English Renaissance Drama*. Ed. A. R. Braunmuller and Michael Hattaway. Cambridge: Cambridge University Press, pp. 301–51.

Wayne, Valerie 1985: "Refashioning *The Shrew.*" *Shakespeare Studies* 17, 159–87.

——1998: "The Sexual Politics of Textual Transmission." In *Textual Formations and Reformations*. Ed. Laurie E. Maguire and Thomas L. Berger. Newark, DE: University of Delaware Press, pp. 179–210.

Weidhorn, Manfred 1969: "The Rose and its Name: On Denomination in *Othello, Romeo and Juliet, Julius Caesar.*" *Texas Studies in Literature and Language* 11, 671–86.

Weimann, Robert 1996: *Authority and Representation in Early Modern Discourse*. Baltimore, MD: Johns Hopkins University Press.

Wells, Stanley and Taylor, Gary, with Jowett, John and Montgomery, William 1987: *William Shakespeare: A Textual Companion*. Oxford: Clarendon Press.

White, Michael 2000a: "PM's Wife under Fire from Tories." *Guardian*, August 8.

——2000b: "Tories Aim Barbs at PM's 'Lady Macbeth.'" *Guardian*, August 9.

White, R. S. 1991: *The Merry Wives of Windsor*. London: Harvester Wheatsheaf.

Wilcox, Lance 1985: "Katherine of France as Victim and Bride." *Shakespeare Studies* 17, 61–88.

Wilde, Oscar 1980: *The Importance of Being Ernest*. Ed. Russell Jackson. London: Ernest Benn.

Williams, Arnold 1948: *The Common Expositor: An Account of the Commentaries on Genesis 1527–1633*. Chapel Hill: University of North Carolina Press.

Williams, Laurence n.p. "Composing Males: Conception as a Basis for Male Authority in *Macbeth.*" Unpublished paper.

Williamson, Jane 1975: "The Duke and Isabella on the Modern Stage." In *The Triple Bond*. Ed. Joseph G. Price. University Park, PA: Penn State University Press, pp. 149–69.

Wilson, K. J. 1997: *When Violence Begins at Home*. Alameda, CA: Hunter House.

Wimsatt, W. K. 1960: *Dr. Johnson on Shakespeare*. Harmondsworth: Penguin.

Winterson, Jeanette 2001: "Art – Not Propaganda." *Guardian*, November 13, *G2 Review*, p. 9.

Wixson, Douglas C. 1981: "Calm Words Folded Up in Smoke: Propaganda and Spectator Response in Shakespeare's *King John.*" *Shakespeare Studies* 14, 111–27.

Woodeson, Nicholas 1993: "King John." In *Players of Shakespeare 3*. Ed. Russell Jackson and Robert Smallwood. Cambridge: Cambridge University Press, pp. 87–98.

Zitner, Sheldon P. 1974: "Aumerle's Conspiracy." *Studies in English Literature* 14, 239–57.

Index